m

Ilhas das Cobras

Ilhas
Fiscal

Baía de Guanabara

Ferry to Niterói & Ilha de Paquetá

Estação das Barcas

▼ 18

(Perimetral)

da Misericórdia

28 🏛

CASTELO

Santa Luzia

Avenida Churchill

Avenida General Justo

Ave Franklin Roosevelt

▪ 40

41 ▪

Trevo dos Estudantes

*Aeroporto
Santos Dumont*

Avenida Alm. Silvio de Noronha

*Enseada da
Glória*

Map 1 Central Rio
(see previous page)

PLACES TO STAY

5   Guanabara Palace Hotel
36   Nelba Hotel
38   Itajuba Hotel
41   Aeroport Othon Hotel
49   Hotel Marajó

PLACES TO EAT

11   Miako
12   English Bar
18   Restaurante Alba Mar
21   Confeitaria Colombo
24   Bar Luis
31   Suco (Juice) Bars
34   Hotel Ambassador
35   Outdoor Cafés & Political Debating
48   Restaurante Ernesto

OTHER

1   Polícia Federal (Visa Extensions)
2   Mosteiro de São Bento
3   Palácio da Conceicao
4   Fortaleza da Conceicao
6   Igreja NS de Candelária
7   Palácio Itamaraty
8   Post Office
9   Igreja e Museu da Santa Cruz dos Militares
10   Igreja da Lapa
13   Chafariz da Piramide
14   Praça Quinze de Novembro
15   Igreja e Museu do Carmo
16   Paço Imperial
17   Museu Naval e Oceanográfico
19   Igreja de São José

20   TurisRio & Riotur (State & City) Tourist Offices
22   Riotur Booth
23   Hospital Estadual Souza Aguiar
25   Casa Oliveira
26   Convento de Santo Antônio
27   Crafts Market
28   Museu Histórico Nacional
29   Museu Nacional de Belas Artes
30   Teatro Municipal
32   Bilbioteca Nacional
33   Praça Ana Amelía
37   Catedral de San Sebastian
39   Buses to Southern Suburbs: Flamengo, Copacabana etc
40   French Consulate
42   Praça Floriano
43   US Consulate
44   Varig Airlines Main Office
45   Praça Mahatma Gandhi
46   Circo Voador
47   Escola da Música
50   Museu de Arte Moderna
51   Monumento Nacional dos Mundial

Rio de Janeiro

a Lonely Planet city guide

Andrew Draffen

Rio de Janeiro
1st edition

Published by
Lonely Planet Publications
Head Office: PO Box 617, Hawthorn, Vic 3122, Australia
Branches:　　155 Filbert St, Suite 251, Oakland,
　　　　　　CA 94607, USA
　　　　　　10 Barley Mow Passage, Chiswick,
　　　　　　London W4 4PH, UK
　　　　　　71 bis rue du Cardinal Lemoine,
　　　　　　75005 Paris, France

Printed by
SNP Printing Pte Ltd., Singapore

Photographs by
John Maier, Jr, Andrew Draffen, Guy Moberly (Retna Pictures), Chris Beall (Retna Pictures)

Front cover: Towel rack in Rio sidewalk (John Maier, Jr)
Front gatefold: Top: Pão de Açúcar (Andrew Draffen)
　　　　　　　　Bottom: Ipanema beach (Andrew Draffen)
Back gatefold: Mauá (Andrew Draffen)
Title page: Having fun in Búzios (John Mair, Jr)

First Published
November 1995

National Library of Australia Cataloguing in Publication Data

Draffen, Andrew
　Rio de Janeiro

1st ed.
Includes index.
ISBN 0 86442 315 2.

1. Rio de Janeiro (Brazil) – Guide-books.
I. Title (Series: Lonely Planet city guide).

918.1530464

Andrew Draffen

Australian-born Andrew has travelled and worked his way around Australia, Asia, North America and the Caribbean, settling just long enough in Melbourne to complete an Arts degree, majoring in history. During his first trip to South America in 1984, Andrew fell in love both with Brazil and his future wife, Stella. They have since toured extensively in Brazil, Europe and Asia, and today travel with their young children, Gabriela and Christopher, whose great-great-grandfather introduced football to Brazil. Andrew is co-author of LP's guide to *Brazil*. He also contributed to the LP guide to *South America*.

From the Author

Muito obrigado to the following for their support, advice and/or insider tips: Peter Bolgarow, the Brazilian mosquitoes' favourite gringo; Riotur; Embratur; John and Masai; Mike and Ivandy; and Terry and Sloane – two of Mangueira's finest sea monsters.

Special thanks to my Brazilian family, especially Vera Miller – my favourite mother-in-law – and Dona Heloisa Alves de Lima e Motta; Iara Costa da Pinto for her hospitality on many Brazil trips; Frank and Helen Draffen for their support over the years; and Stella, Gabriela and Christopher Draffen, who make it all worthwhile.

From the Publisher

This book was coordinated at the Lonely Planet head office in Melbourne, Australia, by Mary Neighbour, who also did some of the proofing. Lynn McGaurr and Jenny Missen edited and proofed the book. Lou Callan edited the Language section. Chris Wyness did some additional proofing and took the book through layout. Rachel Black drew the maps and did the design and layout. Simon Bracken designed the cover and Andrew Tudor drew the back cover map. Kerrie Williams produced the index.

Warning & Request

Things change – prices go up, schedules change, good places go bad and bad places go bankrupt – nothing stays the same. So if you find things better or worse, recently opened or long since closed, please write and tell us and help make the next edition better.

We greatly appreciate all information that is sent to us by travellers. Back at Lonely Planet we employ a hard-working readers' letters team to sort through the many letters we receive. The best ones will be rewarded with a free copy of the next edition or another Lonely Planet guide if you prefer. We give away lots of books, but, unfortunately, not every letter/postcard receives one.

Stop Press

Prices in Rio have increased dramatically since this book was researched. The strength of the Brazilian currency, the real, is a major factor; after years of steady decline against the US dollar, the real has actually been appreciating. In Rio prices have increased by about 50% on average. Following are some examples, comparing the prices quoted in this book to the prices charged in September 1995 (with the percentage increase in brackets):

Pre-paid taxi from Aeroporto Galeão to Copacabana: from US$24 to US$42 (+ 75%)

Ferry from Centro to Niterói: from 30c to 50c (+ 67%)

Corcovado funicular railway: from US$11 to US$16.50 (+ 50%)

Pão de Açúcar cablecar: from US$8 to US$11.50 (+ 45%)

Double rooms in Copacabana hotels: Santa Clara from US$25 to US$40 (+ 60%); Biarritz Hotel from US$35 to US$44 (+ 25%); Lancaster Othon from US$90 to US$122 (+ 35%); Copacabana Palace Hotel from US$160 to US$220 (+ 40%)

Food: at Bar Largoa in Ipanema meals were US$7 to US$10 and are now US$13 to US$18 (+ 80%); at an Arataca restaurant, a serve of vatapá was US$4 and is now US$12 (+ 300%).

Lonely Planet books provide independent advice. Accredited Lonely Planet writers do not accept discounts or payment in exchange for positive coverage.

Contents

Maps

Introduction

Flying into Rio is exciting. Forget the black-and-white images of chorus lines dancing samba on the wings of an aeroplane. The real thing is much better. Flying in along the coast you clearly see the escarpment, a 2000-metre wall rising sharply a few km from the coast. As the plane starts to come in for a landing you can make out the famous granite outcrops you've seen so often on travel posters: Pão de Açúcar (Sugar Loaf) and Corcovado topped by Cristo Redentor (Christ the Redeemer) with his arms outstretched. You can almost touch the famous mosaic pavements of Copacabana as you pass its sweeping curve and enter Baía de Guanabara. In this gloriously exuberant tropical setting, sandwiched between the mountains and the sea, Rio de Janeiro has seduced travellers for centuries.

The people who live here are called Cariocas. They call their city the Cidade Maravilhosa – the Marvellous City. More than seven million of them are squeezed into the world's most beautiful setting. This makes Rio one of the world's biggest tropical cities and one of the most densely populated places on earth. This thick brew of Cariocas pursues pleasure like no other people: beaches, bossa nova and the body beautiful; samba and *cerveja* (beer); football and *cachaça* (the popular local alcoholic beverage).

Rio has its problems, and they are enormous. A fifth of the people live in the *favelas* (shantytowns) that blanket many of the hillsides. The poor have no schools, no doctors, no jobs. Drug abuse and violence are endemic. Police corruption and brutality are commonplace. Nevertheless, in Rio everything ends with samba – football games, weddings, work, political demonstrations and, of course, a day at the beach. There's a lust for life, and a love of romance, music, dance and talk that seem to distinguish the Carioca from everyone else. For anyone coming from the developed capitalist world, with its efficiency and rationality, this is potent stuff. The sensuality of Carnaval is the best known expression of this Dionysian spirit, but there's plenty more.

In the last few years, the city that was once the capital of the United Kingdom of Portugal, Brazil and the Algarve has recovered some of its glitter. It never lost its natural beauty, yet there's a new vitality and sense of optimism and pride in the city. Restoration projects have halted the decay of many elegant old buildings, and projects are underway to deal with more serious problems, like providing the favelas with basic services and cleaning up Baía de Guanabara.

Rio may no longer be the political capital of the nation, but it remains the international face of Brazil and a city of dreams for poor Brazilians searching for a better life. And with more than 80 km of beach and lots of sun, Rio de Janeiro is a wonderful place to visit. There are restaurants and hotels to suit every budget. The beaches are free and democratic. There's lots to explore in the city centre and in several other neighbourhoods with their parks and museums. Mass transportation is fast and easy. And if you can meet some locals – not nearly so hard as in New York, London or Sydney – well, then you're on Easy Street.

Facts about Rio de Janeiro

HISTORY

Gaspar de Lemos set sail from Portugal for Brazil in May 1501 and entered a huge bay in January 1502. Mistaking the bay for a river, he named it Rio de Janeiro. It was the French, however, who first settled along the great bay. Like the Portuguese, the French had been harvesting brazil wood along the Brazilian coast, but unlike the Portuguese they hadn't attempted any permanent settlements until Rio de Janeiro.

As the Portuguese colonisation of Brazil began to take hold, the French became concerned that they'd be pushed out of the colony. Three ships of French settlers reached the Baía de Guanabara in 1555. They settled on a small island in the bay and called it Antarctic France. Almost from the start the town seemed doomed to failure. It was torn by religious divisions, isolated by harsh treatment of the Indians and demoralised by the puritanical rule of the French leader, Nicolas de Villegagnon. Antarctic France was weak and disheartened when the Portuguese attacked and drove the French from their fortress after a prolonged seige lasting from 1565 to 1567.

ANDREW DRAFFEN

Pão de Açúcar (Sugar Loaf)

A greater threat to the Portuguese were the powerful Tamoio Indians, who had allied with the French. A series of battles occurred, but the Portuguese were better armed and better supplied than the French, whom they finally expelled. They drove the Tamoio from the region in a series of bloody battles.

The First Town

The Portuguese set up a fortified town on the Morro Castelo in 1567 to maximise protection from European invasion by sea and Indian attack by land. They named it São Sebastião do Rio de Janeiro, after King Sebastião of Portugal. The founding 500 Cariocas built a typical Brazilian town: poorly planned, with irregular streets in the medieval Portuguese style. By the end of the century the small settlement was, if not exactly prosperous, surviving on the export of brazil wood and sugar cane, and from fishing in the Baía de Guanabara.

In 1660 the city had a population made up of 3000 Indians, 750 Portuguese and 100 Blacks. It grew along the waterfront and what is now Praça 15 de Novembro. Religious orders came – the Jesuits, the Franciscans and the Benedictines – and built austere, closed-in churches.

Economic Growth

With its excellent harbour and good lands for sugar cane, Rio became Brazil's third most important settlement (after Salvador de Bahia and Recife-Olinda) in the 17th century. Slaves were imported and the sugar plantations thrived. The owners of the sugar estates lived in the protection and comfort of the fortified city.

The gold rush in Minas Gerais at the beginning of the 18th century changed Rio forever. In 1704 the Caminho Novo, a new road to the Minas gold fields, was opened. Until the gold began to run out, half a century later, a golden road went through the ports of Rio.

Rio was now the prize of Brazil. In 1710 the French, who were at war with Portugal and raiding its colonies, attacked the city. The French were defeated, but a second expedition succeeded and the entire population abandoned the city in the dark of night. The occupying French threatened to level the city unless a sizeable ransom in gold, sugar and cattle was paid. The Portuguese obliged. During the return voyage to an expected heroes' welcome in France, the victors lost two ships and most of the gold.

Rio quickly recovered from the setback. Its fortifications were improved, many richly decorated churches were built and by 1763 its population had reached 50,000. With international sugar prices slumping and the sugar economy in the doldrums, Rio replaced Salvador de Bahia as the colonial capital in 1763. The city expanded south toward Botafogo, and north to São Cristovão. Main streets were paved and swampy areas were filled.

Growth of the Modern City

In 1808 the entire Portuguese monarchy and court – fleeing an imminent invasion by Napoleon's armies – arrived in Rio. The city thus came to house the court of the Portuguese Empire – or at least what was left of it. With the court came an influx of money and talent that helped build some of the city's lasting monuments, like the palace at the Quinta da Boa Vista and the Jardim Botânico (a pet project of the king). Within a year of his arrival, Dom João (the king) also created the School of Medicine, the Bank of Brazil, the Law Courts, the Naval Academy and the Royal Printing Works. Talented French exiles, such as the architect Jean de Montigny and the painters Jean Baptiste Debret and Nicolas Antoine Taunay, had a profound influence on Rio's cultural life. During Dom João's 13-year stay in Brazil, Rio was transformed from a colonial outpost into the capital of the United Kingdom of Portugal, Brazil and the Algarve. The coffee boom in the mountains of São Paulo and Rio revitalised Brazil's economy during the 19th century. Rio took on a new importance as a port and commercial centre, and coffee commerce modernised the city. By 1860, Rio had become the largest city in South America, with a population of more than 250,000. A telegraph system and gas street lights were installed in 1854. Regular passenger ships began sailing to London (1845) and Paris (1851). The ferry service to Niteroí began in 1862.

Population Explosion & the 20th Century

At the end of the 19th century the city population exploded because of European immigration and internal migration (mostly ex-slaves from the declining coffee and sugar regions). By 1890 there were more than a million inhabitants of Rio, a quarter of them foreign-born. The city spread rapidly between the steep hills, bay and ocean. The first tunnel through the mountains to Copacabana was built in 1892 and the Leme Tunnel was

ANDREW DRAFFEN

Rio is a mix of architectural styles

completed in 1904. The rich started to move further out, in a pattern that continues today.

Radical changes took place in the city centre. In 1904, almost 600 buildings were cleared to make way for Avenida Central (later renamed Rio Branco) which became the Champs Elysées of Rio, an elegant boulevard full of sidewalk cafés and promenading Cariocas.

The early '20s to the late '50s is remembered by many as Rio's golden age. With the inauguration of the grand luxury resort hotels, the Glória in 1922 and the Copacabana Palace in 1924, Rio became a romantic, exotic destination for Hollywood celebrities and international high society. They came to play and gamble at the casinos and dance or perform at the nightclubs. Visitors included Lana Turner, Jayne Mansfield, Josephine Baker, Maurice Chevalier, Eva Peron and Ali Khan. Orson Welles stayed at the Copacabana Palace in 1942, and partied hard. He even threw furniture out the window in a jealous rage – years before rock stars would follow the trend.

The face of Rio continued to change. Three large landfill projects were undertaken to ease the strain on a city restricted by its beautiful surroundings. The first was to become Aeroporto Santos Dumont, near the Centro. The second resulted in Flamengo Park and the third created the strand at Copacabana.

1960 to the Present

Rio remained the political capital of Brazil until 1960, when the capital was moved to Brasília (and thousands of public servants went into deep depression). Rio became the city-state of Guanabara, before merging with the state of Fluminense in 1975 to form the state of Rio de Janeiro, of which Rio is the capital.

During the '60s, lots of modern skyscrapers went up in the city, and some of Rio's most beautiful buildings were lost. A hotel building boom along the beaches saw the rise of the big hotels like the Sheraton, Rio Palace and the Meridien. During the same period, the favelas (shantytowns) of Rio were becoming overcrowded with immigrants from poverty-stricken areas of the north-

JOHN MAIER, JR.

The beach at Copacabana

east and interior, who swelled the number of urban poor in the city. The 'marvellous city' began to lose its gloss, as urban crime and violence began to increase.

The last 10 years of the military dictatorship in Brazil, from 1975 to 1985, were not kind to the city. The politicians governing Rio opposed the military, who responded by witholding vital federal funding. The administration was forced to tighten its belt, and infrastructure deteriorated as decay set in.

The turning-point for Rio came when it was chosen as host city for Eco 92, the United Nations Conference on Environment and Development. In the build-up to the conference, major projects, financed by federal grants, were undertaken to improve Rio's roads and restore many old buildings and parks. This trend has continued, and efficient management of the city's finances by the progressive mayor, César Maia, has meant long-awaited projects can be financed.

Rio remains the cultural and tourist capital of Brazil. It still sets the fashion and the pace for the rest of the nation and should continue to do so for many years to come.

GEOGRAPHY

Rio is blessed by nature. Its location between the mountains and the sea, bathed by the sun, has entranced visitors for centuries. Darwin called it '...more magnificent than anything any European has ever seen in his country of origin'.

It all started millions of years ago, when the movement of the earth pushed the rock crystal and granite, already disturbed by faults, fractures and cleavage, into the sea. Low-lying areas were flooded and the high granite peaks became islands.

The plains and swamps on which the city is built rose slowly, after many centuries of erosion from the peaks and the gradual build-up of sediments from rivers and the ocean.

The mountains, their granite peaks rounded and worn by intense erosion, their slopes covered with Atlantic rainforest, form three ranges: the Tijuca-Carioca massif, the Rural da Pedra Branca massif, and the Rural Marapicu-Gericinó massif.

The Tijuca-Carioca massif has the most important influence on the geographical beauty of the city. It can be seen from almost everywhere in Rio and is responsible for the coastline, which alternates between bare granite escarpments and Atlantic beaches. Its most famous peaks are the Pão de Açucar (Sugar Loaf), the Morro do Leme, the Ponta do Arpoador, Morro Dona

Marta, Corcovado and the Dois Irmãos at the end of Leblon beach.

The sea has also played its part. The stretch of coast between Dois Irmãos and Arpoador was once a large spit, and Lagoa Rodrigo de Freitas a bay which stretched up to the botanical gardens. Between Arpoador and Morro do Leme, the sea created the beautiful curved beach of Copacabana, and between Leme and Urca, Praia Vermelha, the smallest of Rio's Atlantic beaches and the only one with yellow sand instead of white. Inside Baía de Guanabara, river sediment and reclamation projects formed the present bay rim.

The most important river, historically, is the Rio Carioca, which begins near Corcovado and meets the sea between Flamengo and Glória. Today it's completely channelled, but to the Tamoio Indians it was a sacred river, capable of endowing women with beauty and poets and singers with good voices.

It's also how the inhabitants of Rio got their name. Carioca is a Tamoio word meaning 'house of the white' or 'house of stones', after a small hut built at the falls of the river by the first settlers, who used the water to supply ships.

CLIMATE

Rio sits close to the Tropic of Capricorn, so it has a classic tropical climate. Expect some rain. In the summer, from December to March, it gets hot and humid. Daily top temperatures range from 25°C to 40°C. There's more rain than at other times but it rarely lasts for too long. In the winter, temperatures range from around 20°C to 30°C or so, with plenty of good days for the beach.

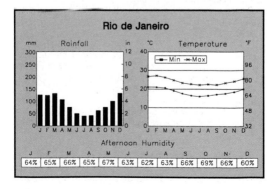

Rio de Janeiro

	J	F	M	A	M	J	J	A	S	O	N	D
Afternoon Humidity	64%	65%	66%	65%	67%	63%	62%	63%	66%	69%	66%	60%

CHRIS BEALL

JOHN MAIER, JR.

CHRIS BEALL

Top: Copacabana from Pão de Açúcar
Middle: Ipanema
Bottom: Botafogo with Corcovado in the distance

ENVIRONMENT

Since Eco 92, the United Nations Conference on Environment and Development, Rio has billed itself as the ecological capital of the world. The Earth Summit may not have been a turning-point in world history, but it certainly helped the city. In the build-up to the conference, the federal government poured in almost US$1 billion to improve Rio's infrastructure. US$18 million was spent on satellite communications alone, and a huge, new convention centre, Riocentro, was built.

Long-awaited projects are now being financed. The biggest is the *favela-bairro* project, which aims to integrate 66 favelas with the rest of the city. This includes providing basic sanitation, and planning leisure areas, health clinics, schools, pre-schools and community centres. In early 1995, the green light was given (and more importantly, finance was provided) for treatment plants to stop effluent flowing into Baía de Guanabara.

GOVERNMENT

The state of Rio (one of Brazil's 24 states) has a governor, elected for a four-year term, and then there's the city council, headed by the mayor. Rio politics is colourful, to say the least. When the state assembly met recently at Palácio Tiradentes, the old federal assembly building, a search of politicians uncovered so many revolvers that they decided to install a metal detector at the entrance.

The excessive number of public servants, around 5500, is a huge burden on the state. It means that 70% of the budget is already earmarked just for wages.

Corruption is rife. Some examples: the previous head of the legislative house is accused of tax evasion, of illicit enrichment, and of buying 70 new cars for political allies; the nine deputies controlling the Secretariat of Health are alleged to have devastated the state's hospitals through overbilling and fictitious billing.

The biggest breakdown over the last few years has been in the area of law and order. Things got so bad with corruption in the Polícia Civil and the Polícia Militar that the state government was forced to ask the federal government to send the army into the favelas in an attempt to fight the drug traffickers in December 1994.

Government at the city level is, fortunately, a little better. Mayor César Maia is committed to 'trimming the fat' in city spending, and this policy has been so successful that the city has around one billion dollars in its coffers. Maia plans to use the money to finance several large projects. These include the construction of a 24-km expressway from Barra da Tijuca to Ilha do Fundão, the restoration and recuperation of 19 historic areas in the city centre, and the favela-bairro project (see Environment).

ECONOMY

As well as being the most popular tourist destination in Brazil, Rio is also a thriving shipping, banking, cultural, publishing and administrative centre. Within 500 km of the city is 32% of Brazil's population, 65% of its industries and 40% of its agricultural production. Its port trades more than 30 million tonnes of goods each year. More than 80% of Brazil's visitors arrive and leave from the city's airports. Most of Brazil's main film and record companies are based in the city, alongside Globo and Manchete, the country's largest and most influential TV networks.

For information about Brazil's currency, see the Money section in the Facts for the Visitor chapter.

POPULATION & PEOPLE

Jammed into an area of almost 1200 sq km, Rio de Janeiro is one of the fastest growing and most crowded cities in Brazil. Its population of over 10 million inhabitants – six million in the city itself and four million in the surrounding areas – makes Rio the second largest city in Brazil. And the population density is one of the highest in the world.

Rio's population is a reflection of its past; a mix of Africans, Europeans and Indians who have intermarried freely since colonial times. Despite claims of racial tolerance in Brazil, Cariocas are very particular about skin colour, with a vocabulary to match. A *moreno* is a dark White, a *caboclo* is a European/Indian mix, whereas *cabo verdes* are straight-haired Blacks. And of course, the light-skinned Black is the famous *mulato*.

It's economics, though, that separates Rio's population, two-thirds of whom are Black. At least one in five Cariocas lives in a favela. The favelas close to the city cling to the hillsides, creating a highly visible class distinction.

The *zona sul* (south zone) of the city is home to one in six Cariocas. Copacabana, with its high population density of more than 4000 people per block, has been called a rich 'ghetto'. The apartments along the beachfront in Copacabana and Ipanema are some of the most expensive in the world.

Rio's Favela Dwellers

Favelas (shanty towns) are a highly visible aspect of Rio's urban life. At last count there were 661 favelas in the greater metropolitan area. Aside from ignoring them, governments over the years have done very little for favela dwellers. For years the solution was to raze the favelas and the hills they were built on and cart away the soil for landfill projects.

Tax receipts from favelas are minimal, but then so is the service they get from the government. There are no paved roads, no running water and no health or education services provided.

Favela dwellers are left to do it themselves. Most have a well-organised social structure, including schools, churches and medical centres. And the number of parabolic antennae is increasing daily.

Government law and order has for many years stopped at the entrance to the favela. The first law of the favela is to see nothing, hear nothing, ask no questions and keep your mouth shut.

Drug traffickers gain a reputation as benevolent figures within the favela, helping out with donations for community projects and money for samba schools. Theirs is a violent and often short life. Most of the drug kings are barely out of their teens. Heavily armed, they battle with rival gangs for control of the favela's *boca* (the point where drugs, marijuana and cocaine are sold and literally mean 'mouth'). It's estimated that 1300 kilos of cocaine passes through the favelas each week.

In the past few years, the lawlessness has gotten out of hand. The gang of drug traffickers known as the *Command Vermelho* (Red Command) has been at war with the police. Favela dwellers traditionally fear the police because they tend to shoot first and ask questions later. They may kill some criminals, but they kill innocent victims as well. Things got so bad that in November 1994, federal troops were called in to 'cleanout' the favelas. Drug traffickers took the opportunity to take a holiday away from the city and the price of drugs went up. Most favela-dwellers believe that when the army leave the favelas, things will get back to the way they were. Many are hoping the new favela-bairro project will be the start of something better.

If you don't want to spoil your postcard view of Rio, you need never visit a favela. But if you're interested in how one fifth of the city's population lives, take a favela tour – it really is the other side of Rio (see the Getting Around chapter). English urbanist John Turner describes favelas as: "...a group of live cells growing in a disorderly way – not a cancer – but a sign of life". ■

JOHN MAIER, JR.

JOHN MAIER, JR.

The faces of Rio

GUY MOBERLY

JOHN MAIER, JR.

The faces of Rio

Cariocas

Known throughout Brazil as pleasure-seeking hedonists (especially by the hard-working Paulistas from São Paulo), Cariocas have a lust for life and love of romance. Like New Yorkers, they love their city and wouldn't dream of living anywhere else. Theirs is the Cidade Maravilhosa.

Cariocas often describe themselves as having a bit of the *moleque* and *malandro* in them. Both are mythical characters in Rio folklore. The moleque is the swift-footed street urchin; a happy-go-lucky type who's always grinning. The malandro is the fixer, the good-natured troublemaker who lives from day-to-day, trying to avoid working. When he does work, it is in bursts of frenzied activity followed by long periods of idleness. The malandro parties and fights with equal enthusiasm. His ideal life is days filled with football and nights filled with samba, all accompanied by *chopp* (draught beer) and mulatas.

To the first-time visitor to the city, the Carioca lifestyle may come as a shock. There are a couple of aspects to bear in mind. The first is that Rio is the most informal city in the world; dress is light, colourful and casual. In the zona sul, Cariocas will walk around wearing their bathing suits without a second thought.

The next thing to remember is that Cariocas are not known for punctuality. In fact, many argue they have no sense of time whatsoever. In a city with so many distractions, the Carioca will always choose the most pleasurable option. If they do decide to turn up, they are invariably an hour or two late. If you are invited to a party, make sure you turn up late too, or you'll embarass your hosts. By the way, Cariocas would never risk offense by refusing an invitation. They believe it's much easier to invent a creative excuse later on.

Cariocas also consider body contact an essential part of the communication process. On greeting, it's customary for men to kiss women on both cheeks, starting with their right cheek. Women also kiss women, but men do not kiss men. A handshake with a few pats on the back is the way to go. Cariocas like to stand close and look you in the eye while conversing. They also frequently touch you on the arm. This is perfectly normal, so don't think that this closeness signifies any hidden intentions – then again, you never know with Cariocas!

Listen and watch their expressive way of communicating; go to a football game and watch the intensity and variety of emotions, both on the field and in the stands; hang out on the beach; experience the bacchanal of Carnaval and attempt to dance the samba, and you may begin to understand what it is to be a Carioca. ■

ARTS

Music

Rio is synonymous with samba and bossa nova. Samba is the music of the masses. It is the music of the corner bars, the favelas, the street. It is the music of Carnaval. Bossa nova celebrates the beauty of the city and the Carioca lifestyle. It is the music of the middle class, of intimate cocktail bars and nightclubs with glittering views of the Cidade Maravilhosa.

Rio is also home to a large jazz fraternity, with clubs like Mistura Fina, Jazzmania and People showcasing international stars and local favorites. Rio also hosts jazz and rock festivals each year.

Samba *Tudo dá samba*: everything makes for a samba. The most popular Brazilian rhythm, samba was first performed at the Rio Carnaval in 1917, though its origins go back much further.

It is intimately linked with African rhythms; notably the Angolan tam-tam, which provided the basis for its music and distinctive dance steps. It caught on quickly after the advent of radio and records and has since become a national symbol. It is the music of the masses.

The 1930s is known as the Golden Age of Samba. By then, samba canção had also evolved, as had *choro*, a romantic, intimate music with a ukulele or guitar as its main instrument, playing off against a recorder or flute.

The most famous Brazilian singer of this period, perhaps of all time, is Carmen Miranda. A star of many Hollywood musicals of the period, she was known for her fiery, Latin temperament and her 'fruity' costumes. She has since become a cult figure among Rio's gay community, and Carnaval in Rio sees many of them impersonating her.

Samba keeps developing. In recent years, *pagode* has been a popular form, and samba funk is becoming popular, with many *funkeiros* joining the newer samba schools.

Bossa Nova In the '50s came bossa nova, and the democratic nature of Brazilian music was altered. Bossa nova was new, modern and intellectual. It also became an international hit. The middle class stopped listening to the old interpretations of samba and other regional music like the *forró* of the Northeast.

Bossa nova was more than a musical style or movement. It initiated a new style of playing instruments and singing. The more operatic, florid style of singing was replaced by a quieter, more relaxed sound. Its founders, Antônio Carlos (Tom) Jobim, João Gilberto and lyricist/poet Vinicius Moraes slowed down and played around with the basic samba rythm to create bossa nova's intimate, harmonic style. It was a big international success, and was recorded by Frank Sinatra and saxophonist Stan Getz, among others.

Great bossa nova singers include Gal Costa and Beth Carvalho, but Elis Regina is the eternal queen. Known to her public as *furacão* (the hurricane), she sang with intense emotion. Her death by accidental overdose in 1982, at the peak of her career, was a national tragedy.

Bossa nova was associated with the rising middle class of urban, university-educated Brazil. It was a musical response to other modernist movements of the '50s and '60s such as the Cinema Novo, the Brazilian Modern architecture of Oscar Niemeyer et al, and other aspects of the cultural life of the nation during the optimistic presidency of Juscelino Kubitschek from 1956 to 1960.

Tropicalismo At the end of the '60s the movement known as tropicalismo burst onto the scene. Tropicalismo provoked a kind of general amnesty for all the forgotten musical traditions of the past. The leading figures – Gilberto Gil, Caetano Veloso, Rita Lee, Macalé, Maria Betânia, Gal Costa – said that all musical styles were important and relevant. All the styles and traditions in Brazilian music could be freely mixed. This kind of open thinking led to innovations like the introduction of the electric guitar and the sound of electric samba.

Música Popular Brasileira Paralleling these musical movements are several incredibly popular musicians who are hard to categorise: they are simply known as exponents of MPB – Música Popular Brasileira (Popular Brazilian Music).

Chico Buarque de Holanda, who mixes traditional samba with a modern, universal flavour, is immensely popular, as is Paulinho da Viola, a master *sambista* who also bridges the gap between traditional samba and pop music. Jorge Bem comes from a particular Black musical tradition of the Rio suburbs, but plays an original pop samba without losing its characteristic Black rhythms. Another example is Luis Melodia, who combines the samba rhythms of the Rio hills with more modern forms from the '70s and '80s, always with beautiful melody.

Milton Nascimento was elected by readers of *Down-Beat* magazine as the number one exponent of World music. He has long been famous in Brazil for his fine voice, stirring anthems and ballads.

Brazilian Rock Derived more from English than American rock, this is the least Brazilian of all the Brazilian music. It's all the rage with the youngsters. Groups like Titãs, Kid Abelha, Legião Urbana, Capital Inicial and Plebe Rude are all worth a listen if you like rock music. Heavy metal bands like Sepultura and Ratos do Porão have huge followings. Brazilian rap music is popular, with groups like MRN (Movimento e Ritmo Negro) and Racionais MC with their hard-edged lyrics about life in the favelas.

Cazuza was a Carioca rock singer from the zona sul who died of AIDS in 1990. Openly bisexual, he sang about the hypocritical elements of Brazilian society. After finding out he had AIDS in 1987, Cazuza kept performing. His last two albums are classics.

Recent Trends *Pagode*, a type of samba that has existed for some time, was recently picked up and promoted by the record producers. For some of the best of pagode, listen to Bezerra da Silva, who was popular in the favelas before ever recording. Pagode, samba, frevo and forró all have corresponding dances – perhaps a reflection of the African influence on Brazilian music and the Brazilian use of music as a celebration of communication.

Lambada is a rhythm with a sensual dance that has become another international success story. Originating in Belém, and influenced by various Caribbean rhythms like rumba, merengue and salsa, lambada became really popular in Porto Seguro, which today is considered its home. From there it spread to the cities of Brazil and eventually to Europe and the USA. It even inspired a couple of terrible Hollywood movies.

The most successful lambada artist is Beto Barbosa and her group Kaoma, made up of Brazilian, Argentine and French musicians. Other Brazilian musicians who have recorded some lambada tracks include Lulu Santos, Pepeu Gomes and Moraes Moreira, and even Caetano Veloso.

Also hugely popular is *sertanejo*, a kind of Brazilian country and western music. It has long been a favourite with truckdrivers and cowboys, but has only recently entered the mainstream of popular Brazilian music. Usually sung by male duets wearing cowboy hats, fringe jackets and large belt-buckles, sertanejo is characterised by its soaring harmonies and, of course, its lyrics about broken hearts, life on the road, etc. Popular exponents are: José Rico and Millionario, Chitãozinho and Xororó, and Leandro e Leonardo.

Axé, a samba-inspired, pop/rock/reggae/funk music from Salvador, has also become well-known thanks to the music of the flamboyant and sexy Daniela Mercury.

Theatre & Dance

The Teatro Municipal is the showcase of the higher performing arts, and is reserved for opera, ballet, and classical music. It's the home of the city's world-class ballet troupe and opera company. There are dozens of other theatres in Rio, and performances range from intermational hit musicals to plays with Brazilian themes.

Cinema

Rio has been the home of Brazilian cinema since the turn of the century, when it was, appropriately, the city itself which starred in the first film made in the country – a slow pan of Baía de Guanabara. From 1942 until 1962, Rio was the home of Atlântida Productions, which churned out musicals, comedies and romances. Rio starred again in Marcel Camus' 1959 film, *Black Orpheus*, with its wonderful bossa nova soundtrack. The realism of Cinema Novo and the films of Glauber Rocha received international acclaim, and in 1980 Hector Babenco's *Pixote*, the tale of a street kid in Rio, won the Golden Palm award at Cannes.

In recent years, filmmaking in Brazil has taken a backseat to the production of *telenovelas*, soap operas that are watched religiously by all Brazilians and in many other countries. All the big money is there, so the best scriptwriters, directors and actors all work in the genre. Most of the high-quality novelas are made at the Rio studios of Rede Globo.

Fine Arts

Rio has always inspired landscape painters, which is easy to understand. The French artists Jean-Baptiste Debret and Nicholas Taunay made good use of the exuberant landscape around the city. They arrived with a French artistic mission to the city in 1816, and taught in the Academía de Belas Artes, which organised classes, expositions and art awards. The influence of the French neoclassicists remained strong until the turn of the century, when the Impressionists in France began to influence Brazilian artists like Eliseu d'Angelo Visconti.

Tom Jobim – King of Bossa Nova

Antonio Carlos Jobim, or Tom Jobim as he was known, was Brazil's greatest composer. When he died from a blood clot in the heart in New York in December 1984, aged 67, he had already written more than 300 songs in a career spanning five decades.

Tom Jobim was born in the northern Rio suburb of Tijuca, but it's with Ipanema that he'll be eternally associated. Together with poet/lyricist Vinicius de Morais, he wrote the famous bossa nova tune that put the suburb/bairro on the map – *The Garota de Ipanema (The Girl from Ipanema)*. Together with guitarist João Gilberto, Tom played Chega da Saudade and defined a style that came to be known world-wide as bossa nova.

A classically-trained pianist, Jobim paid his dues in the clubs of the zona sul, joints with names like the Mocambo, Acapulco and Vogue, playing everything from tango and bolero to foxtrot while smoking four packs a day. He also got work doing arrangements for the popular vocalists for the day. Tom enjoyed his infamous status as one of the best session men in Ipanema. Later when he came to play in front of 30,000 people at a stadium festival, he expressed horror. He preferred the smaller, intimate venues.

Within two years, from 1956 to 1958, Tom became famous. He teamed up with Vinícius de Morais, in what was to become a fruitful composing partnership, to write *Orfeu da Conceição*, and he and João Gilbert backed Elisete Cardoso on *Chega de Saudade*. Bossa nova was born, and it charmed the world.

Frank Sinatra invited him to New York to record. Tom took the call while he was having a chopp in Bar Veloso (today it's known as Garota de Ipanema). But in New York, they wouldn't let him play piano, his usual instrument. In the eyes of the Americans, a Latin lover had to play a guitar! On Tom's death, Sinatra said, "The world has lost one of its most talented musicians, and I have lost a marvellous friend".

During his life, Tom had seven, million-selling records: *Garota de Ipanema* with 4.2 million copies sold, *Meditação*, *Wave*, *Corcovado*, *Desafinado*, *Insensatez* and *Samba de uma Nota Só*.

It's often said that Tom and his music were inspired by cool jazz and American bebop, but this is not true. He preferred the standards of the Glenn Miller Orchestra to the experimentations of Charlie Parker. According to Tom, his major influences were Debussy, Villa-Lobos, Stravinsky and Chopin.

Tom Jobim's smooth and innovative sound can be heard at jazz concerts and in bars, restaurants, supermarkets and elevators all over the world. He was a specialist at what he dedicated his life to – seducing and fascinating his audience with excellent popular music. ■

Modern art in Rio gained a home in 1948 with the founding of the Museu de Arte Moderna. It has a permanent exhibition of works by Brazilian artists, including Cândido Portinari, the most famous Brazilian artist.

Architecture

The city is a mix of architectural styles from the 17th, 18th, 19th and 20th centuries, as any visitor will quickly notice from a stroll downtown. From the colonial buildings around Praça 15 de Novembro to the religious baroque of the Convento de Santo Antônio and Mosteiro de São Bento through to the French Neo-Classical style of the Museu Nacional de Belas Artes and the Teatro Municipal and the modernism of the Catedral Metropolitana and the Museu de Arte Moderna, Rio has it all.

RELIGION

Officially, Brazil is Catholic, claiming the largest Catholic population of any country in the world. However, Brazil is also noted for the diversity and syncretism (blending) of its many sects and religions, which offer great flexibility to their followers.

Historically, the principal religious influences have been Indian animism, Catholicism and African cults brought by the Blacks during the period of slavery. The slaves were prohibited from practising their religions by the colonists in the same way that they were kept from other elements of their culture, such as music and dance, for fear that it would reinforce their group identity. Religious persecution led to religious syncretism. To avoid persecution the slaves gave Catholic names and figures to all their African gods. This was generally done by finding the similarities between the Catholic images and the *orixás* (gods). Thus, the slaves worshipped their own gods behind the representations of the Catholic saints.

Under the influence of liberalism in the 19th century, Brazilians wrote into their constitution the freedom to worship all religions. But the African cults continued to suffer persecution by the White elites for many years. The spectrum of Brazilian religious life was gradually broadened by the addition of Indian animism to Afro-Catholic syncretism, and by the increasing fascination of Whites with the spiritualism of Kardecism, introduced by French spiritual master Allan Kardec in the 19th century. Kardec's teachings incorporated some Eastern

JOHN MAIER, JR.

Cristo Redentor on the summit of Corcovado

religious ideas into a European framework, emphasising spiritism associated with parlour seances, multiple reincarnations and speaking to the dead. Kardecism is now followed by large numbers of Brazilians.

Today Catholicism retains its status as the official religion, but it is declining in popularity. Throughout Brazil, churches are closing or falling into disrepair for lack of funds or priests, and attendance at services is dwindling to attendance at the basics: baptism, marriage, and burial. The largest numbers of converts are being attracted to Afro-Brazilian cults, and spiritist or mystic sects. Nowadays, the intense religious fervour of Brazilians extends across gradations and subdivisions of

Afro-Brazilian Cults

African cults were brought to Brazil by Black slaves in the 16th to 19th centuries. In Rio, followers of Afro-Brazilian cults still turn out in huge numbers to attend a series of festivals around New Year.

These cults do not follow the ideas of the major European or Asian religions; nor do they use doctrines to define good and evil. One of the greatest shocks to Europeans in their first contact with African images and rituals was the cult of Exú. This entity was represented by combined human and animal images, complete with an erect penis. Europeans identified Exú as the devil, but for Africans Exú represents the transition between the material and spiritual worlds and acts as a messenger between the gods and human beings. For example, money, love, and protection against thieves all come under the watchful eye of Exú.

Macumba

This is the most orthodox of the cults brought from Africa by the Nago, Yoruba, and Jeje peoples.

Rituals are practised in a *casa-de-santo* or *terreiro* directed by a *pai* or *mãe de santo* (literally, father or mother of the saint), the priest or priestess. This is where the initiation of novices takes place, as well as consultations and rituals. Ceremonies are conducted in the Yoruba tongue. If you attend a Macumba ceremony, it's best to go as the invited guest of a knowledgeable friend or commercial guide.

Each person's orixá (see below) is identified after a pai or mãe de santo makes successive throws with a handful of *búzios* (shells). The position of the shells is used to interpret your luck, your future, and your past relation with the gods.

numerous sects: from purist cults to groups that worship Catholic saints, African deities and the Cabóclos of the Indian cults simultaneously.

LANGUAGE

When they settled Brazil in the 16th century, the Portuguese encountered the diverse languages of the Indians. These, together with the various idioms and dialects spoken by the Africans brought in as slaves, extensively changed the Portuguese spoken by the early settlers. Along with Portuguese, Tupi-Guaraní, an Indian language which was written down and simplified by the

Orixás According to Macumba, each person has an orixá which attends from birth and provides protection throughout life. Like the gods in Greek mythology, each orixá has a personality and history. Although orixás are divided into male and female types, some can switch sexes. One example is Logunedé, son of two male gods, Ogun and Oxoss. Another example is Oxumaré, who is male for six months of the year and female the other months.

To keep themselves strong and healthy, followers of Macumba give food to their orixá. Each orixá has particular preferences. In the ritual, Exú is given food first because he is the messenger. He likes *cachaça* and other alcoholic drinks, cigarettes and cigars, strong perfumes and meats. To please Iemanjá, the goddess/queen of the sea, one should give perfumes, white and blue flowers, rice and fried fish.

Each orixá is worshipped at a particular time and place. Oxósse, god of the forests, should be revered in a forest or park, but Xangô, god of stone and justice, receives his offerings in rocky places.

Umbanda

Umbanda, or white magic, is a mixture of Macumba and spiritism. It traces its origins from various sources, but in its present form it is a religion native to Brazil. The African influence is more Angolan/Bantu. The ceremony, conducted in Portuguese, incorporates figures from all the Brazilian races: *preto velho*, the old Black slave, *o caboclo* and other Amerindian deities, *o guerreiro*, the White warrior, etc. Umbanda is less organised than Macumba and each pai or mãe de santo modifies the religion.

Quimbanda is the evil counterpart to Umbanda. It involves lots of blood, animal sacrifice and nasty deeds. The practice of Quimbanda is illegal. ∎

Jesuits, became widely used and understood. It was spoken by the general public until the middle of the 18th century, but its usage diminished with the great number of Portuguese gold-rush immigrants and a royal proclamation in 1757 prohibiting its use. With the expulsion of the Jesuits in 1759, Portuguese was well and truly established as the national language.

Still, many words remain from the Indian and African languages. From Tupi-Guaraní come lots of place names (eg Guanabara, Carioca, Tijuca and Niterói), animal names (eg *piranha, capivara* and *urubu*) and plant names (eg *mandioca, abacaxí, caju* and *jacarandá*). Words from the African dialects, mainly those from Nigeria and Angola, are used in Afro-Brazilian religious ceremonies (eg Orixá, Exú and Iansã), cooking (eg *vatapá, acarajé* and *abará*) and general conversation (eg samba, moleque and mocambo).

Within Brazil, accents, dialects and slang *(gíria)* vary regionally. For example, Cariocas insert the 'sh' sound in place of 's'.

Portuguese is similar to Spanish on paper, but sounds completely different. You will do quite well if you speak Spanish in Brazil, although in general, Brazilians will understand what you say, but you won't get much of what they say. So don't think studying Portuguese is a waste of time. Listen to language tapes. Develop an ear for Portuguese – it's a beautiful-sounding language.

Unfortunately, most Cariocas speak little or no English. This is changing, however, as English is now taught in schools. All the same, don't count on finding an English speaker outside of the tourist hotels and restaurants. The more Portuguese you speak, the more you will derive from your trip, so take time to learn some of the language.

Most phrasebooks are not very helpful; their vocabulary is often dated and contains the Portuguese spoken in Portugal, not Brazil. Notable exceptions are Lonely Planet's *Brazilian Phrasebook*, and a Berlitz phrasebook for travel in Brazil. Make sure any English-Portuguese dictionary you use is a Brazilian Portuguese one.

If you're more intent on learning the language, try the US Foreign Service Institute (FSI) tape series. It comes in two volumes, and the total cost is US$245. For fluent Spanish speakers, FSI also has: *Portuguese – from Spanish to Portuguese*. This one costs US$20. To get hold of these, write to or call the National Audiovisual Centre (tel) (301) 763-1896), Information Services PF, 8700 Edgeworth Drive, Capitol Heights, Maryland, USA, 20743-3701.

In Australia, most foreign language and travel bookstores stock a range of material, from the basic travel pack with a phrasebook and two tapes for A$35, to a condensed version of the FSI tapes. Twelve 90-minute tapes cost A$200. The Living Language course is inbetween, with phrases, vocabulary, grammar and conversation. The manual and CD cost A$50.

Combine these with a few Brazilian samba tapes and some Jorge Amado novels and you're ready to begin the next level of instruction, on the streets of Brazil. If that doesn't suffice, it's easy to arrange tutorial instruction at the IBEU (Instituto Brazil Estados Unidos) in Rio.

ANDREW DRAFFEN

ANDREW DRAFFEN

ANDREW DRAFFEN

Rio's colourful billboards

Useful Words & Phrases

Brazilian Portugese, like Spanish, has masculine and feminine forms. This means words will have different endings, depending on their gender. These endings appear separated by a slash, the masculine form first (*o/a*).

Greetings & Civilities

Hello.	*Oi.*
Goodbye.	*Tchau.*
Good morning.	*Bom dia.*
Good afternoon/evening.	*Boa tarde/noite.*
Please.	*Por favor.*
Thank you (very much).	*(Muito) obrigado.* (males)
	(Muita) obrigada.
	(females)
Yes.	*Sim.*
No.	*Não.*
Maybe.	*Talvez.*
Excuse me.	*Com licença.*
I am sorry.	*Desculpe (me perdoe).*
	(lit: forgive me)
How are you?	*Como vai você?/Tudo bem?*
I'm fine thanks.	*Vou bem, obrigado/a.*
	Tudo bem, obrigado/a.

Language Difficulties

Please write it down.
  Escreva por favor.
Please show me (on the map).
  Por favor, me mostre (no mapa).
I (don't) understand.
  Eu (não) entendo.
I (don't) speak Portuguese.
  Eu (não) falo português.
Do you speak English?
  Você fala inglês?
Does anyone speak English?
  Alguem fala inglês?
How do you say ... in Portuguese?
  Como você fala ... em português?

Paperwork

I have a visa/permit.
  Eu tenho um visto/uma licença.

passport	*passaporte*
surname	*sobrenome*

given name	*nome*
date of birth	*data de nascimento*
place of birth	*local de nascimento*
nationality	*nacionalidade*
male/female	*masculino/feminino*

Small Talk

What is your name?
 Qual é seu nome?
My name is ...
 Meu nome é ...
I'm a tourist/student.
 Eu sou um turista/estudante.
Where/What country are you from?
 Aonde/ Da onde voce é?
I am from ...
 Eu sou ...
How old are you?
 Quantos anos voce tem?
I am ... years old
 Eu tenho ... anos.
Are you married?
 Você é casado/a?
Do you like ...?
 Você gosta de ...?
I (don't) like ...
 Eu (não) gosta de ...
I like it very much.
 Eu gosta muito.
Just a minute.
 Só um minuto.
May I?
 Posso?
It's all right/No problem.
 Está tudo bem/ não há problema.

Getting Around

I want to go to ...
 Eu quero ir para ...
I want to book a seat for ...
 Eu quero reservar um assento para ...

What time does ... leave/arrive?	*A que horas ... sai/chega?*
Where does the ... leave from?	*Da onde o/a ... sai?*
bus	*onibus*
tram	*bonde*
train	*trem*

boat	*barco*
ferry	*ferry* (sometimes called *balsa*)
aeroplane	*avião*

The train is ...	*O trem está ...*
delayed	*atrasado*
cancelled	*cancelado*
on time	*na hora*
early	*adiantado*

How long does the trip take?
Quanto tempo a viagem demora?
Do I need to change?
Eu precisa trocar?
You must change trains/platform
Você precisa trocar de trem/plataforma.

one-way (ticket)	*passagem de ida*
return (ticket)	*passagem de volta*
left luggage locker	*guarda volumes*
station	*estação*
ticket	*passagem*
ticket office	*bilheteria*
timetable	*horário*

I would like to hire a ...	*Eu gostaria de alugar um/uma ...*
bicycle	*bicicleta*
motorcycle	*moto*

JOHN MAIER, JR.

Men playing chess in Copacabana

car	*carro*
guide	*guia*
horse	*cavalo*

Directions

How do I get to ...?
  Como eu chego a ...?
Where is ...?
  Aonde é ...?
Is it near/far?
  É perto/longe?

What ... is this?	*O que é ... isto?*
street/road	*rua/estrada*
house number	*numero da casa*
suburb	*bairro*
town	*cidade*

Go straight ahead.	*Vá em frente.*
Turn left.	*Vire a esquerda.*
Turn right.	*Vire a direita.*
at the traffic lights	*no farol*
at the next corner	*na próxima esquina*
up/down	*acima/abaixo*
behind/opposite	*atrás/em frente*
here/there	*aqui/lá*
east	*leste*
west	*oeste*
north	*norte*
south	*sul*

Accommodation

I'm looking for the ...	*Eu estou procurando o/a ...*
youth hostel	*albergue da juventude*
camping ground	*camping*
hotel	*hotel*
guesthouse	*pousada*
manager/owner	*gerente/dono*

What is the address?
  Qual é o endereço?

Do you have a ...	*Você tem um/a ...*
available?	*para alugar?*
bed	*cama*
cheap room	*quarto barato*
single room	*quarto de solteiro*
double room	*quarto de casado*
room with two beds	*quarto com duas camas*

for one/two nights
para uma/duas noites
How much is it per night/per person?
Quanto é por noite/por pessoa?
Is service/breakfast included?
O serviço/café de manha está incluído?
Can I see the room?
Posso ver o quarto?

It is very ...	*É muito ...*
dirty	*sujo*
noisy	*barulhento*
expensive	*caro*

Do you have (a) ...?	*Você tem (um/uma) ...?*
clean sheet	*lençol limpo*
hot water	*água quente*
key	*chave*
shower	*chuveiro*

Where is the toilet?
Aonde é o banheiro?
I am/We are leaving now.
Eu estou/Nós estamos saindo agora.

Around Town

Where is the/a ...?	*Aonde é o/a ...?*
bank/exchange office	*banco/casa de câmbio*
city centre	*centro da cidade*
embassy	*embaixada*
hospital	*hospital*
market	*mercado/feira*
post office	*correio*
public toilet	*banheiro público*
restaurant	*restaurante*
telephone centre	*telefônica*
tourist information office	*posto de informações turísticas*

I want to make a telephone call.
Eu quero fazer uma ligação.

I'd like to change some ...	*Eu gostaria de trocar um pouco de ...*
money	*dinheiro*
travellers' cheques	*cheques de viagem*

beach	*praia*
bridge	*ponte*
cathedral	*catedral*

church	*igreja*
fort	*forte*
island	*ilha*
lake	*lago*
main square	*praça principal*
old city	*cidade velha*
palace	*palácio*
ruins	*ruínas*
sea	*mar*
square	*praça*
tower	*torre*

Useful Signs

CAMPING	CAMPING GROUND
ENTRADA	ENTRANCE
SAIDA	EXIT
CHEIO	FULL
ABERTO	OPEN
FECHADO	CLOSED
MULHERES	LADIES
HOMENS	GENTS
POUSADA	GUESTHOUSE
HOTEL	HOTEL
ALBERGUE DA JUVENTUDE	YOUTH HOSTEL
QUARTOS PARA ALUGAR	ROOMS AVAILABLE
INFORMAÇÃO	INFORMATION
POLÌCIA	POLICE
DELEGACIA	POLICE STATION
PROIBIDO	PROHIBITED
BANHEIROS	TOILETS
ESTAÇÃO DE TREM	RAILWAY STATION

Food

breakfast	*café da manhá*
lunch	*almoço*
dinner	*jantar*
set menu	*refeição*
food stall	*barraca de comida*
grocery store	*mercearia*
delicatessen	*confeitaria*
market	*feira*
restaurant	*restaurante*

I am hungry/thirsty.
  Eu estou com fome/sede.
I would like the set lunch please.
  Eu gostaria do prato feito por favor.

Is service included in the bill?
O serviço esta incluído na conta?
I am a vegetarian.
Eu sou vegetariano/a.
I would like some.
Eu gostaria de algum/a.
Another ... please.
Outro/a ... por favor.
I don't eat ...
Eu não como ...

beer	*cerveja*
bread	*pão*
chicken	*frango*
coffee	*café*
eggs	*ovos*
fish	*peixe*
food	*comida*
fruit	*frutas*
meat	*carne*
milk	*leite*
mineral water	*água mineral*
pepper	*pimenta*
pork	*porco*
salt	*sal*
soup	*sopa*
sugar	*açucar*
tea	*chá*
vegetables	*verduras*
wine	*vinho*

Shopping
How much does it cost?
Quanto custa?
I would like to buy it.
Eu gostaria de comprar.
It's too expensive for me.
É muito caro para mim.
Can I look at it?
Posso ver?
I'm just looking.
Só estou olhando.

I'm looking for ...	*Estou procurando ...*
a chemist	*uma farmácia*
clothing	*roupas*
souvenirs	*lembanças*

JOHN MAIER, JR.

Taking time to watch the temperature

Do you take travellers' cheques/credit cards?
Você aceita cheques de viagem/cartões de crédito?
Do you have another colour/size?
Você tem outra cor/tamanho?

big/bigger	*grande/maior*
small/smaller	*pequeno/menor*
more/less	*mais/menos*
cheap/cheaper	*barato/mais barato*

Times & Dates
What time is it?
Que horas são?

Facts about Rio de Janeiro

It's ...	*São ...*
1.15	*uma e quinze*
1.30	*uma e meia*
1.45	*uma e quarenta e cinco*

o'clock	*horas*
in the morning	*da manhã*
in the evening	*da noite*
When?	*Quando?*
yesterday	*ontem*
today	*hoje*
tonight	*hoje de noite*
tomorrow	*amanhã*
the day after tomorrow	*depois de amanhã*
morning	*a manhã*
afternoon	*a tarde*
night	*a noite*
all day	*todos o dia*
every day	*todos os dias*

Sunday	*domingo*
Monday	*segunda-feira*
Tuesday	*terça-feira*
Wednesday	*quarta-feira*
Thursday	*quinta-feira*
Friday	*sexta-feira*
Saturday	*sábado*

January	*Janeiro*
February	*Fevereiro*
March	*Março*
April	*Abril*
May	*Maio*
June	*Junho*
July	*Julho*
August	*Agosto*
September	*Setembro*
October	*Outubro*
November	*Novembro*
December	*Dezembro*

Numbers

0	*zero*
1	*um/uma*
2	*dois/duas*
3	*três*
4	*quatro*
5	*cinco*

6	*seis* (when quoting phone or house numbers, Brazilians often say *meia* instead)
7	*sete*
8	*oito*
9	*nove*
10	*dez*
11	*onze*
12	*doze*
13	*treze*
14	*catorze*
15	*quinze*
16	*dezesseis*
17	*dezessete*
18	*dezoito*
19	*dezenove*
20	*vinte*
30	*trinta*
40	*quarenta*
50	*cinqüenta*
60	*sessenta*
70	*setenta*
80	*oitenta*
90	*noventa*
100	*cem*
1000	*mil*
one million	*um milhão*

first	*primeiro*
last	*último*

Health

I'm allergic to antibiotics/penicillin.
Eu sou alérgico a antibióticos/penicilina.

I'm ...	Eu sou ...
diabetic	*diabético*
epileptic	*epilético*
asthmatic	*asmático*

antiseptic	*antiséptico*
aspirin	*aspirina*
condoms	*camisinhas*
contraceptive	*contraceptivo*
diarrhoea	*diarréia*
medicine	*remédio*
nausea	*nausea*

| sunblock cream | *creme de proteção solar* |
| tampons | *absorventes internos* |

Emergencies

Help!	*Socorro!*
Go away!	*Va embora!*
Call a doctor!	*Chame o médico!*
Call the police!	*Chame a polícia!*

Slang

Brazilians pepper their language with strange oaths and odd expressions (literal translations in parentheses):

Hello.	*Oi.*
Everything OK?	*Tudo bem?*
Everything's OK.	*Tudo bom.*
That's great/Cool!	*Chocante!*
That's bad/Shit!	*Merda!*
Great/Cool/OK!	*'ta lógico/ 'ta ótimo/ ta legal*
It's crazy/You're crazy.	*'ta louco*
My God!	*Meu Deus*
Gosh!	*Nossa!* (Our Lady!)
Whoops!	*Opa!*
Wow!	*Oba!*
You said it!	*Falou!*
(curse word)	*Palavrão!*
Shooting the breeze.	*Batendo um papo.*
I'm mad at ...	*Eu estou chateado com ...*
Is there a way?	*Tem jeito?*
There's always a way.	*Sempre tem jeito.*

JOHN MAIER, JR.

Train surfers riding the rails

guy	*cara*
girl	*garota*
money	*grana*
bum	*bum-bum/bunda*
bald	*careca*
a fix/troublesome problem	*abacaxí*
a mess	*bagunça*
the famous Brazilian bikini	*fio dental* (dental floss)
marijuana	*fumo* (smoke)

Body Language

Brazilians accompany their oral communication with a rich body language, a sort of parallel dialogue. The thumbs up of *tudo bem* is used as a greeting, or to signify 'OK' or 'Thank you'. Never use the American OK sign with the thumb and forefinger forming a circle. It's a very rude gesture. The authoritative *não, não* finger-wagging is most intimidating when done right under a victim's nose, but it's not a threat. The sign of the *figa*, a thumb inserted between the first and second fingers of a clenched fist, is a symbol of good luck derived from an African sexual charm. It's more commonly used as jewellery than as a gesture.

To indicate *rápido!* (speed and haste), thumb and middle finger touch loosely while rapidly shaking the wrist. If you don't want something (*não quero*), slap the back of your hands as if ridding yourself of the entire affair.

Touching a finger to the outer corner of the eye means 'I'm wise to you'.

Facts for the Visitor

ORIENTATION

Rio is divided into a *zona norte* (north zone) and a *zona sul* (south zone) by the Serra da Carioca, steep mountains that are part of the Parque Nacional da Tijuca. These mountains descend to the edge of the city centre, where the zonas norte and sul meet. From Corcovado, one of these mountain peaks, there are views of both zones.

Rio is a tale of two cities. The upper and middle classes reside in the zona sul; the lower class, except for the favela dwellers, in the zona norte. Favelas (slums or shanty towns) cover steep hillsides on both sides of town – Rocinha, Brazil's largest favela with somewhere between 150,000 and 300,000 residents, is in Gávea, one of Rio's richest neighbourhoods. Most industry is in the zona norte, as is most of the pollution. The ocean beaches are in the zona sul.

Unless they work in the zona norte, residents of the zona sul rarely go to the other side of the city. The same holds true for travellers, unless they head north to the Maracanã football stadium, the Quinta da Boa Vista, with the national museum, or the international airport, which is on the Ilha do Governador.

MAPS

In the USA, Maplink (☎ (805) 965-4402), 25 E Mason St, Dept G, Santa Barbara, CA 93101, is an excellent and exhaustive source for maps of Brazil and just about anywhere else in the world. A similarly extensive selection of maps is available in the UK from Stanfords (☎ (071) 836-1321), 12-14 Long Acre, London WC2E 9LP.

Within Brazil, the maps used by most Brazilian and foreign travellers are produced by Quatro Rodas, which also publishes the essential *Guia Brasil*, an annually updated travel guide in Portuguese.

The Rio city maps provided in *Guia Brasil* help with orientation. Riotur also provides an excellent map of the city with detailed street layout.

TOURIST OFFICES

Local Tourist Offices

Riotur (☎ 297-7177; fax 531-1872) is the Rio city tourism agency. The main office is at Rua da Assembléia 10, 8th floor, Centro, but the special 'tourist room' is in Copacabana at Avenida Princesa Isabel 183. There, you'll find free brochures (in Portuguese and English), which include maps. It's open Monday to Saturday from 9 am to 6 pm.

You can also get the brochures at Riotur's information booths at the main *rodoviária* (bus terminal – open daily from 6 am to 11 pm); Pão de Açúcar (daily, from 8 am to 7 pm); the international airport at Galeão (daily, from 5 am to 11 pm); Cosme Velho at the Corcovado railway station (daily, from 7 am to 7 pm); the Instituto Brasileiro da Pâtrimonio Cultural at Avenida Rio Branco 44 (daily, from 10 am to 5 pm); and sometimes in your hotel.

If you are arriving in Rio by bus, the Riotur booth at the rodoviária can save you a lot of time by calling around town to find a vacant hotel and making a reservation. The staff only have lists of the mid-range to top-end hotels, but if you give them the phone number of a cheaper one they're happy to call it. Riotur also operates a tourist information hotline (☎ 541-7522). Call them from 9 am to 5 pm Monday to Friday with any questions. The receptionists speak English and more often than not they'll be able to help you.

TurisRio (☎ 531-1922; fax 531-2506) is the Rio state tourism agency. Its office is in the same building as Riotur's (metro stop Carioca), on the 7th floor. Embratur (☎ 273-2212; fax 273-9290) is Brazil's national tourism agency. The main office is in Brasília, but there's a branch at Rua Mariz e Barros 13 near Praça da Bandeira on the north side of town. For the average traveller, neither of these agencies is worth a special trip.

Tourist Offices Abroad

Brazilian embassies and consulates provide limited information about their country.

DOCUMENTS

Visas

At the time of writing, Brazilian visas were necessary for citizens of countries that required visas for visitors from Brazil. American, Canadian, French, Australian and NZ citizens needed visas, but UK citizens did not. Tourist visas are issued by Brazilian diplomatic offices and are valid for arrival in Brazil within 90 days of issue and then for a 90-day stay in Brazil. They are renewable in Brazil for an additional 90 days.

It should only take about three hours to issue a visa. You need a passport valid for at least six months, a single passport photograph (either B&W or colour) and either a return ticket or a statement from a travel agent, addressed to the Brazilian diplomatic office, stating that you have the required ticketing. If you only have a one-way ticket they may accept a document from a bank or similar organisation proving that you have sufficient funds to stay and buy a return ticket, but it's probably easier to get the necessary letter from a travel agent.

Visitors under 18 years of age must submit a notarised letter of authorisation from their parents or legal guardian.

Visa Extensions If you need to renew your visa for another three months, go to the Polícia Marítima building (☎ 203-2142, *ramal* (extension) 37) at Avenida Venezuela 2, Centro (near the far end of Avenida Rio Branco). It's open from 8 am to 4 pm for visa extensions. Bring a passport, money and airline ticket (if you have one). The fee is around US$12.

Tourist Card When you enter Brazil, you will be asked to fill out a tourist card, which has two parts. Immigration officials will keep one part, and the other one will be attached to your passport. When you leave Brazil, this will be detached from your passport by immigration officials. Make sure you don't lose your part of the card while travelling around or your departure could be delayed until officials have checked your story. For added security, make a photocopy of your section of the tourist card and keep this in a safe place, separate from your passport.

Driver's Licence & Permits To rent a car you must be at least 25 years old, and have a credit card and a valid driver's licence. You should also carry an International Driver's Permit or Inter-Americas licence. The rental car company won't ask for it, but cops will.

Other Documents By law you must carry a passport with you at all times, but many travellers opt to carry a photocopy (preferably certified). A credit card is handy, as is an International Youth Hostel card if you plan to use the *albergues de juventude* (youth hostels). The International Student Identity Card is practically useless.

It's convenient to have several extra passport photographs for any documents or visas you might acquire in Brazil. As a backup for emergencies, it's handy to have

ANDREW DRAFFEN

ANDREW DRAFFEN

Decorative pavements in Copacabana

photocopies of the following: your passport (including relevant visas), tourist card (provided when entering Brazil), travellers' cheque numbers, and airline tickets. (See also suggestions under Dangers & Annoyances in this chapter.)

EMBASSIES

Brazilian Embassies & Consulates Abroad

Brazilian embassies and consulates are maintained in the countries listed here. New Zealanders must apply to the Brazilian embassy in Australia for their visas; this can be done easily through a travel agent.

Australia
    19 Forster Crescent, Yarralumla, ACT 2600 (☎ (062) 732-372)
Canada
    255 Albert St, Suite 900, Ottawa, Ontario K1P-6A9 (☎ (613) 237 1090
France
    34 Cours Albert, 1er, 75008 Paris (☎ (1) 259-9250)
Germany
    Kurfürstendamm 11, 1 Stock, 1 Berlin 15 (☎ (30) 883-1208)
UK
    32 Green St, London W1Y 4AT (☎ (071) 499-0877)
USA
    630 Fifth Ave, Suite 2720, New York, NY 10111 (☎ (212) 687-0530); there are also consulates in Atlanta (☎ (404) 659-0660), Chicago (☎ (312) 372-2179), Houston (☎ (713) 961-3063), Los Angeles (☎ (213) 382-3133), Miami (☎ (305) 374-2263), and San Francisco (☎ (212) 981-8170)

Foreign Embassies & Consulates in Rio

The following countries have embassies or consulates in Rio de Janeiro:

Argentina
    Praia de Botafogo 228, 2nd floor, Botafogo (☎ 551-5198; fax 552-4191); open Monday to Friday, noon to 5 pm
Austria
    Avenida Atlântica 3804, Copacabana (☎ 227-0040; fax 227-1734); open Monday to Friday, 9 am to 12.30 pm
Belgium
    Rua do Ouvidor 60, room 803, Centro (☎ 252-2967; fax 232-8339); open Monday to Friday, 10 am to 1 pm
Bolivia
    Avenida Rui Barbosa 664, No 101, Botafogo (☎ 551-1796; fax 551-3047); open Monday to Friday, 8.30 am to 1 pm
Canada
    Rua Lauro Muller 116, 1104 Botafogo (☎ 275-2137; fax 541-3898); open Monday to Friday, 9 am to 1 pm
Chile
    Praia do Flamengo 344, 7th floor, Flamengo (☎ 552-5349); open Monday to Friday, 8.30 am to 12.30 pm
Colombia
    Praia do Flamengo 284, No 101, Flamengo (☎ 552-6248; fax 552-5449); open Monday to Friday, 9 am to 1 pm
Ecuador
    Avenida NS de Copacabana 788, 8th floor, Copacabana (☎ 235-6695; fax 255-2245); open Monday to Friday, 8.30 am to 1 pm

France
    Avenida Presidente Antônio Carlos 58, 8th floor, Centro
    (☎ 210-1272; fax 220-4779]; open Monday to Friday, 9 am
    to 12.30 pm
Germany
    Rua Presidente Carlos de Campos 417, Laranjeiras (☎ 553-
    6777; fax 553-0814); open Monday to Friday, 8.30 to 11.20
    am
Israel
    Avenida NS de Copacabana 680, Copacabana, (☎ 255-
    5432; fax 235-6048); open Monday to Friday, 9 am to 4 pm
Japan
    Praia do Flamengo 200, 10th floor, Flamengo (☎ 265-5252;
    fax 205-7135); open Monday to Friday 9 am to 5 pm
    (closed for lunch)
Netherlands
    Praia de Botafogo 242, 7th floor, Botafogo (☎ 552-9028; fax
    552-8294); open Monday to Friday, 9 am to noon
Paraguay
    Avenida NS de Copacabana 538, No 404, Copacabana
    (☎ 255-7572; fax 255-7532); open Monday to Friday, 9 am
    to 1 pm
Peru
    Avenida Rui Barbosa 314, 2nd floor, Botafogo (☎ 551-
    6296; fax 551-9796); open 9 am to 1 pm
South Africa
    Avenida Presidente Antonio Carlos 607, 3rd floor, Centro
    (☎ 533-0158; fax 533-0150); open Monday to Friday, 2 to
    4.30 pm
Sweden
    Praia do Flamengo 344, 9th floor, Flamengo (☎ 552-2422;
    fax 551-9091); open Monday to Friday, 9 am to noon
Switzerland
    Rua Candido Mendes 157, 11th floor, Glória (☎ 242-8035;
    fax 263-1523); open Monday to Friday, 9 am to noon
Uruguay
    Rua Arthur Bernardes 30, Catete (☎ 225-0089); open
    Monday to Friday, 9 am to 1 pm
UK
    Praia do Flamengo 284, 2nd floor, Flamengo (☎ 552-1422;
    fax 552-5796); open Monday to Thursday, 9 to 11.30 am
    and 1.30 to 3.30 pm (on Friday, open in the morning)
USA
    Avenida Presidente Wilson 147, Centro (☎ 292-7117; fax
    220-0439); open Monday to Friday, 8 am to 4.30 pm
Venezuela
    Praia de Botafogo 242, 5th floor, Botafogo (☎ 551-5398; fax
    551-5248); open Monday to Friday, 9 am to 1 pm

CUSTOMS

Travellers entering Brazil are allowed to bring in one
radio, tape player, typewriter, video and still camera.

Personal computers are allowed. Duty free goods to the value of US$250 are permitted.

At Rio airport, customs use the random check system. After collecting your luggage you pass a post with two buttons; if you have nothing to declare, you push the appropriate button. A green light means walk straight out; a red light means you've been selected for a baggage search.

MONEY

Since 1986 the name of the currency has changed five times, from cruzeiro to cruzado to cruzado novo and back to cruzeiro. Then it became the cruzeiro real and, in July 1994, the real.

At the moment, the monetary unit of Brazil is the real (pronounced HAY-ow); the plural is reais (pronounced HAY-ice). It's made up of 100 centavos. The frustratingly similar coins are 1, 5, 10, 25 and 50 centavos. There's also a one-real coin as well as a one-real note. Notes are different colours, so there's no mistaking them. As well as the green one-real note there's a blue/purple five, a red 10, a brown 50 and a blue 100.

Exchange Rates

There are currently three types of exchange rate operating in Brazil: official (also known as *comercial* or *câmbio livre*), turismo and *paralelo*.

Until recently, the official rate has always been much lower than the parallel rate. But thanks to a certain

JOHN MAIER, JR.

Collectors meet on Sunday in the Passeio Publico

amount of deregulation in an attempt to wipe out black market trading it's now possible to change cash dollars and travellers' cheques at banks using the turismo rate, which is only slightly less than the parallel rate. Credit cards now get billed at the turismo rate.

Since the introduction in mid-1994 of the Plano Real, a new economic plan to cut inflation, the difference between the official and parallel rates has been minimal anyway, although full parallel rates are usually available only at borders and in the larger cities like Rio and São Paulo.

Exchange rates are written up every day on the front page and in the business section of the major daily papers, *O Globo, Jornal do Brasil* and the *Folha de São Paulo*, and are announced on the evening TV news.

Approximate bank rates as at June 1995 were as follows:

USA	US$1	=	R$ 0.90
UK	UK£1	=	R$ 1.44
Australia	A$1	=	R$ 0.65
New Zealand	NZ$1	=	R$ 0.60
Canada	C$1	=	R$ 0.65
Germany	DM1	=	R$ 0.64
France	FFr1	=	R$ 0.18
Switzerland	SwFr1	=	R$ 0.78
Japan	Y100	=	R$ 1.07

Cash & Travellers' Cheques

US cash dollars are easier to trade and are worth a bit more on the parallel market, but travellers' cheques are an insurance against loss, and now that they can be exchanged at the turismo rate it's good value and good sense to use them. But since they can be hard to change sometimes, you might prefer to carry a Visa card. (See Credit Cards.)

American Express is the most recognised brand of travellers' cheques, but they charge 1% of the face value of the cheque (on top of the interest that your money makes while sitting in their banks), and sometimes, with all the non-accidental losses of cheques, they're a little squirrelly about giving your money back on the spot. Thomas Cook, Barclays and First National City Bank are also good. Get travellers' cheques in US dollars and carry some small denominations for convenience. Have some emergency US cash to use when the banks are closed.

Changing Money

Changing money in Rio is easy, especially if you have cash. Have a look at the exchange rates posted on the front page of *O Globo* or *Jornal do Brasil*. The exchange houses should give you the turismo rate for cash and a few points less for travellers' cheques.

In the centre of the city, there are several travel agencies/casas de câmbio on Avenida Rio Branco, a couple of blocks before and after the intersection with Avenida Presidente Vargas (be cautious carrying money in the city centre). The Casa Piano office at Avenida Rio Branco 88 is one of the best places to change. There's also an office in Ipanema at Visconde de Pirajá 365. Cambitur has several offices: Rua Visconde de Pirajá 414, Ipanema; Avenida NS de Copacabana 1093, Copacabana; and Avenida Rio Branco 31, Centro. Another is Exprinter at Avenida NS de Copacabana 371, Copacabana, and Avenida Rio Branco 128 and 57, Centro.

The major banks with currency exchange facilities include:

Banco do Brasil
Rua Senador dantas 105, 11th floor and Rua do Acre 15 in the Centro (☎ 276-4384) and Avenida NS de Copacabana 619/A, Copacabana (☎ 255-8992). They're open weekdays from 10 am to 4.30 pm
Banco do Boston
Avenida Rio Branco 110, Centro (☎ 291-6123)
Banco Mitsubishi Brasileiro
Avenida Presidente Vargas 642, Centro (☎ 203-1243)
Citibank
Rua da Assenbléia 100, Centro (☎ 276-3636)
Francês e Brasileiro
Avenida Rio Branco 193, Centro (☎ 292-0123)

At the international airport there is a Banco do Brasil open 24 hours a day; the two exchange houses Cambitur and Avipam are open daily from 6.30 am to 11 pm. Both change at the turismo rate. Porters and cleaners at the airport will also offer to change money. They don't change travellers' cheques, but change cash at the 'gringo rip-off' rate.

Don't change money on the streets, follow exchangers into unfamiliar areas, or give money or unsigned cheques up front.

Cabling Money

Cabling money is difficult, time-consuming and expensive. You must know the name and address of both the bank sending (record this and keep this with your documents) and the bank receiving your money. In Rio, Casa Piano on Avenida Rio Branco is the most experienced with overseas transactions. The Brazilian American Cultural Center (BACC), which has offices in the USA and Brazil, provides a special remittance service for members – for details and main address of BACC, refer to the Useful Organisations section in this chapter.

Credit Cards

International credit cards like Visa, American Express and MasterCard are accepted by many expensive hotels, restaurants and shops. But it's surprising how many don't accept them. Make sure you ask first if you plan to use one.

Visa is the most versatile credit card in Brazil, and using it for getting cash advances is becoming easier. International Visa card-holders can even use the Bradesco bank's automatic teller machines (ATMs). Banco do Brasil and Banco Econômico also do cash advances on Visa, and according to them, it won't be long before Visa card-holders will be able to use the 24-hour, ATM system that has distinctive red booths scattered around town.

American Express card-holders can purchase US dollar travellers' cheques from Amex offices in the large cities. MasterCard and Diners Club card-holders can pay for many goods and services with their card, but cash advances are difficult.

At present, you get billed at the turismo rate in reais. Sometimes the hotel/restaurant/store will try to add an extra charge for using the card. It's illegal to do this and you can make a complaint to the relevant credit card company.

New-style credit card coupons do not have carbon paper inserts and offer more protection against misuse. If you sign an old-style coupon, be sure to ask for the carbon inserts and destroy them after use.

Credit card emergency numbers are: American Express (☎ 552-7299), Diners Club (☎ 220-9090), MasterCard/Credicard (☎ 292-7172), Visa/Chasecard (☎ 532-1244), Visa/Nacional (☎ 292-5354)

American Express The American Express agent in Rio is Kontik-Franstur SA (☎ 235-1396). The address is Avenida Atlântica 2316-A, Copacabana CEP 20040, Copacabana, Rio de Janeiro, Brazil. They do a pretty good job of getting and holding onto mail. Beware of robbers when leaving their office. There's another office at Praia de Botafogo 228, block A, 5th floor, room 514, that's open weekdays from 9 am to 6 pm.

Costs

Because of wild fluctuations in the economy, it's difficult to make any solid predictions about how much you'll spend. Since the introduction of the real, inflation has fallen to less than 2% per month, and although this inflation rate is still well above the US level, the real has appreciated by about 15% against the US$ because of increased US$ inflow into Brazil. As a result, Brazil has become a somewhat expensive destination for foreign travellers.

If you're staying in hotels for US$10 a night, and eating in restaurants and/or drinking in bars every night, US$30 to US$40 a day would be a rough estimate. You should also bear in mind that during the holiday season (December to February) accommodation costs generally increase by around 25 to 30%, sometimes more in popular resorts.

Brazil is not among the kinder destinations for solo travellers. The cost of a single room in a hotel is not much less than for a double, and when you eat, you'll find most dishes in restaurants are priced for two people.

Rio is a city where you can have a good time spending only a little money and a great time if you spend a bit more. With US$100 each to spend every day, a couple could get a good hotel in Copacabana or Ipanema on or near the beach, eat out at fine restaurants for lunch and dinner, and still have some money left for souvenirs.

Tipping

Most services get tipped 10%, and as the people in these services make the minimum wage – which is not enough to live on – you can be sure they need the money. In restaurants the service charge will usually be included in the bill and is mandatory. If a waiter is friendly and helpful you can give more. Even when it is not included in the bill, it's still customary to leave a 10% tip. There are many places where tipping is not customary but is a welcome gesture. The local juice stands, bars, coffee corners, street and beach vendors are all tipped on occasion.

Parking assistants receive no wages and are dependent on tips, usually the equivalent of 50c to US$1. Gas station attendants, shoe shiners and barbers are also frequently tipped. Taxis are not usually tipped.

Bargaining

Bargaining for hotel rooms should become second nature. Before you agree to take a room, ask for a better price. *Tem desconto?* (Is there a discount?) and *Pode fazer um melhor preço?* (Can you make a better price?) are phrases to use. There's often a discount for paying *á vista* (cash) or for staying during the *baixa estação* or *época baixa* (low season) when hotels need guests to cover running costs. It's also possible to reduce the price if you state that you don't want a TV, private bath or air-con. If you're staying longer than a couple of days, ask for a discount. Once a discount has been quoted, make sure

JOHN MAIER, JR.

Beach vendors sell just about everything

it is noted on your bill at the same time – this avoids 'misunderstandings' at a later date. You should also bargain in markets and unmetered taxis.

WHEN TO GO

The big decision for travellers to Rio is whether to come for Carnaval, as if there should be any doubt! Carnaval sees Rio in full party mode, and travellers who want to make the most of it should get used to snatching a bit of sleep during the day and staying up all night. During Carnaval, the city is full of travellers and tourists, so prices go up and accomodation becomes scarce.

At other times, Rio is a bit calmer – though one could never describe it as a calm place – and it's easier for the visitor to concentrate on other attractions of the marvellous city: its beautiful scenery, world-famous beaches and the warm, happy-go-lucky Cariocas themselves.

WHAT TO BRING

Pack light. With its warm climate and informal dress standards, you don't need to bring many clothes to Rio. Unless you're planning an excursion into the mountains, where it gets cold in the evening, the only weather you need to contend with is heat and rain, and whatever you're lacking you can purchase while travelling.

You don't need more than a pair of shorts, trousers, a couple of T-shirts, a long-sleeved shirt, bathing suit, towel, underwear, walking shoes, thongs and some raingear. Quick-drying, light cotton clothes are most convenient. Suntan lotion and sun protection cream are readily available in Rio. Most other toiletries are also easy to get.

COMMUNICATIONS

Post

Postal services are pretty good in Brazil. Most mail seems to get through, and airmail letters to the USA and Europe usually arrive in a week or so. For Australia, allow two weeks. The cost, however, is ridiculously high for mail leaving Brazil, around US$1 for an international letter or postcard. Rates are raised very frequently, and are now among the highest in the world.

There are mail boxes on the street but it's a better idea to go to a post office. Most post offices (correios) are open 8 am to 6 pm Monday to Friday, and on Saturday until noon. The branch at the international airport is open 24 hours a day.

Any mail addressed to Posta Restante, Rio de Janeiro, Brazil, ends up at the post office at Rua Primeiro de Março 64, in the city. They hold mail for 30 days and are reasonably efficient. A reliable alternative for American Express customers is to have mail sent to one of its offices.

Telephone

International Calls Phoning abroad from Brazil is very expensive, and charges continue to be revised upwards at frequent intervals. To the USA and Canada, allow approximately US$2.50 a minute. Prices are 25% lower from 8 pm to 6 am daily and all day Sundays. To the UK and France the charge is US$3 a minute, and to Australia and New Zealand, US$4 a minute. There are no cheaper times to these last two countries.

International phone calls can be made from the following locations in Rio:

Aeroporto Santos Dumont
    6 am to 11 pm
Centro
    Praça Tiradentes 41, open 24 hours
Copacabana
    Avenida NS de Copacabana 540 (upstairs), open 24 hours
Ipanema
    Rua Visconde de Pirajá 111, 6 am to 11 pm
Rodoviária Novo Rio
    open 24 hours
Méier
    Dias da Cruz 182, 6.30 am to 11 pm

If you're calling direct from a private phone dial 00, then the country code number, then the area code, then the phone number. So to call New York, you dial 001-212-(phone number). For information on international calls dial 000333. Some of the country code numbers are: UK 44, USA 1, Australia 61, New Zealand 64, Canada 1, France 33, Argentina 54, Chile 56, Peru 51, Paraguay 595.

Embratel, the Brazilian telephone monopoly, now offers Home Country Direct Services for the following countries:

Australia (☎ 000-8061)
Canada (☎ 000-8014)
France (☎ 000-8033)
Germany (☎ 000-8049)

Israel (☎ 000-8097)
Italy (☎ 000-8039)
Japan (☎ 000-8081)
Netherlands (☎ 000-8031)
UK (☎ 000-8044)
USA (☎ 000-8010 for AT&T, ☎ 000-8012 for MCI and ☎ 000-8016 for Sprint)

International collect calls *(a cobrar)* can be made from any phone. To get the international operator dial 000111 or 107 and ask for the *telefonista internacional*.

JOHN MAIER, JR.

Public phone on Ipanema beach

Making International Collect Calls
If the telephone operator doesn't speak English, experiment with some of the following phrases:

I would like to make an international call to...
    Quero fazer uma ligação internacional para...
I would like to reverse the charges.
    Quero fazê-la a cobrar.
I am calling from a public (private) telephone in Rio de Janeiro.
    Estou falando dum telefone público (particular) no Rio de Janeiro.
My name is...
    Meu nôme é...
The area code is...
    O código é...
The number is...
    O número é...

National Long-Distance Calls National long-distance calls can also be made at the local phone company office, unless you're calling collect. All you need is the area code and phone number, and a few dollars. For calling collect within Brazil dial 9 – area code – phone number. A recorded message in Portuguese will ask you to say your name and where you're calling from, after the beep.

Local Calls Brazilian public phones are nicknamed *orelhões* (big ears). They use *fichas*, coin-like tokens, which can be bought at many newsstands, pharmacies, etc. They cost less than 5c, but it's a good idea to buy a few extra fichas as phones often consume them liberally.

On almost all phones in Brazil you wait for a dial tone and then deposit the ficha and dial your number. Each ficha is generally good for a couple of minutes, but the time can vary considerably. When your time is up, you will be disconnected without warning, so it's a good idea to deposit an extra ficha. To call the operator dial 100; for information call 102.

Phonecards, *cartão telefônico*, are now widely available. They cost US$1.20 and are good for around 20 local calls.

Fax, Telex & Telegram

Faxes can be sent from any large post office. Telexes can be sent from major post offices or by calling 135. To send a telegram, go to any post office or call 135 (national) or 000222 (international).

BOOKS

Guidebooks

There are several guidebooks to Rio. *Guia Rio* by Quatro Rodas has the most comprehensive list of restaurants, hotels, bars and activities. It's well worth buying if you understand Portuguese and are going to be in Rio a long time; it's sold at newsstands. However, it covers only the upper end of the price spectrum. *Rio – The Guide* by Christopher Pickard covers a lot of ground, has detailed descriptions of Rio's fine restaurants and is in English. You can find it in hotel souvenir shops.

If you're a student of colonial architecture and plan on seeing the remains of old Rio, the Riotur office at Assembléia sells a book in Portuguese entitled *Guia do Patrimônio Cultural Carioca Bens Tomados*, filled with detailed maps and descriptions of the city's historic buildings. Also in Portuguese is the renowned Michelin guide *Rio de Janeiro – Cidade e Estado*. Museum buffs may want to get hold of a copy of the *Guia Museus do Rio* by AGIR, in both Portuguese and English.

During Carnaval, *The Rio Carnaval Guide*, by Felipe Ferreira, in both Portuguese and English, is a detailed and often humorous read. Speaking of humour, you must buy a copy of Priscilla Ann Goslin's hilarious *How to be a Carioca – The Alternative Guide for the Tourist in Rio*. As well as containing a lot of laughs, her insights into the Carioca lifestyle are right on the mark.

History

Rio has a fascinating and fantastic history. As the centre of empire and government from 1763 until 1960, the city figures prominently in any book about Brazilian history. The most famous book on Brazil's colonial period is Gilberto Freyre's *The Masters & the Slaves: A Study in the Development of Brazilian Civilization* (University of California Press 1986). There's a new paperback edition from the same press, which is also publishing Freyre's other works, *The Mansions & the Shanties: The Making of Modern Brazil* (1986) and *Order & Progress: Brazil from Monarchy to Republic* (1986).

Emília Viotti da Costa has a collection of well-written essays in English which is one of the best treatments of 19th-century Brazil. *The Brazilian Empire: Myths & Histories* (University of Chicago Press, 1986) interweaves the ideological and economic components of Brazilian history, and the results are illuminating and suggestive.

Fiction

José de Alençar is one of Brazil's famous romantic-era writers. Many of his works are set in Rio. They include *Cinco Minutos* and *Senhora*, both published in 1875. Joaquim Manoel de Macedo was a great chronicler of the customs of his time. As well as romances such as *A Moreninha*, he wrote *Um Passeio pela Cidade do Rio de Janeiro*, published in 1863, and *Memórias da Rua do Ouvidor* in 1878.

Machado de Assis was a Carioca who used the city as the background for most of his works in the late 19th century. His understanding of human relations was both subtle and deeply cynical, as the terse titles of books like *Epitaph of a Small Winner* (Avon Bard 1977) and *Philosopher or Dog* (Avon Bard 1982) might suggest. He wrote five major novels; my favourite is *Dom Casmurro* (Avon Bard 1980).

Contemporary Brazilian writers who have found inspiration in Rio include Manuel Bandeira, and Nelson Rodrigues, whose *A Vida Como Ela É...* selection of short stories give a fascinating insight into what makes Cariocas tick.

General

In the 19th century, practically every Westerner who visited Rio seems to have written a travelogue. John Lubbock visited Rio in 1808 and wrote *Notes about Rio de Janeiro and Meridional Parts of Brazil*, published in 1820. It remains one of the most descriptive accounts of Rio during that era.

Samba by Alma Guillermoprieto (Random House 1990), describes a year in the life of Mangueira, one of the most traditional Rio samba schools. The author joined the school and went on to parade with them. An excellent read.

Escolas de Samba by Luis Gardel (Rio de Janeiro 1967), is a detailed description of the Carnaval Guilds of Rio. A bit dated, but very interesting. It's available in good bookshops in Rio.

Rio is God's gift to the 'coffee-table book' industry. In bookshops throughout Rio you'll find plenty of glossy books, unfortunately they are quite expensive. Bruce Weber's *O Rio de Janeiro* (Knopf 1986) has great pictures.

Libraries

Instituto Brasil-Estados Unidos (IBEU; ☎ 255-8939) has an English library with a large fiction collection, many books about Brazil in English and a good selection of current magazines from the USA. To borrow books you have to take classes there or buy a membership, but it's cheap. The library is at Avenida NS de Copacabana 690, 3rd floor.

With an American passport you can get into the American Consulate, which has a fantastic periodical room. It's on the corner of Avenida Presidente Wilson and Rua México; open 8 am to 4 pm Monday to Friday.

MEDIA

Brazil's media industry is concentrated in the hands of a few organisations. The companies that own the two major TV stations, O Globo and Manchete, also control several of the nation's leading newspapers and magazines. Both are based in Rio.

Newspapers & Magazines

English & French In Rio you will find three daily newspapers in English: the *Miami Herald, USA Today* and the *International Herald Tribune.* They are usually on the newsstands by noon.

Time and *Newsweek* magazines are available throughout Brazil. What can one say about these icons? Their coverage is weakest where the *Miami Herald* is strongest: Latin America and sports. The *Economist* is sold in Rio and São Paulo, but it costs about US$4.

In Rio you can find all sorts of imported newspapers and magazines at some newsstands, but they are very expensive. The newsstands on Avenida Rio Branco in the Centro have large selections of foreign newspapers and magazines. In Ipanema, the newsstand in front of Casa Piano has French and English newspapers and magazines.

Portuguese The *Jornal do Brasil* and *O Globo* are Rio's main daily papers. Both have entertainment listings. *Balcão* is a Rio weekly with only classified advertisements, a good source for buying anything. *O Nacional* is a weekly paper that has some excellent critical columnists. *O Povo* is a popular daily with lots of gory photographs.

Among weekly magazines, *Veja*, the Brazilian *Time* clone, is the country's best-selling magazine. In Rio, it comes with the *Veja Rio* insert, which details the weekly entertainment options. It's easy reading if you want to practise your Portuguese. *Isto É* has the best political and economic analysis, and reproduces international articles from the British *Economist*, but it's not light reading. It also provides good coverage of current events.

Environmental and ecological issues (both national and international) are covered in the glossy monthly magazine, *Terra*. It seems genuine about environmental concerns as well as having some great photos.

Radio

FM radio stations are plentiful in Rio, and by law at least a third of the music they play must be Brazilian. 'Channel surfing' is a great way to get to hear what the Cariocas are listening to.

For the latest Brazilian and Foreign hits, try Jovem Pan (94.9), 98 (98.1), RPC (100.5), Transamérica (101.3) and Cidade (102.9). For jazz, tune into Globo (92.5) or MEC (98.9).

For Brazilian *pagode* and pop, switch to Roquette (94.1), O Dia (90.3), JB (99.7), Tropical (104.5) or Universidade (107.9).

Between 7 and 8 pm the government news hour is broadcast over every channel.

TV

English If you are having second thoughts about visiting Brazil because you don't want to miss the Superbowl, Wimbledon or, perhaps, the Miss Teen America pageant, go ahead and make those reservations. All the major American TV events are shown in Rio.

Portuguese Many of the worst American movies and TV shows are dubbed into Portuguese and shown on Brazilian TV. Brazil's most famous TV hosts are Xuxa and Faustão. Xuxa, the queen of kiddy titillation, has coquettishly danced and sung her way into the hearts of tiny Brazilians everywhere. Faustão hosts *Domingão de Faustão*, a seemingly endless bump'n'grind variety show on Sunday afternoons.

What is worth watching? On Sunday night, starting at 9 or 10 pm, you can see the highlights of soccer matches played that day. And there's a good comedy show that starts daily at 5.30 pm called *Escolinha do Professor Raimundo*. The most popular programmes on Brazilian TV are the *novelas* (soap operas), which are followed religiously by many Brazilians. They go on the air at various times from 7 to 9 pm.

O Globo and Manchete, the two principal national networks, both have rather pedestrian national news shows. *Aqui Agora* (Here Now) is a sensational news show on SBT that is worth a look, even if you don't understand Portuguese.

Cable TV is a recent addition to the airwaves, with ESPN (the sports network), CNN (Cable News Network), RAI (Radio Televisione Italia), and, of course, MTV (music television) available to those few who can afford them.

PHOTOGRAPHY & VIDEO

Photographic equipment and accessories are expensive in Brazil and you'd be well advised to buy your film and equipment before arrival. However, Kodak and Fuji print film is sold and processed almost everywhere. You can only get Ektachrome or Kodachrome slide film developed in the big cities and it's expensive to buy. If you're shooting slides it's best to bring film with you and have it processed back home. Heat and humidity can ruin film, so remember to keep it in the coolest, driest place available. Use a lead film bag to protect film from airport X-ray machines. This is especially important for the sensitive high-ASA films.

If you must get your film processed in Rio, have it done at Kronokroma Foto (☎ 285-1993) at Rua Russel 344, Loja E, near Praia do Flamengo's Hotel Glória. Bring in exposed film in the morning, when the chemical baths are fresh. The Fomar Photo Store (☎ 221-2332) at Rua São Jose 90 off Avenida Rio Branco sells some camera accessories. Their friendly staff do quick camera cleaning. If your Nikon is on the blink, speak to Louis (☎ 220-1127) at Franklin Roosevelt 39 on the 6th floor near the US Consulate. Also recommended for camera repairs is Technica Miyazaki (☎ 227-4894), at Rua Djalma Ulrich 110, shop 214 in Copacabana (enter from Avenida NS de Copacabana 1063).

All video tapes manufactured in Brazil use the American (NTSC) system. Most of the tourist videos, however, are available in both NTSC and the European Pal system. Video 8 cassettes are widely available in Rio.

Some Macumba temples do not permit photography. Respect the wishes of the locals and ask permission before taking photos of them.

TIME

Brazil has four official time zones. The standard time zone covers the eastern, north-eastern, southern, and south-eastern parts of Brazil, including Rio. This zone is three hours behind GMT. So when it is noon in Rio it is 3 pm in London; 10 am in New York; 7 am in San Francisco; 1 am the next day in Sydney or Melbourne; and 11 pm in New Zealand. Summer time runs from October to February.

ELECTRICITY

Electrical current is not standardised in Brazil, so it's a good idea to carry an adaptor if you can't travel without your hairdryer. In Rio de Janeiro and São Paulo, the current is almost exclusively 110 or 120 volts, 60 cycles, AC. Salvador and Manaus have 127 volt service. Recife, Brasília and various other cities have 220 volt service. Check before you plug in.

Speaking of plugs, the most common power points have two round sockets.

LAUNDRY

There are laundromats in Copacabana at Rua Miguel Lemos 56 and Avenida NS de Copacabana 1226. In Flamengo, there's one at Rua Marquês de Abrantes 82. All are open Monday to Saturday from 8 am to 10 pm.

If you don't want to wash your own clothes, enquire at your hotel, as often the housekeepers wash clothes at home to make a few extra reais.

WEIGHTS & MEASURES

Brazil uses the international metric system for weights and measures.

HEALTH

Predeparture Preparations

Some vaccinations are necessary to protect against diseases you may encounter along the way. A yellow fever vaccination and related documentation is strongly recommended for every traveller in Brazil. In addition, Brazilian authorities will not grant entrance, especially in Amazônia, without it. The vaccination certificate remains effective for 10 years. Other commonly recommended jabs for travel to South America are typhoid, tetanus DPT, polio, and meningitis vaccines as well as gamma globulin as protection against hepatitis. Some physicians will also recommend a cholera vaccine but its effectiveness is minimal.

JOHN MAIER, JR.

JOHN MAIER, JR.

Over 5000 varieties of plants are on display at the
Jardim Botânico

Take a needle and syringe pack with you overseas – it is a cheap insurance package against infection with HIV or hepatitis.

Travel insurance is recommended to cover possible medical or dental costs – the latter are particularly high.

Medical Problems & Treatment

Some medical problems that travellers in Rio may experience or need to be aware of include:

Sunburn, Prickly Heat & Heat Exhaustion Rio lies in the humid tropics, where the sun's rays are more direct and concentrated than in temperate zones. All these complaints result from insufficient respect for and precautions against excessive sun and heat. Use a sunscreen, wear a hat and loose cool clothing and get plenty of liquids to drink. You may need to eat salty food or take salt tablets to replace what you lose by sweating or from the vomiting and diarrhoea caused by upset travellers' tummy.

If you feel exhausted or irritable from the heat take the commonsense precautions of resting in the shade, having a cool swim or retreating to air-conditioning for a while.

Heatstroke This serious, sometimes fatal, condition can occur if the body's thermostat breaks down and body temperature rises to dangerous levels. Continuous exposure to high temperatures can leave you vulnerable to heatstroke. Alcohol intake and strenuous activity can increase chances of heatstroke, especially in those who've recently arrived in a hot climate.

Symptoms include minimal sweating, a high body temperature (39 to 40°C), and a general feeling of unwellness. The skin may become flushed and red. Severe throbbing headaches, decreased coordination, and aggressive or confused behaviour may be signs of heatstroke. Eventually, the victim will become delirious and go into convulsions. Get the victim out of the sun, if possible, remove clothing, cover with a wet towel and fan continually. Seek medical help as soon as possible.

Fungal Infections Fungal infections occur more frequently in hot weather. They are most often found on the scalp, between the toes or fingers (athlete's foot), in the groin (jock itch or crotch rot) and on the body (ringworm). You get ringworm (which is a fungal infection, not a worm) from infected animals or by walking on damp areas, like shower floors.

To prevent fungal infections wear loose, comfortable clothes, avoid artificial fibres, wash frequently and dry carefully. If you do get an infection, wash the infected area daily with a disinfectant or medicated soap and water, and rinse and dry well. Apply an antifungal powder like the widely available Tinaderm. Try to expose the infected area to air or sunlight as much as possible and wash all towels and underwear in hot water as well as changing them often.

Diarrhoea A change of water, food or climate can all cause the runs; diarrhoea caused by contaminated food or water is more serious. Despite all your precautions you may still have a mild bout of travellers' diarrhoea but a few rushed toilet trips with no other symptoms is not indicative of a serious problem. Moderate diarrhoea, involving half-a-dozen loose movements in a day, is more of a nuisance. Dehydration is the main danger with any diarrhoea, particularly for children where dehydration can occur quite quickly. Fluid replacement remains the mainstay of management. Weak black tea with a little sugar, soda water, or soft drinks allowed to go flat and diluted 50% with water are all good.

With severe diarrhoea it is important to consult a doctor or pharmacist, especially if there is blood and mucus in the stool, if you have a fever or if the diarrhoea persists for more than five days.

HIV/AIDS HIV, the Human Immunodeficiency Virus, may develop into AIDS, Acquired Immune Deficiency Syndrome. It is a very serious problem in Brazil to a degree unfamiliar to most Western travellers and should be a major concern to all visitors. Any exposure to blood, blood products or bodily fluids may put the individual at risk. In South America, transmission is predominantly through heterosexual sexual activity. This is quite different from industrialised countries where transmission is mostly through contact between homosexual or bisexual males, or via contaminated needles shared by IV drug users. Apart from abstinence, the most effective preventative is always to practise safe sex using condoms. It is impossible to detect the HIV-positive status of an otherwise healthy-looking person without a blood test.

HIV/AIDS can also be spread through infected blood transfusions; most developing countries cannot afford to screen blood for transfusions. It can also be spread by dirty needles — vaccinations, acupuncture, tattooing and ear or nose piercing can potentially be as dangerous as intravenous drug use if the equipment is not clean. If you do need an injection, ask to see the syringe unwrapped in front of you, or use your own.

Fear of HIV infection should never preclude treatment for serious medical conditions. Although there may be a risk of infection, it is very small indeed.

Medical Services

The Rio Health Collective (☎ 325-9300 extension 44) offers a free telephone referral service. The staff speak English and can hook you up with an English-speaking doctor or specialist in any part of the city. They're open from 9 am to 2 pm.

Some private medical facilities in Rio de Janeiro are on a par with US hospitals. UK and US consulates have lists of English-speaking physicians.

Brazilian blood banks don't always screen carefully. Hepatitis B is rampant, so if you should require a blood transfusion, do as the Brazilians do: have your friends blood-typed and choose your blood donor in advance.

Hospitals & Pharmacies

Pharmacies in Brazil are known as *farmácias* and medicines are called *remédios*. The word for doctor is *doutor* or *médico*; and medicine tablets are known as *comprimidos*.

These hospitals have 24-hour emergency services and doctors who speak English: Miguel Couto (☎ 274-2121), Rua Mario Ribeiro 117, Gavea, and Souza Aguiar (☎ 296-41140, Praça da República 111, Centro.

Rio's 24-hour pharmacies include Farmácia Piauí at: Avenida Ataulfo de Paiva 1283, Leblon (☎ 274-8448); Rua Barata Ribeiro 646, Copacabana (☎ 255-6249); Rua Ministro Viveiros de Castro 32, Leme (☎ 275-3847); and Praia do Flamengo 224, Flamengo (☎ 284-1548).

Pharmacies stock all kinds of drugs and sell them much more cheaply than in the West. However, when buying drugs anywhere in South America, be sure to check expiry dates and storage conditions. Some drugs available there may no longer be recommended, or may even be banned, in other countries. In addition, travellers should be aware of any drug allergies they may have and avoid using such drugs or their derivatives while travelling in Brazil. Since common names of prescription medicines in South America are likely to be different from the ones you're used to, ask a pharmacist before taking anything you're not sure about.

Some pharmacists will give injections (with or without prescriptions). This is true of the Drogaleve pharmacy chain. Sometimes hygiene is questionable, so always purchase fresh needles.

WOMEN TRAVELLERS

In Rio, foreign women without travelling companions will scarcely be given a sideways glance.

Although *machismo* is an undeniable element in the Brazilian social structure, it is manifested less overtly than in Spanish-speaking Latin America. Perhaps because attitudes toward sex and pornography are quite liberal in Brazil, males feel little need to assert their masculinity or prove their prowess in the eyes of peers. Flirtation – often exaggerated – is a prominent element in Brazilian male/female relations. It goes both ways and is nearly always regarded as amusingly innocent banter. If unwelcome attention is forthcoming, you should be able to stop it by merely expressing disgust or displeasure.

Once you've spent an hour in Copacabana or Ipanema, where some women run their errands wearing *fio dental*, the famous Brazilian skimpy bikini, you'll be aware that dress restrictions aren't as strict as they could be.

It's a good idea to keep a low profile in the city at night and avoid going alone to bars and nightclubs if you'd rather not chance being misconstrued. Similarly, women should not hitch either alone or in groups.

GAY & LESBIAN TRAVELLERS

Rio is the gay capital of Latin America. There is no law against homosexuality in Brazil. During Carnaval, thousands of expatriate Brazilian and gringo gays fly in for the festivities. Ipanema beach, in front of Rua Farme do Amoedo, is standing room only during the day. Transvestites steal the show at all carnival balls, especially the gay ones. Outside of Carnaval, the gay scene is active, but less visible than in cities like San Francisco and Sydney.

Available at newsstands, the *Guia gay* is a small booklet with a lot of useful information.

Groups and organisations for gays include:

Atoba
    Rua Professor Carvalho e Melo 471, Magalhoes Bastos (☎ 332-0787; fax 205-4796)
Grupo de Atuacão e Afirmacão Gay (GAAG)
    PO BOX 135, Duque de Caixas, RJ 20001
ABIA – Associação Brasileira Interdisciplinar de Aids
    Rua Sete de Stembro 48, sala 12 (☎ 224-1654; fax 224-3414)

JOHN MAIER, JR.

JOHN MAIER, JR.

Top: Beachwear is often worn on the street
Bottom: Machismo is an undeniable element in Brazil

DISABLED TRAVELLERS

In Rio the Centro de Vida Independente (☎ 257-0019), Rua Marques de São Vincente 225, Gavea, can give advice about travel in Brazil.

Disabled travellers in the USA might like to contact the Society for the Advancement of Travel for the Handicapped (☎ (718) 858-5483), 26 Court St, Brooklyn, New York, NY 11242. In the UK, a useful contact is the Royal Association for Disability & Rehabilitation (☎ (071) 242-3882), 25 Mortimer St, London W1N 8AB.

RIO FOR CHILDREN

Brazilians are very family oriented. Many hotels let children stay free, although the age limit varies. Babysitters are readily available and most restaurants have high chairs. Some of the sights and places of interest described in the Things to See & Do chapter are good places to take kids. They will love the cog train that winds up through the forest at **Corcovado**, although the steps at the top are tiring for little ones. **Ilha da Paquetá**, the small island in Baía de Guanabara, where the only means of transport are bicycles and horse-drawn carriages, is a nice change of pace. The **Jardim Zoológico** has more than 2500 animals, as well as snack bars and picnic areas. At **Pão de Açucar**, as well as the cable-car ride, there are small playgrounds on Morro da Urca and on Sugar Loaf itself. **Parque do Flamengo** has lots of space for kids to run around. You might also like to try the following places:

Fazenda Alegria
> Fazenda Alegria (☎ 342-9066) is a small children's farm. It's on the Estrada da Boca do Mato in Vargem Pequena and is open on weekends and holidays from 10 am to 5 pm.

Lokau
> Lokau in Barra da Tijuca is an expensive restaurant facing the Lagoa da Marapindi. It's on a small estate with a few animals, like monkeys and peacocks. Kids are allowed to wander around.

Mini-Rio Barra Shopping
> Mini-Rio, (☎ 325-5611), located in Barra Shopping on the first floor is a small amusement area, with dodgem cars, boat and plane rides for the tiny tots. It's open daily from 10 am to 10 pm.

Tivoli Parque
> Tivoli Parque (☎ 274-1846) in Lagoa on Avenida Borges de Medeiros, is a popular amusement park for adults and children. It's open on Thursday and Friday from 2 to 8

pm, Saturday from 2 to 10 pm, and Sunday from 10 am to 10 pm.

Planetário

The Planetário(☎ 274-0096) at Rua Padre Leonel Franca 240 in Gávea, shows the southern sky accompanied by a classical music soundtrack. Older kids will enjoy it.

Wet'n Wild

Barra becomes more like California each year. It now has a franchise of the American Wet'n Wild aquatic park. It includes Surf Lagoon, a pool with a wave-making machine and other rides with names like Black Hole, Raging Rapids and Mach 5. Entry is US$15 for adults and US$12 for children.

USEFUL ORGANISATIONS

The Brazilian American Cultural Center (BACC; ☎ (212) 7301010; or toll-free (1-800) 222-2746), 16 West 46th St, New York, NY 10036, is a tourism organisation which offers its members discounted flights and tours. Members also receive a monthly newspaper about Brazil and the Brazilian community in the USA, and can send money to South America using BACC's remittance service. The organisation can also secure tourist visas for members through the Brazilian Consulate in New York.

For information about the growing network of Brazilian youth hostels, contact the Federação Brasileira dos Albergues de Juventude (FBAJ; ☎ (021) 252-4829), Rua da Assembléia 10, sala 1211 Centro, Rio de Janeiro, CEP 20011, RJ. Include an envelope and postage.

For information about gay and lesbian and disabled travellers, see those sections earlier in this chapter.

Business Travellers

Business travellers will find the Rio Convention & Visitors Bureau (☎ 259-6165; fax 511-2592) most helpful. It's in Ipanema at Rua Visconde de Pirajá 547 on the 6th floor. As well as seeking assistance from the commercial section of your consulate you may also find it useful to approach one of the many international chambers of commerce in Rio.

Both Telerj (☎ 263-2509), at Avenida Presidente Vargas 2560, Centro, and Locacell (☎ 224-2551; fax 224-3049) rent mobile phones. They have representatives at both airports, in the Centro at Rua da Assembléia 87, 8th floor, and in Copacabana at Avenida NS de Copacabana 1417, suite 209. Varig also has a cellular phone service for passengers in various Brazilian cities. If you plan to fly with Varig, ask for details.

DANGERS & ANNOYANCES

Emergency Services

To call emergency telephone numbers in Rio you do not need fichas (tokens). The numbers include:

Tourist Police Office (☎ 511-5112) at Rua Afrânio de Melo Franco (in front of Scala), Leblon
Radio Police (☎ 190)
Ambulance (☎ 192)
Fire (☎ 193)
Detran (☎ 194) for road accidents
Maritime & Aerial Police (☎ 263-3747)

Security

Rio gets a lot of bad international press about its violence and high crime rate. There are four kidnappings a week. Homicides have increased 22.6% in the last two years. 1080 street children under 17 were killed between January 1991 and July 1993. Over 55% of the population has been assaulted at least once. Not surprisingly, a recent official survey of foreign visitors to Brazil reported that concern about safety and security was one of the major reasons for feeling apprehensive about travelling to Brazil.

Don't let this stop you from coming. Travellers to Rio have as much chance of getting mugged as in any big city with a high crime rate, so the same precautions apply here. This section has been written in detail to heighten awareness, but that doesn't mean you should get too paranoid to leave the hotel room. By following a few common-sense precautions, you're unlikely to suffer anything more than sunburn.

Predeparture Precautions

If you work on the elements of vulnerability, you can significantly reduce the risks. For starters, you should take with you only those items which you are prepared to lose or replace. Travel insurance is essential for replacement of valuables and the cost of a good policy is a worthwhile price to pay for peace of mind. Loss through petty theft or violence is an emotional and stressful experience which can be reduced if you think ahead. The less you have, the less you can lose. Don't bring any jewellery, chains, or expensive watches, and if you have to wear a watch, then use a cheapie worth a few dollars.

Be prepared for the worst – make copies of your important records: a photostat of your passport (page with passport number, name, photograph, location where issued and expiration date; all visas); tourist card (issued on entry to Brazil); travellers' cheque numbers; credit card numbers; airline tickets; essential contact addresses, etc. Keep one copy on your person, one copy with your belongings and exchange one with a travelling companion.

Security Precautions in Rio

Leave your watch and any other jewellery in the hotel room; there are large digital clocks all over Rio if you must know the time. Leave all important documents, like passport and travellers' cheques, at the hotel. Get used to keeping small change and a few banknotes in a shirt pocket so that you can pay bus tickets and small expenses without extracting large amounts of money which could quickly attract attention. Better still, carry only the cash you think you'll need. If you do take your wallet, keep it in your front pocket.

Most travellers carry a daypack. Whether you're in a bus station, restaurant, shop, or elsewhere, whenever you have to put your daypack down, *always* put your foot through the strap. It makes things more difficult for furtive fingers or bag-slashers.

If you have a camera with you, never wander around with it dangling over your shoulder or around your neck - keep it out of sight as much as possible. It's also unwise to keep it in a swanky camera bag, which is an obvious target. We sometimes carried a camera in a sturdy plastic bag from a local supermarket.

At night, don't walk into any alleys, narrow streets, underpasses or wherever there are trees and bushes that may be used as hiding places.

Credit cards are useful in emergencies, for cash advances and for regular purchases. Make sure you know the number to call if you lose your credit card and be quick to cancel it if lost or stolen.

Never change money on the street; always ignore itinerant moneychangers who whisper favourable rates into your ear as you pass; and never follow any of these types into a side street for such a transaction. No exceptions: never means never.

Favourite Scams Distraction is a common tactic employed by street thieves. The 'cream technique' is now very common throughout South America, and Brazil is no exception. The trick commences when you're walking down the street or standing in a public place, and someone surreptitiously sprays a substance on your shoulder, your daypack or anything else connected with you. The substance can be anything from mustard to chocolate or even dog muck. An assistant (young or old; male or female) then taps you on the shoulder and amicably offers to clean off the mess...if you'll just put down your bag for a second. The moment you do this, someone makes off with it like a flash.

Another distraction technique involves one or more people working to divert you or literally throw you off balance. This trick usually happens when you're standing in the street or somewhere busy like a bus station. One or more characters suddenly ask you a question, 'bump' into you or stage an angry discussion or fight around you, and whilst you are off balance or diverted, there'll be an attempt to pick your pockets or whip your gear.

Druggings have also been reported. Exercise caution when you are offered cigarettes, beer, sweets etc. If the circumstances make you suspicious or uneasy, the offer can be tactfully refused by claiming stomach or other medical problems.

On the Beach Don't bring anything to city beaches apart from just enough money for lunch and drinks. No camera, no bag and no jewellery. If you want to photograph the beach, return the camera to your room before staying on the beach. Don't hang out on deserted city beaches at night.

The favourite beach rip-off scam (apart from the fast snatch and grab) is where the thieves wait for you to be alone on the beach guarding you (because you decided to take it in turns to go in the water). One thief approaches from one side and asks you for a light or the time. While you're distracted, the thief's partner grabs your gear from the other side.

Streets, Buses & Taxis Thieves watch for people leaving hotels, car-rental agencies, American Express offices, tourist sights – places with lots of foreigners. If you notice you are being followed or closely observed, it helps to pause and look straight at the person(s) involved or, if you're not alone, simply point out the person(s) to your companion. This makes it clear that the element of surprise favoured by petty criminals has been lost.

Always have enough money on hand to appease a mugger (about US$2 to US$5). Don't carry weapons: in many cases this could make matters much worse.

If you ride the buses, have your change ready before boarding. Avoid the super-crowded buses. If you talk out loud, it's easier for thieves to identify you. If you have valuables, take taxis rather than buses.

When entering or leaving a taxi, it's advisable (particularly for solo travellers) to keep a passenger door open during the loading or unloading of luggage – particularly if this is being done by someone other than the driver. This reduces the ease with which a taxi can drive off with your luggage, leaving you behind! A neater solution for those who travel light is to fit luggage inside the taxi rather than in the boot.

Also, when entering or leaving a taxi, always remember to watch your luggage (slip your foot or your arm through the appropriate strap).

Before starting, immediately question the presence of any 'shady' characters accompanying the driver, and don't hesitate to take another taxi if you feel uneasy. If there are mechanical or orientation problems en route, do not allow yourself to be separated from your luggage. When you arrive at your destination, *never* hand over your luggage to a person who tries to help you out of the car and offers to carry something, unless you are quite positive about their identity.

Hotels If you consider your hotel to be reliable (as a rough guide in Rio I'd say any place with three stars or more), place valuables in its safe and get a receipt. Make sure you package your valuables in a small, double-zippered bag which can be padlocked, or use a large envelope with a signed seal which will easily show any tampering. Count money and travellers' cheques before and after retrieving them from the safe – this should quickly identify any attempts to extract single bills or cheques which might otherwise go unnoticed.

Check the door, doorframe, and windows of your room for signs of forced entry or unsecured access. Don't leave your valuables strewn around the room. It's too much of a temptation to cleaners and other hotel staff.

The Police

If something is stolen from you, you can report it to the tourist police (see Emergency Services earlier in this section). No big investigation is going to occur but you will get a police form to give to your insurance company. All police aren't to be trusted, however. Brazilian police are known to plant drugs and sting gringos for bribes, and this is still said to be going on in Copacabana.

ANDREW DRAFFEN

Rio's Tourist Police

Drugs

Marijuana and cocaine are plentiful in Brazil, and very illegal. The military regime had a rather pathological aversion to drugs and enacted stiff penalties, which are still in force. Nevertheless, marijuana and cocaine are widely used, and, like many things in Brazil, everyone except the military and the police has a rather tolerant attitude towards them.

Drugs provide a perfect excuse for the police to get a fair amount of money from you, and Brazilian prisons are brutal places. A large amount of cocaine is smuggled out of Bolivia and Peru through Brazil. Be very careful with drugs. Don't buy from strangers and don't carry anything around with you.

If you're coming from one of the Andean countries and have been chewing coca leaves, be especially careful to clean out your pack before arriving in Brazil.

BUSINESS HOURS

Most shops and government services (eg the post office) are open Monday to Friday from 9 am to 6 pm and Saturday from 9 am to 1 pm. Because many Cariocas have little free time during the week, Saturday mornings are usually spent shopping. Some shops stay open later than 6 pm in the cities and the huge shopping malls often stay open until 10 pm and open on Sunday as well. Banks, always in their own little world, are generally open from 10 am to 4.30 pm. Câmbios often open an hour later, when the daily dollar rates are available.

PUBLIC HOLIDAYS

National holidays observed in Rio fall on the following
dates:

1 January
New Year's Day
6 January
Epiphany
February or March (four days before Ash Wednesday)
Carnaval
March or April
Easter & Good Friday
21 April
Tiradentes Day
1 May
Labour Day
June
Corpus Christi
7 September
Independence Day
12 October
Our Lady of Aparecida Day
2 November
All Souls' Day
15 November
Proclamation Day
25 December
Christmas Day

FESTIVALS & CULTURAL EVENTS

Major festivals celebrated in Rio de Janeiro include the
following:

1 January
New Year & Festa de Iemanjá (see below)
20 January
Dia de São Sebastião The day of the patron saint of the city
is commemorated with a procession carrying the image
of São Sebastião from the Igreja de São Sebastião dos
Capuchinos in Tijuca (Rua Haddock Lobo 266) to the
Catedral Metropolitana, where it's blessed in a celebra-
tory mass by the Archbishop of Rio de Janeiro.
February
Carnaval (see below)
1 March
Dia da Fundação da Cidade Founded by Estácio de Sá in
1565, the city commemorates the date with a mass in the
church of its patron saint, São Sebastião, in Tijuca.

March or April
> *Sexta-Feira da Paixão* Good Friday is celebrated throughout the city. The most important ceremony is a re-enactment of the Via Sacra under the Arcos da Lapa, with more than 100 actors.

June
> *Festas Juninas* One of the most important folkloric festivals in Brazil. In Rio, it's celebrated in various public squares, principally on 13 June (Dia de Santo Antônio), 24 June (São João) and 29 June (São Pedro).

3 July
> *Festa da São Pedro do Mar* Fisherfolk pay homage to their patron saint in a maritime procession. Their decorated boats leave from the fishing community of Caju and sail to the statue of São Pedro in Urca.

15 August
> *Festa de NS da Glória do Outeiro* A solemn mass and procession from the church into the streets of Glória mark the Feast of the Assumption. The church is ablaze with decorated lights. The festa includes music and colourful stalls set up in the Praça NS da Glória. Festivities start at 8 am and go all day.

7 September
> *Dia de Independência do Brasil* Independence day is celebrated with a big military parade down Avenida Presidente Vargas. It starts at 8 am at Candelária and goes down just past Praça XI.

October
> *Festa da Penha* One of the largest religious and popular festivals in the city. It takes place every Sunday in October and the first Sunday in November, at Igreja NS da Penha de França, Largo da Penha 19. It's very lively.

31 December
> *Celebração de Fim de Ano & Festa de Iemanjá* (see below)

Rio's two major festivals are New Year's Eve and Carnaval.

New Year's Eve & Festa de Iemanjá

In 1994, New Year's Eve in Copacabana was celebrated by 3.5 million people. For 13 minutes, tonnes of fireworks exploded in the sky over Copacabana. At the end of the beach, near the fort, a dirigible launched a cascade of fireworks over the sea. For 10 minutes, a glittering cascade covered the entire 30-floor facade of the Meridien Hotel. The year before, crowd estimates were 3 million.

New Year's Eve also coincides with the Festival de Iemenja, the goddess of the sea. According to African legend, Iemenja, daughter of the sky god Obtala and the earth god Odudua, bore 15 children. To Brazilian macumba and umbanda followers, she is the 'Mother of All'.

Believers, all wearing white, carry Iemenja's statue to the beach and launch offerings into the sea for her. These include bunches of flowers and small boats containing perfumes, champagne and talcum powder to beautify the goddess. If the boat goes out to sea, all is well, but if it's swept back to shore, it means the owners have displeased Iemenja. On New Year's Day, thousands of these rejected offerings are strewn along the shoreline.

Carnaval

Carnaval is a pagan holiday originating perhaps in the Roman bacchanalia celebrating Saturn or in the ancient Egyptian festival of Isis. Carnaval was a wild party during the Middle Ages until tamed in Europe by Christianity, but the sober church of the Inquisition could not squelch Carnaval in the Portuguese colony, where it came to acquire African rhythms and Indian costumes.

People speculate that the word carnaval derives from the Latin carne-vale, meaning 'goodbye meat'. The reasoning goes something like this: for the 40 days of Lent, nominally Catholic Brazilians give up liver or flank steaks. To compensate for the big sacrifices ahead, they rack up sins in a delirious carnal blow-out in honour of King Momo, the king of Carnaval.

Every year wealthy and spaced-out foreigners descend on Rio en masse, get drunk, get high, bag some sunrays and exchange exotic diseases. Everyone gets a bit unglued at this time of year and there are lots of car accidents and murders. Some of the leaner and meaner Cariocas can get a little ugly with all the sex, booze and flash of money. Apartment rates and taxi fares triple and quadruple and some thieves keep to the spirit of the season by robbing in costume.

The excitement of Carnaval builds all year and the pre-Lenten revelry begins well before the official dates of Carnaval. A month before Carnaval starts, rehearsals at the escolas de samba (samba clubs) are open to visitors on Saturdays. The rehearsals are usually in the favelas. They're fun to watch, but for your safety go with a Carioca. Tourist Carnaval shows are held all year round at Scala in Leblon, up top at Pão de Açúcar, and at Plataforma 1.

The escolas de samba are actually predated by bandas (marching bands, nonprofessional equivalents of the escolas de samba), which are now returning to the Carnaval scene as part of the movement to return Rio's Carnaval to the streets. Riotur has all the information in a special Carnaval guide.

JOHN MAIER, JR.

GUY MOBERLY

JOHN MAIER, JR.

The costumes of Rio's Carnaval

JOHN MAIER, JR.

GUY MOBERLY

JOHN MAIER, JR.

The costumes of Rio's Carnaval

Carnaval Balls Carnaval balls are surreal and erotic events. In one ball at Scala we saw a woman (transsexual?) bare her breasts and offer passers-by a suck while rickety old ladies were bopping away in skimpy lingerie. A young and geeky rich guy was dancing on tables with whores past their prime, young models and lithe young nymphets, all in various stages of undress. Breasts were painted, stickered with adhesive tattoos, covered with fish-net brassieres or left bare. Bottoms were spandexed, G-stringed or mini-skirted.

More action took place on the stages. One stage had a samba band, the other was crushed with young women. They didn't dance, but ground their hips and licked their lips to the incessant, hypnotic music and the epileptic flashing of the floor lights. Throngs of sweaty photographers and video crews mashed up to the stage. Everyone played up for the camera, vying for space and the attention of the photographers. The Vegas headdresses, the pasty-faced bouncers and the rich men in private boxes overlooking the dance floor lent a mafiosi feel to the place.

Carnaval is the holiday of the poor. Not that you could tell from the price of the tickets to the balls. Some of them cost more than the monthly minimum wage. There are snooty affairs like the ones at the Copacabana Palace (☎ 255-7070, US$80), Hotel Intercontinental (☎ 322-2200, US$150) or the new venue in Barra, the Metropolitan (☎ 385-0515, US$80 plus a stiff cab fare). Raunchier parties are held in Leblon at Scala (☎ 239-4448, US$40), Canecão (☎ 295-3055, US$40) in Botafogo and Help disco in Copacabana (US$20). Tickets go on sale about two weeks beforehand and the balls are held nightly for the preceding week and all through Carnaval. Buy a copy of the *Veja* magazine with the *Veja Rio* insert. It has details of all the balls and bandas.

There are three rules of thumb: beautiful, flirtatious and apparently unescorted women are either escorted by huge, jealous cachaça-crazed men wielding machetes, or else they are really men dressed up as women; everything costs several times more within the club than outside; and, finally, don't bring more money than you're willing to lose – the club bouncers are big, but not that effective.

Street Carnaval What do Cariocas do in the afternoon and early evening during Carnaval? They dance in the streets behind *bandas* (marching bands with brass and percussion instruments), which pump out the banda theme song and other Carnaval marching favourites

The Samba Parades

The parades begin with moderate mayhem, then work themselves up to a higher plane of frenzy. The announcers introduce the escola, the group's colours and the number of wings. Far away the lone voice of the *puxador* starts the samba. Thousands more voices join him, and then the drummers kick in, 200 to 400 per school. The booming drums drive the parade. This samba do enredo is the loudest music you're ever likely to hear in your life. The samba tapes flood the air waves for weeks prior to the beginning of Carnaval. From afar the parade looks alive. It's a throbbing beast – and slowly it comes closer, a pulsing, Liberace-glittered, Japanese-movie-monster slimemould threatening to engulf all of Rio in samba and vibrant, vibrating mulatas.

The parades begin with a special opening wing or *abre alas*,which always displays the name of the school and the theme of the escola. The whole shebang has some unifying message, some social commentary, economic criticism or political message, but it's usually lost in the glitter. The abre alas is then followed by the *commissão de frente*, who greet the crowds. The escola thus honours its elderly men for work done over the years.

Next follow the main wings of the escola, the big allegorical floats, the children's wing, the drummers, the celebrities and the bell-shaped Baianas twirling in their elegant hoop skirts. The Baianas honour the history of the parade itself, which was brought to Rio from Salvador de Bahia in 1877. The *mestre-sala* (dance master) and *porta-bandeira* (flag bearer) waltz and whirl. Celebrities, dancers and tambourine players strut their stuff. The costumes are fabulously lavish: 1½-metre-tall feathered headdresses, flowing sequin capes, rhinestone-studded G-strings.

The floats gush neo-baroque silver foil and gold tinsel. Sparkling models sway to the samba, dancing in their private Carnavals. All the while the puxador leads in song, repeating the samba do enredo for the duration of the parade. Over an hour after it began, the escola makes it past the arch and the judges' stand. There is a few minutes' pause. TV cranes stop bobbing up and down over the Pepsi caps and bibs of the foreign press corps. Now garbage trucks parade down the runway clearing the way for the next escola. Sanitation workers in orange jumpsuits shimmy, dance and sweep, gracefully catch trash thrown from the stands and take their bows. It's their Carnaval, too. The parade continues on through the night and into the morning, eight more samba schools parade the following day, and the week after, the top eight schools parade once more in the parade of champions. ■

while they move along. To join in the fun, all you need to do is jump in when you see the banda pass. Bandas are one of the most traditional aspects of Carnaval in Rio. Banda de Ipanema is a traditional banda that parades two Saturdays before Carnaval from Praça General Osório in Ipanema. It's full of drag queens and party animals. It starts around 5 pm and goes until around 9 pm. The banda also parades again on Carnaval Saturday. Banda Carmen Miranda, with its famous gay icon, is also a lot of fun, not only for gays but everyone. It parades through Ipanema around 4 pm on the Sunday before Carnaval. There are lots of bandas in Copacabana before and during Carnaval too.

The street parades in Avenida Rio Branco in the Centro and Boulevard 28 de Setembro in Vila Isabel, both on Carnaval Saturday, are really worth checking out. You won't see many other tourists there, but just carry a few dollars in your pocket for beers and a snack, and you'll have nothing to worry about.

Sambódromo Parades In the *sambódromo*, a tiered street designed for samba parades, the Brazilians harness sweat, noise and confusion and turn it into art. The 16 top-level samba schools prepare all year for an hour of glory in the sambódromo. The best escola is chosen by a hand-picked set of judges on the basis of many components including percussion, the *samba do enredo* (theme song), harmony between percussion, song and dance, choreography, costume, storyline, floats and decorations. The championship is hotly contested; the winner becomes the pride of Rio and Brazil.

Getting tickets at the legitimate prices can be tough. Many tickets are sold 10 days in advance of the event; check with Riotur on where you can get them, as the outlet varies from year to year. People queue up for hours and travel agents and scalpers snap up the best seats. Riotur reserves seats in private boxes for tourists for US$200.

If you do happen to buy a ticket from a scalper (don't worry about finding them – they'll find you), make sure you get both the plastic ticket with the magnetic strip and the ticket showing the seat number. Different days have different coloured tickets, so check the date as well.

But don't fret if you don't get a ticket. It's possible to see the show without paying an arm and a leg. The parades last eight to 10 hours each and no one can or wants to sit through them that long. Unless you're an aficionado of an escola that starts early, don't show up at the sambódromo until midnight, three or four hours into the show. Then you can get tickets at the grandstand

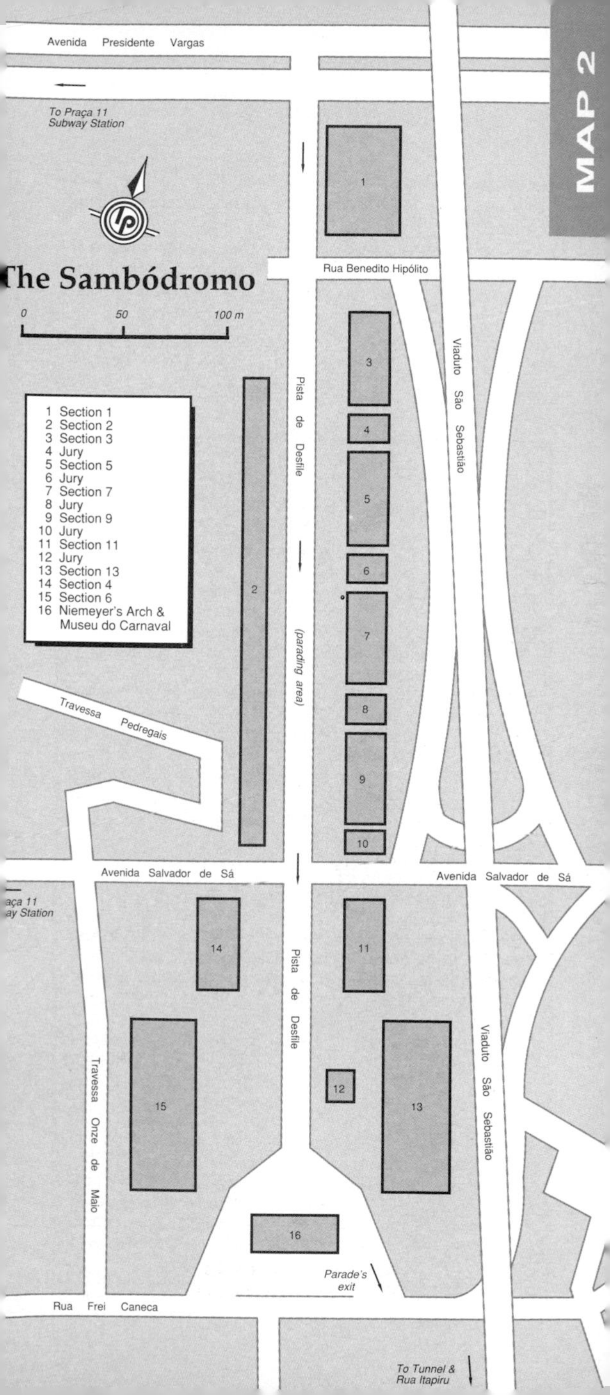

MAP 2

Avenida Presidente Vargas

To Praça 11
Subway Station

The Sambódromo

0   50   100 m

1	Section 1
2	Section 2
3	Section 3
4	Jury
5	Section 5
6	Jury
7	Section 7
8	Jury
9	Section 9
10	Jury
11	Section 11
12	Jury
13	Section 13
14	Section 4
15	Section 6
16	Niemeyer's Arch & Museu do Carnaval

Rua Benedito Hipólito

Viaduto São Sebastião

Pista de Desfile

(parading area)

Travessa Pedregais

Avenida Salvador de Sá

aça 11
ay Station

Avenida Salvador de Sá

Travessa Onze de Maio

Pista de Desfile

Viaduto São Sebastião

Parade's exit

Rua Frei Caneca

To Tunnel &
Rua Itapiru

for about US$10. And if you can't make it during Carnaval, there's always the cheaper (but less exciting) parade of champions the following week.

If you can avoid it, don't take the bus to or from the sambódromo; it's safer to take the mêtro, which is open 24 hours a day during Carnaval. It's also fun to check out the paraders in their costumes on the train.

By the way there's nothing to stop you taking part in the parade. Most samba schools are happy to have foreigners join one of the alas. All you need is between

Sambódromo Glossary

Alas (wings) – are groups of samba school members responsible for a specific part of the theme samba. Special alas include the *bahianas*, women dressed as bahian 'aunts' in full skirts and turbans. The *abre-ala* of each school is the opening wing or float.

Bateria – is the drum section. It's the driving beat behind the school's samba. The 'soul' of the school.

Carnavalescos – are the artistic directors of each school, and are responsible for the overall layout and design of the school's theme.

Carros allegoricos – are the dazzling floats, usually decorated with near-naked mulatas. The floats are pushed along by the school's maintenance crew.

Desfile – All the schools are divided up and the most important ones *desfilar* (parade) on the Sunday and Monday night of Carnaval. Each school's desfile is judged on its samba, drum section, master of ceremonies and flag bearer, the floats, the leading commission, costumes, dance coordination and harmony.

Destaques – are the richest and most elaborate costumes. The heaviest ones usually get a spot on one of the floats.

Diretores de harmonia – are the school organisers, usually dressed in white or the school colours, and running around yelling and 'pumping up' the wings and making sure there aren't any gaps in the parade.

Enredo – the enredo is the central theme of each school, and the *samba do enredo* is the samba that goes with it. Themes vary tremendously. In 1995, they included a tribute to football club Flamengo, the story of the wheel, the discovery of Brazil, the beauty and legends surrounding the island Fernando de Noronha, and the story of an expedition Dom Pedro II made to the state of Cear, to name a few.

Passistas – are the best samba dancers in the school. They roam the parade in groups or alone, stopping to show their fancy footwork along the way. The women are scantily dressed and the men usually hold tambourines. ■

US$200-US$300 for your costume and you're in. It helps to arrive in Rio a week or two in advance to get this organised. Ask at the hotel how to go about it. It usually takes just a few phone calls.

Carnaval Dates Dates for the Carnaval parade in coming years are:

1996	18 & 19 February
1997	9 & 10 February
1998	22 & 23 February
1999	14 & 15 February
2000	5 & 6 March

Carnaval Income
Carnaval generates more than half a billion dollars each year in Brazil.

In 1995, all of the 22,000 hotel rooms in Rio were occupied for the five days of Carnaval (In 1994 occupation rates were 75%). In room rent alone this is almost US$40 million.

Carnaval revenue for TV Rede Globo was US$10 million, including US$8 million from the beer company sponsoring the event.

Costumes for the 130,400 people who took part in the Rio Carnaval parade cost around US$25 million.

Sales from the recording of the samba-enredos, around 800,000 copies, generated almost US$15 million. ■

WORK

Travellers on tourist visas aren't supposed to work in Brazil. The only viable paid work is teaching English in the city, but you need to speak a bit of Portuguese and allow enough time to get some pupils.

To find work, look in the classifieds under 'Professor de Ingles' or 'English Teacher', or ask around at the English schools. Expect to earn around US$10 an hour.

Getting There & Away

Most travellers start their Brazilian odyssey by flying down to Rio, but this is only one of many ways to arrive. Other gateway airports include: Recife, popular with German package tourists on their way to one of the many beach resorts catering to their needs; Fortaleza; Salvador; Manaus, capital of the state of Amazonas; and Belem, capital of the state of Pará, both of which are halfway between Rio and Miami.

Brazil also has land borders with every other country in South America, with the exception of Chile and Ecuador, so while some travellers may be bussing in from Uruguay in the south, others may be arriving via the *trem da morte* (death train) from Bolivia. By river, many travellers take a slow boat down the Amazon from Iquitos in Peru or into the Pantanal via the Rio Paraguay from Asunçion.

However you're travelling, it's worth taking out travel insurance. Work out what you need – you may not want to insure that grotty old army surplus backpack, but everyone should be covered for the worst possible case: an accident, for example, that will require hospital treatment and a flight home. It's a good idea to make a copy of your policy, in case the original is lost. If you are planning to travel for a long time, the insurance may seem very expensive – but if you can't afford it, you certainly won't be able to afford to deal with a medical emergency overseas.

AIR

Buying a Plane Ticket

Your plane ticket will probably be the single most expensive item in your budget, and buying it can be an intimidating business. There is likely to be a multitude of airlines and travel agents hoping to separate you from your money, and it is always worth putting aside a few hours to research the current state of the market. Start early: some of the cheapest tickets have to be bought months in advance, and some popular flights sell out early. Talk to other recent travellers – they may be able to stop you from making some of the same old mistakes. Look at the ads in newspapers and magazines (not forgetting the South American press if you have access to it). Consult reference books and watch for special offers, and then phone round travel agents for bargains. (Airlines can supply information on routes and timetables; however, except at times of inter-airline war they do not supply the cheapest tickets.) Find out the fare, the route, the duration of the journey and any restrictions on the ticket. (See restrictions in the Air Travel Glossary.) Then sit back and decide which is best for you.

You may discover that those impossibly cheap flights are 'fully booked, but we have another one that costs a bit more...' Or the flight is on an airline notorious for its poor safety standards and leaves you in the world's least favourite airport mid-journey for 14 hours. Or they claim only to have the last two seats available for Brazil for the whole of July, which they will hold for you for a maximum of two hours. Don't panic – keep ringing around.

JOHN MAIER, JR.

The Santa Teresa trolley on the Arcos da Lapa

Use the fares quoted in this book as a guide only. They are approximate and based on the rates advertised by travel agents at the time of going to press. Quoted airfares do not necessarily constitute a recommendation for the carrier.

If you are travelling from the UK or the USA, you will probably find that the cheapest flights are being advertised by obscure bucket shops whose names haven't yet reached the telephone directory. Many such firms are honest and solvent, but there are a few rogues who will take your money and disappear, to reopen elsewhere a month or two later under a new name. If you feel suspicious about a firm, don't give them all the money at once – leave a deposit of 20% or so and pay the balance when you get the ticket. If they insist on cash in advance, go somewhere else. And once you have the ticket, ring the airline to confirm that you are actually booked on the flight.

You may decide to pay more than the rock-bottom fare by opting for the safety of a better known travel agent. Firms such as STA, which has offices worldwide, Council Travel in the USA or Travel CUTS in Canada are not going to disappear overnight, leaving you clutching a receipt for a non-existent ticket, but they do offer good prices to most destinations.

Varig, Brazil's international airline, flies to many major cities in the world. From the USA the basic carriers serving Brazil are Varig, American Airlines, United Airlines and Japan Airlines (JAL) (from the west coast); from England, British Airways and Varig; and from Australia, Qantas, and Aerolineas Argentinas.

Discount tickets have restrictions. The most pernicious is the limit on the amount of time you can spend in Brazil. Charter flights often restrict a stay to as little as three weeks. Most other tickets have a 90-day limit. There's usually a premium for tickets valid over 180 days. Although the Brazil Air Pass is no longer the bargain it once was, it's worth mentioning here that you *must* purchase it outside Brazil. (See the Getting Around chapter for more information.)

If you are planning to stay in Brazil for more than 90 days, cheap airline tickets are a big problem. You are required to buy a return ticket before you will be issued with a visa in the USA, but it's not hard to get around this (see the Visa section in the Facts for the Visitor chapter). Unfortunately, the cost of a one-way ticket is more than twice the price of a return economy fare. For example: from Los Angeles to Rio return costs about US$900 if you buy from the airlines, but you may be able to obtain a discount ticket for as little as US$700 from a specialist travel agent. The fare for a one-way ticket is US$850, and for a return ticket valid for over three months the fare is doubled. Absurd! This means it may be cheaper to buy a discounted return ticket with a 90-day limit, bury the return portion ticket and then buy a ticket in Brazil when you are ready to go home.

If you plan to stay more than six months in Brazil you also have to consider leaving the country to get a new visa. Ask about package deals. We were able to get a return Aerolineas Argentinas ticket from New York to Buenos Aires with an unlimited stopover in Rio. This gave us a free ride to Buenos Aires to get new visas after several months in Brazil – but check if this is still available.

Once you have your ticket, write its number down, together with the flight number and other details, and keep the information somewhere separate. If the ticket is lost or stolen, this will help you get a replacement.

It's sensible to buy travel insurance as early as possible. If you buy it the week before you fly, you may find, for example, that you're not covered for delays to your flight caused by industrial action.

Air Travellers with Special Needs

If you have special needs of any sort – you've broken a leg, you're vegetarian, travelling in a wheelchair, taking the baby, terrified of flying – you should let the airline know as soon as possible so that staff can make arrangements accordingly. You should remind them when you reconfirm your booking (at least 72 hours before departure) and again when you check in at the airport. It may also be worth ringing round the airlines before you make your booking to find out how they can handle your particular needs.

Airports and airlines can be surprisingly helpful, but they do need advance warning. Most international airports will provide escorts from check-in desk to plane where needed, and there should be ramps, lifts, accessible toilets and reachable phones. Aircraft toilets, on the other hand, are likely to present a problem; travellers should discuss this with the airline at an early stage and, if necessary, with their doctor.

Guide dogs for the blind will often have to travel in a specially pressurised baggage compartment with other animals, away from their owner, though smaller guide dogs may be admitted to the cabin. All guide dogs will be subject to the same quarantine laws (six months in isolation, etc) as any other animal when entering or returning to countries currently free of rabies such as the UK or Australia.

GUY MOBERLY

Rio de Janeiro

Deaf travellers can ask for airport and in-flight announcements to be written down for them.

Children under two travel for 10% of the standard fare (or free, on some airlines), as long as they don't occupy a seat. They don't get a baggage allowance either. 'Skycots' should be provided by the airline if requested in advance; these will take a child weighing up to about 10 kg. Children between two and 12 can usually occupy a seat for half to two-thirds of the full fare, and do get a baggage allowance. Push chairs can often be taken as hand luggage.

To/From the USA

The *New York Times*, the *LA Times*, the *Chicago Tribune* and the *San Francisco Examiner* all produce weekly travel sections in which you'll find any number of travel agents' ads. Council Travel and STA Travel have offices in major cities nationwide. The Brazilian American Cultural Center (BACC; ☎ (1-800) 222-2746) offers its members low-priced flights to Brazil (for more details about BACC, see the section on Useful Organisations in the Facts for the Visitor chapter).

Also highly recommended is the newsletter *Travel Unlimited* (PO Box 1058, Allston, MA 02134) which publishes details of the cheapest airfares and courier possibilities for destinations all over the world from the USA.

From the USA the gateway cities for major carriers are New York, Los Angeles and Miami. All have basically the same fare structure. Economy fares often have to be purchased two weeks in advance and restrictions commonly require a minimum stay of two weeks and a maximum of three months. Varig offers this type of return ticket to Rio at US$726 (ex Miami); US$787 (ex New York); and US$886 (ex Los Angeles). Lineas Aereas Paraguayas (LAP) used to offer a cheap Miami-Asunción-Rio flight, but this has apparently been discontinued. LAP also offers a Miami-Asunción-São Paulo flight for around US$540 (requiring two-week advance purchase for a two-week minimum stay or three months maximum).

Some of the cheapest flights from Brazil to the USA are charters from Manaus to Miami (the Disneyworld express!). Manaus, which lies halfway between Rio and Miami, is a useful gateway city if you plan to make a long circuit around Brazil.

To/From Canada

Travel CUTS has offices in all major cities. The *Toronto Globe & Mail* carries travel agents' ads, and the magazine *Great Expeditions* (PO Box 8000-411, Abbotsford BC V2S 6H1) is useful. Travellers interested in booking flights with Canadian courier companies should obtain a copy of the newsletter published by Travel Unlimited (see the USA section for details).

To/From the UK

Look for travel agents' ads in the Sunday papers, the travel magazine *Complete Traveller*, and listings magazines such as *Time Out* and *City Limits*. Also look out for the free magazines widely available in London – start by looking outside the main railway stations.

To initiate your price comparisons, you could contact travel agents such as Journey Latin America (JLA; ☎ (081) 747-3108) which publishes a very useful *Flights Bulletin*; Travel Bug (☎ (061) 721-4000); Trailfinders (☎ (071) 938-3444); STA (☎ (071) 937-9962); and South American Experience (☎ (071) 379-0344). For courier flight details, contact Polo Express (☎ (081) 759-5383) or Courier Travel Service (☎ (071) 351-0300).

The Globetrotters Club (BCM Roving, London WC1N 3XX) publishes *Globe*, a newsletter for members which covers obscure destinations and can help find travelling companions.

Prices for discounted flights between London and Rio start at around £300 one way or £550 return – bargain hunters should have little trouble finding even lower prices.

To/From Europe

The newsletter *Farang* (La Rue 8 á 4261, Braives, Belgium) deals with exotic destinations, as does the magazine *Aventure au Bout du Monde* (116 Rue de Javel, 75015 Paris). One reader from Germany quoted us these prices for return tickets to Brazil: British Airways US$1000; Varig/Lufthansa US$1200; United US$1100, with stops in New York and/or Washington.

To/From Australia & New Zealand

Aerolineas Argentinas flies Sydney-Auckland-Buenos Aires-Rio de Janeiro via the South Pole once a week (twice during peak periods) for A$3207. This ticket is valid for six months. If you shop around, you should be able to pick up a fare for approximately A$2500. Aerolineas has some other interesting fares: a Circle Americas fare to South and North America for A$2969; Circle Pacific fares via South America for A$3455; a Two-Continents fare that includes Africa and South America for A$3500; and a Round-the-World (RTW) fare via South America for A$3199 that's valid for one year. It also has some winter specials you should keep an eye out for, like its A$1699 fare to Brazil for up to 45 days.

Qantas flies Sydney-Rio de Janeiro via Los Angeles for A$4200. The LA-Rio leg is on Varig; a maximum of two stopovers is allowed in the Pacific, in places like Honolulu and Tahiti. A Qantas/Varig RTW fare costs A$3700. United Airlines flies Sydney-Auckland-Los Angeles-New York-Rio for A$2749.

To/From Asia

Hong Kong is the discount plane ticket capital of the region. Its bucket shops, however, are at least as unreliable as those of other cities. Ask the advice of other travellers before buying a ticket.

STA, which is reliable, has branches in Hong Kong, Tokyo, Singapore, Bangkok and Kuala Lumpur.

From the Orient, the hot tickets are JAL and Singapore Airlines. JAL flies Tokyo-Los Angeles-Rio de Janeiro-São Paulo, and it often has the best fares to Rio from the west coast of the USA.

Round-the-World Tickets & Circle Pacific Fares

RTW tickets that include a South American leg have become very popular in the last few years. These tickets are often real bargains, and can work out no more expensive or even cheaper than an ordinary return ticket. From the UK, a RTW ticket including Rio starts at around UK£1300. From the USA, a RTW ticket including Rio starts at around US$2500.

Official airline RTW tickets are usually made available by cooperation between two airlines which permit you to fly anywhere you want on their route systems, as long as you don't backtrack. Other restrictions are that you (usually) must book the first sector in advance and cancellation penalties then apply. There may be restrictions on how many stopovers you are permitted and usually the tickets are valid from 90 days up to a year. An alternative type of RTW ticket is one put together by a travel agent using a combination of discounted tickets.

Circle Pacific tickets use a combination of airlines to circle the Pacific – combining Australia, New Zealand, South America, North America and Asia. As with RTW tickets there are advance purchase restrictions and limits to how many stopovers you can take.

Arriving in Rio by Air

Almost all flights into Rio – domestic and national – arrive at Aeroporto Galeão on Ilha do Governador. Shuttle flights from São Paulo arrive at the conveniently located Aeroporto Santos Dumont, in the city centre along the bay.

Incoming visitors at Galeão pass through customs and then continue into a large lobby where there's a tourist information counter run by a private company called RDE which can arrange hotel and taxi reservations. The staff also try to palm off a 'travellers passport' for the outrageous sum of US$25, and attempt to pressure befuddled travellers with the argument that government regulations require purchase of this junk package. This is a load of nonsense and a blatant rip-off attempt.

Leaving Rio by Air

All three major Brazilian airlines have their main offices in the centre (metro stop Cinelândia). You can also walk over to the ticket counters at Aeroporto Santos Dumont and make reservations from there.

Varig/Cruzeiro (☎ 292-6600 for reservations or 292-5220 for information) has its main office in Centro at Avenida Rio Branco 277 (☎ 220-3821). There are also offices at Rua Rodolfo Dantas 16 in Copacabana (☎ 541-6343), and Rua Visconde de Pirajá 351, Ipanema (☎ 287-9040). The city office is much more reliable and knowledgeable than the other Varig offices.

VASP (☎ 292-2080) has a city office at Rua Santa Luzia 735. It also has offices at Aeroporto Santos Dumont (☎ 292-2112), at Avenida NS de Copacabana 262 (☎ 292-2112) in Copacabana, and at Rua Visconde de Pirajá 444 (☎ 292-2112) in Ipanema.

Transbrasil (☎ 297-4422) is in the centre at Avenida Calógeras 30. The other office is at Avenida Atlântica 1998 (☎ 236-7475) in Copacabana.

Nordeste Linhas Aéreas (☎ 220-4366) is at Aeroporto Santos Dumont. It goes to Porto Seguro, Ilhéus and other smaller cities in the Northeast. Rio Sul (☎ 262-6911) does the same for the south and is also at Aeroporto Santos Dumont.

JOHN MAIER, JR.

On the beach

International airlines with offices in Rio include:

Aeroflot
  Avenida NS de Copacabana 249 A/B, Copacabana
  (☎ 275-0440; fax 541-9542)
Aerolineas Argentinas
  Rua da Assembléia 100, 29th floor, Centro (☎ 292-4131; fax
  224-4931)
Aero Peru
  Praça Mahatma Gandhi 2, Centro (☎ 210-3124; fax 262-
  5065)
Air France
  Avenida Presidente Antônio Carlos 58, 9th floor, Centro
  (☎ 212-6226; fax 532-1284)
Alitalia
  Avenida Presidente Wilson 231, 21st floor, Centro (☎ 240-
  7822; fax 240-7493)
American Airlines
  Avenida Presidente Wilson 165, 5th floor, Centro (☎ 220-
  0603; fax 220-1022)
Avianca
  Avenida Presidente Wilson 165, No 801, Centro (☎ 220-
  7697; fax 220-9848)
British Airways
  Avenida Rio Branco 108, 21st floor, Centro (☎ 221-0922;
  fax 242-2889)
Canadian Airlines International
  Rua da Ajuda 35, 29th floor, Centro (☎ 220-5343; fax 398-
  3604)
Cathay Pacific
  Avenida Rio Branco 181/3303, Centro (☎ 220-1484; fax
  220-3214)
Continental
  Rua da Assembléia 2316, 10th floor, Centro (☎ 531-1761;
  fax 531-1984)
Delta Airlines
  Avenida Nilo Peçanha 50/1009, Centro (☎ 262-3782; fax
  240-9201)
El Al
  Avenida Rio Branco 181/1706, Centro (☎ 220-6098; fax
  220-3230)
Iberia
  Avenida Presidente Antônio Carlos 51, 8th floor, Centro
  (☎ 282-1336; fax 240-9842)
Japan Air Lines
  Avenida Rio Branco 156, No 2014, Centro (☎ 220-6414; fax
  220-6091)
KLM
  Avenida Rio Branco 311A, Centro (☎ 292-7747; fax 240-
  1595)
Korean Airlines
  Rua Siqueira Campos 43/303, Copacabana (☎ 236-5787;
  fax 256-7960)

Lan Chile
    Avenida Nilo Peçanha 50, 13th floor, Centro (☎ 220-9722; fax 532-1420)
LAP-Lineas Aereas Paraguayas
    Avenida Rio Branco 245, 7th floor, Centro (☎ 220-4148; fax 240-9577)
Lloyd Aero Boliviano
    Avenida Calógeras 30, Centro (☎ 220-9548; fax 533-2835)
Lufthansa
    Avenida Rio Branco 156 D, Centro (☎ 282-1253; fax 262-8845)
Qantas
    Avenida Ataulfo de Paiva 226, 5th floor, Leblon (☎ 511-0045; fax 239-8349)
SAS
    Avenida Presidente Wilson 231, 6th floor, Centro (☎ 210-1222; fax 220-9494)
Singapore Airlines
    Avenida Rio Branco 143, 3rd floor, Centro (☎ 252-5604; fax 252-5325)
South African
    Avenida Rio Branco 245, 4th floor, Centro (☎ 262-6002; fax 262-6120)
Swissair
    Avenida Rio Branco 108, 10th floor, Centro (☎ 297-5177; fax 224-9205)
United Airlines
    Avenida Presidente Antônio Carlos, Centro (☎ 240-5068; fax 220-9946)
USAir
    Avenida Presidente Wilson 165/715, Centro (☎ 240-3644; fax 533-0439)

To buy a ticket out of Brazil, non-resident foreigners have to change at a bank the equivalent in US dollars of the price of the ticket. After you present the receipt given by the bank to the travel agent or airline company, your ticket can be issued. Another option is to use an international credit card, which is then debited by calculating the real at the turismo rate.

In the past, the official dollar rate was much less than the parallel rate. This meant that travellers, who required a bank receipt to purchase tickets out, effectively had to pay more for flights than locals, who could change dollars at the parallel rate.

At the time of writing, the official dollar rates and the parallel rates were very close and it appeared that these discrepancies would end. Unfortunately that hasn't happened. Here's why.

Travel agents now offer a number of discounted tickets, but to buy one a foreigner has to go to the bank and change the US dollar equivalent of a full-price ticket.

With the receipt, the ticket can be issued at the discount price, but it leaves the buyer with a couple of hundred dollars worth of reais. The alternatives are to spend them or to buy US dollars from a casa de câmbio.

It should be stressed that this situation could change at any time, so find out about any restrictions well before you plan on buying a ticket.

From Rio to Madrid it costs about US$900 return. Other European cities cost a little more. To the USA, Rio-Miami costs US$700 return. To Australia the cheapest flights are the trans-polar Aerolineas Argentina flights, which cost around US$2000 one way. Discounts are available and worth hunting around for, even if you do have to go through the papershuffling described above.

At the time of writing, the airport tax for domestic flights was about US$7, and for international flights, around US$18. The appropriate tax is usually added to the price of your ticket.

BUS

From Rio, there are buses going everywhere. They all arrive and depart from the loud Novo Rio Rodoviária (☎ 291-5151 for information), Avenida Francisco Bicalho in São Cristóvão, about five minutes north of the centre. At the rodoviária you can get information on transport and lodging if you ask at the Riotur desk on the ground floor.

If you arrive in Rio by bus, it's a good idea to take a taxi to your hotel, or at least the general area you want to stay. Travelling on local buses with all your belongings is a little risky. A small booth near the Riotur desk organises the yellow cabs in the rank out front. Tell them where you want to go and they'll write a price on a ticket you give to the driver of the first cab on the rank. If you just grab the cab the driver will try to add a bit extra.

Excellent buses leave every 15 minutes or so for São Paulo (six hours). Most major destinations have *leito* (executive) buses leaving late at night. These are very comfortable. Many travel agents in the city sell bus tickets. It's a good idea to buy a ticket a couple of days in advance if you can.

Duration of Bus Trips within Brazil

Angra dos Reis	2¾ hours
Belém	60 hours
Belo Horizonte	7 hours
Brasília	18 hours
Cabo Frio	3 hours

Curitiba	11 hours
Florianópolis	20 hours
Foz do Iguaçu	22 hours
Goiânia	18 hours
Ouro Preto	7 hours
Parati	4 hours
Petrópolis	1½ hours
Porto Alegre	27 hours
Recife	38 hours
Salvador	28 hours
São João del Rei	5½ hours
Vitória	8 hours

Duration of International Bus Trips

Asunción, Paraguay	25 hours
Buenos Aires, Argentina	46 hours
Montevideo, Uruguay	39 hours
Santiago, Chile	74 hours

CAR & MOTORBIKE

Drivers of cars and riders of motorbikes entering Brazil will need the vehicle's registration papers, and an international driver's permit in addition to their domestic licence. You should also carry liability insurance. You may also need a *carnet de passage en douane*, which is effectively a passport for the vehicle, and acts as a temporary waiver of import duty. The carnet may need to have listed any more expensive spares that you're planning to carry with you,

JOHN MAIER, JR.

Peak-hour traffic in Rio

such as a gearbox. This is necessary when travelling in many countries, including those in South America, and is designed to prevent car import rackets.

Another document used in South America is the *libreta de pasos por aduana*, a booklet of customs passes. It supposedly takes the place of the carnet, but since the refundable bond for the libreta is only US$100, it doesn't seem much of a deterrent to selling a vehicle.

Some travellers recently reported that the only documents they required were the title of the vehicle and a customs form issued on arrival which must be presented upon departure. Contact your local automobile association for details about all documentation. Remember that it's always better to carry as much as you can.

Anyone planning to take their own vehicle with them needs to check in advance what spares and petrol are likely to be available. Lead-free is not on sale worldwide, and neither is every little part for your car. Brazil has plenty of Volkswagen spares.

BICYCLE

You don't see many long-distance cyclists in Brazil. We wouldn't recommend cycling there, as conditions are very dangerous. Crazy drivers who only respect vehicles larger than themselves, lots of trucks on the main roads spewing out unfiltered exhaust fumes, roads without shoulder room and the constant threat of theft are just some of the reasons. In short, it seems a downright dangerous thing to do.

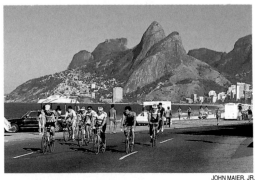

JOHN MAIER, JR.

Cyclists in Ipanema

If you're still determined to tackle Brazil by bike, before you leave home, go over your bike with a fine-toothed comb and fill your repair kit with every imaginable spare. As with cars and motorbikes, you won't necessarily be able to buy that crucial gizmo for your machine when it breaks down somewhere in the back of beyond as the sun sets.

Bicycles can travel by air. You *can* take them to pieces and put them in a bike bag or box, but it's much easier simply to wheel your bike to the check-in desk, where it should be treated as a piece of baggage. You may have to remove the pedals and turn the handlebars sideways so that it takes up less space in the aircraft's hold; check all this with the airline well in advance, preferably before you pay for your ticket.

HITCHING

Hitching in Brazil, with the possible exception of the Amazon and Pantanal, is difficult. The word for hitching in Portuguese is *carona*, so *pode dar carona* is 'can you give (me/us) a lift'. The best way to hitch – practically the only way if you want a ride – is to wait at a petrol station or a truck stop and talk to the drivers. But even this can be difficult. A few years back there were several assaults by hitchhikers and the government began to discourage giving rides in public service announcements.

TRAVEL AGENTS

Expeditours (☎ 287-9697; fax 521-4388) is one of the largest ecological tour operators in Brazil. It specialises in the Amazon and Pantanal, but runs many other programmes for the special interest traveller, as well as tours in Rio itself. It's highly recommended.

Diana Turismo (☎ 255-2296; fax 235-7570), at Avenida NS de Copacabana 330, has an extensive itinerary of city tours and short excursions to other areas in the state. It also organises packages for the Amazon and Pantanal. Kontik Franstur (☎ 253-5111; fax 263-1093) has all the city tours, including Rio by night, Dine Around and Floresta da Tijuca. It also does trips to the mountain town of Petrópolis.

ORGANISED TOURS

The following listing of organisations and tour agencies provides a sample of the tour options available for independent travellers with special interests. Any tour to

Brazil will include Rio de Janeiro on its itinerary. To visit Brazil without seeing Rio would be sheer lunacy.

From the UK

The boom in ecotourism worldwide has prompted the creation of groups and organisations in the UK and elsewhere to monitor the effects of tourism and provide assessments and recommendations for those involved. For more information on ecotours, try contacting: the Centre for the Advancement of Responsible Travel (☎ (0732) 35-2757); Tourism Concern (☎ (081) 878-9053); and Green Flag International (☎ (0223) 89-3587). If you're just interested in flying down to Rio for a couple of weeks holiday, there are lots of packages available. Try any travel agent.

From the USA

Assessments and information about ecological and other types of tours can be obtained from: the North American Coordinating Center for Responsible Tourism, 2 Kensington Rd, San Anselmo, CA 94960; One World Family Travel Network, PO Box 4317, Berkeley, CA 94703; and Travel Links, Co-op America, 2100 M St NW, Suite 310, Washington DC 20036.

Focus Tours (☎ & fax (612) 892-7830), 14821 Hillside Lane, Burnsville, MN 55306, is rated highly for its dedication to conservation and use of naturalists as guides. Tour destinations include the Pantanal (and Chapada das Guimarães); Minas Gerais; the Amazon; Parque Nacional do Itatiaia; and Serra da Canastra.

Brazilian Views (☎ (212) 472-9539), 201 E 66th St, Suite 21G, New York, NY 10021, is a small agency offering a wide range of special-interest tours based on topics such as horticulture, weaving, birdwatching, arts and crafts, gems and minerals etc.

Brazil Nuts (☎ (800) 553-9959 toll-free), 79 Satanford St, Fairfield CT 06430, offers various packages to Brazil, including a 'Rio like a Native' programme that's been recommended by readers.

From Australia

Inca Tours (☎ (043) 512-133; fax (043) 512-526; toll-free 1800-024-955) specialises in travel to South America. Lew Pullbrook, who runs it, has been visiting the continent for years and really knows his way around. Lew organises trips for small or larger groups, and he's happy for backpackers to call for a bit of advice. His office is at 5 Alison Road, Wyong, NSW 2259.

JOHN MAIER, JR.

Ferry from Rio to Niterói

Getting Around

TO/FROM THE AIRPORT

All international and nearly all domestic flights use Aeroporto Galeão, 15 km north of the city centre on Ilha do Governador.

Aeroporto Santos Dumont is in the heart of the city on the bay. It's used for the São Paulo shuttle and some flights to a variety of other destinations like Porto Seguro or Belo Horizonte. You can take the same bus as for Aeroporto Galeão or get to the city and take a taxi, or simply walk to the airport from Centro.

Bus

Air-Conditioned There are two routes with air-con airport buses operating from Aeroporto Galeão from 5.20 to 12.10 am, every 40 minutes to one hour (about US$4). One route goes to the centre and to Aeroporto Santos Dumont, the other route goes to the city centre and along the beaches of Copacabana, Ipanema, Leblon, Vidigal, and São Conrado. The driver will stop wherever you ask along the route. On both routes, you can stop at the rodoviária if you want to catch a bus out of Rio immediately. If you want to catch the metro, ask the driver to let you off right outside the entrance to Carioca metro station.

You can catch the bus on the 2nd floor (arrivals) of the main terminal, at the Galeão sign. The tourist desk inside the airport has schedule and price information. If you're heading to the airport you can get the bus in front of the major hotels along the beach, but you have to look alive and flag them down. The bus company is Empresa Real. Galeão should be written on the direction sign.

It is safer to catch one of these buses or a taxi than to take a local bus if you have many valuables.

Local On the far corner, to your right as you leave the main terminal at Galeão, there is a small terminal for local buses on Rua Ecuador. There are bus numbers and routes posted, so it's pretty easy to get oriented.

For Copacabana, the best is bus No 126, 127 or 128. The best bus to Ipanema and Leblon is No 128, but you can also take No 126 or 127 to Copacabana and then catch another bus to Ipanema and Leblon.

For the budget hotels in Catete and Glória, take bus No 170 ('Gávea – via Jóquei'), which goes down Rua do Catete and then turns up Rua Pedro Americo and along Rua Bento Lisboa. If you want the Catete budget hotels, get off at the stop near the corner of Bento Lisboa and Rua Silveira Martins and walk a block down to Rua Catete.

An alternative is to take any bus that goes to the centre on Avenida Rio Branco. Get off near the end of Avenida Rio Branco and hop on the metro. Get off the metro at Catete station, which is in the heart of the budget hotel area.

Taxi

Many taxis from the airport will try to rip you off. The safe course is to take a radio-dispatched taxi, where you pay a set fare at the airport. This is also the most expensive way to go. A yellow-and-blue *comum* (common) taxi is about 20% cheaper if the meter is working and if you pay what is on the fare schedule. A sample fare from the airport to Copacabana is US$18 in a yellow-and-blue taxi versus US$24 in a radio-dispatched taxi. If you're entering Brazil for the first time and are on a budget, a good compromise is to take a bus to somewhere near your destination and then take a short taxi ride to your hotel.

Sharing a taxi from the airport is a good idea. Taxis will take up to four people. To ensure a little bit of security, before entering the taxi at the airport you can usually get a receipt with the licence plate of your taxi and a phone number to register losses or complaints. If you're heading to Leblon or Ipanema, the Tunnel Reboucas is more direct than the beach route.

BUS

The buses are a real mixture of the good, the bad and the ugly. The good: Rio's buses are fast, frequent and cheap and, because Rio is long and narrow, it's easy to get the right bus and usually no big deal if you're on the wrong one. The bad: Rio's buses are often crowded, slowed down by traffic and driven by raving maniacs who drive the buses as if they were motorbikes. The ugly: Rio's buses are the scene of many of the city's robberies. Locals like to joke that getting on a bus is better than going to an amusement park: you get the toboggan, roller coaster and haunted train rides all for the one low price.

In Rio, you get on at the back and exit from the front. Usually there's a money collector sitting at a turnstile at the rear of the bus, with the bus price displayed above his or her head. If you're unsure if it's the right bus, it's easy to hop on the back and ask the money collector if the bus is going to your destination – *você vai para...?* If it's the wrong bus no-one will mind if you hop off, even if the bus has gone a stop or two.

In addition to their number, buses have their destinations, including the areas they go through, written on the side. Nine out of 10 buses going south from the centre will go to Copacabana and vice versa. All buses have the price displayed above the head of the money collector. The buses you need to catch for specific destinations are listed under individual sights.

Crime can be a problem on buses. Rather than remain at the rear of the bus, it's safer to pay the fare and go through the turnstile. Try to avoid carrying valuables if you can. If you must take valuables with you then keep them well hidden. If you feel paranoid about something on the bus, get off and catch another.

There are also special air-con buses (see To/From the Airport). The Castelo-Hotel Nacional and Castelo-São Conrado buses are good to take for Praia Pepino. From the Castelo station there are buses to Petrópolis and Terosópolis, which saves a trip out to the rodoviária. There is an open-air tourist bus that goes along the beaches and then over to Pão de Açúcar.

If you're staying in the Catete/Flamengo area and want to get to the beaches by bus, you can either walk to the main roadway along Parque do Flamengo and take any bus marked 'Copacabana' or you can walk to Largo do Machado and take the No 570 bus.

METRO

Rio's excellent subway system is limited to points north of Botafogo and is open from 6 am to 11 pm daily, except Sunday. The two air-con lines are cleaner, faster and cheaper than buses (discounts are offered with multiple tickets). The main line from Botafogo to Saens Pena has 15 stops, of which the first 12 are: Botafogo, Flamengo, Largo do Machado, Catete, Glória, Cinelândia, Carioca, Uruguaiana, Presidente Vargas, Central, Cidade Nova and Estácio, which is common to both lines. At Estácio the line splits: the main line continues west towards the neighbourhood of Andarai, making stops at Afonso Pena, Engenho Velho and Tijuca, and the secondary line goes north towards the Maracanã stadium and beyond. The main stops for Centro are Cinelândia and Carioca. Tickets are cheap (35c) and you can buy return tickets (*Ida e Volta*) or tickets for multiple journeys of 10 rides (*multiplo*).

CAR & MOTORBIKE

The number of fatalities caused by motor vehicles in Brazil is estimated at 80,000 per year. The roads can be very dangerous, especially busy highways like the Rio to São Paulo corridor. Most of the problems stem from the Brazilian driver. If you thought the Italians were wild drivers, just wait. This isn't true everywhere, but in general the car owner is king of the road and shows it. Other motorists are treated as unwelcome guests at a private party. Pedestrians are shown no mercy, and certainly no courtesy.

Especially in Rio, the anarchic side of the Brazilian personality emerges from behind the driver's wheel as lane dividers, one-way streets and even sidewalks are disregarded and violated. Driving is unpoliced, traffic violations unheard of.

Despite all appearances to the contrary, Brazil does hold to the convention that a red light means 'stop'. In practice, this old-fashioned, but often useful, concept has been modified to mean 'maybe we'll stop, maybe we'll slow down – but if it's night we'll probably do neither'.

Drivers use their horns incessantly, and buses, which have no horns, rev their engines instead. One of the craziest habits is driving at night without headlights. This is done, as far as we can tell, so that the headlights can be flashed to warn approaching vehicles.

Many drivers are racing fans and tend to drive under the influence, pretending they are Formula One drivers. This cult of speed, a close cousin to the cult of machismo, is insatiable; its only positive aspect is that, unlike grandma driving to church on Sunday, these drivers tend to be very alert and rarely fall asleep at the wheel.

Car & Motorbike Rental

In the city itself, renting a car is pointless. Traffic snarls and parking problems will not make for an enjoyable holiday. If the bus and metro aren't your style there are plenty of taxis. A good alternative to them all is to rent a car with a driver. You'll find most hotels have chauffer-driven cars available. And renting a car with a driver is the same price as renting a car alone. For day trips it's ideal. If you want to go somewhere overnight, you'll have to cover the food and lodging costs of the driver.

Renting a car is expensive, with prices similar to those in the US and Europe. But if you can share the expense with friends it's a great way to explore some of the many remote beaches and national parks near Rio. Several

ANDREW DRAFFEN

JOHN MAIER, JR.

Top: Buses are a mixture of the good, the bad & the ugly
Bottom: Motorbikes are popular in Rio

familiar multinationals dominate the car rental business in Brazil and getting a car is safe and easy if you have a driver's licence, a credit card and a passport. You should also carry an international driver's permit.

Car rental agencies can be found at the airport or clustered together on Avenida Princesa Isabel in Copacabana. Prices are not cheap, at about US$70 a day, but they go down a bit in the off season.

There is little competition between the major rental companies. Prices are usually about the same, although there are occasional promotional deals. Fiat Unos are the cheapest cars to rent, followed by the Volkswagen Golf and Chevette (which has a good reputation). Sometimes the rental companies will claim to be out of these cheaper models; if this is the case, don't hesitate to shop around. Also, when you get prices quoted on the phone, make sure they include insurance, which is required. When looking at the contract, pay close attention to any theft clause which appears to load a large percentage of any loss onto the hirer. Another tricky clause we found was that if you have an accident and get a police statement, you don't have to pay for the damage. But you do have to pay 70% of the daily hire for the number of days it takes the rental company to fix the car!

Car rental agencies include:

Avis
> Avenida Princesa Isabel 150, Copacabana (☎ 295-8041, toll-free 011-800-8787), and Aeroporto Galeão (☎ 398-3083)

Budget
> Avenida Princesa Isabel 254, Copacabana (☎ 295-0040), and Aeroporto Galeão (☎ 398-3831)

Hertz
> Avenida Princesa Isabel 334-B Copacabana (☎ 275-4996), and Aeroporto Galeão (☎ 398-3162)

Interlocadora
> Avenida Princesa Isabel 186 A/B, Copacabana (☎ 275-6546), Aeroporto Galeão (☎ 398-3181), and Aeroporto Santos Dumont (☎ 240-0754)

Localiza National
> Avenida Princesa Isabel 214, Copacabana (☎ 275-3340, toll free 031-800-2322), Aeroporto Galeão (☎ 398-5989), and Aeroporto Santos Dumont (☎ 220-5455)

Locarauto
> Rua Francisco Manoel 81, Benfica (☎ 228-7801, toll free 011-800-8188), and Aeroporto Galeão (☎ 398-3783)

Nobre
> Avenida Princesa Isabel 150, Copacabana (☎ 541-4646, toll-free 011-800-8922), Aeroporto Galeão (☎ 398-3862), and Aeroporto Santos Dumont (☎ 262-5550)

Unidas
Avenida Princesa Isabel 350, Copacabana (☎ 275-8496,
toll free 011-800-3106), Aeroporto Galeão (☎ 398-3844),
and Aeroporto Santos Dumont (☎ 240-9181)

Renting a motorbike is more expensive than renting a
car. If you want to buy a bike, Brazil manufactures its
own, but they are expensive. The most powerful we saw
was 650cc.

Motorbikes are popular in Rio, but theft is a big
problem; you can't even insure them because theft is so
common. Most people who ride keep their bike in a
guarded place, at least overnight. For the traveller this
can be difficult to organise, but if you can manoeuvre
around the practical problems, Rio is a great place to
have a motorbike if you're an experienced rider.

Mar e Moto (☎ 2744398) rents motorbikes but it is
cheaper to rent a car. It's in Leblon at Avenida
Bartolomeu Mitre 1008.

TAXI

Rio's yellow-and-blue taxis are quite reasonably priced,
especially if you're dividing the fare with a friend or two.
Taxis are particularly useful late at night and when
carrying valuables, but they are not a completely safe
and hassle-free ride. First, there are a few rare cases of
people being assaulted and robbed by taxi drivers.
Second, and much more common, the drivers have a
marked tendency to exaggerate fares.

Here's how the taxi is supposed to operate: there
should be a meter and it should work; there should be a
current *tabela* to determine the fare; upon reaching your
destination, check the meter and look that up on the
tabela, usually posted on the passenger window, which
is used to determine the fare.

Now, what to watch out for: most importantly, make
sure the meter works. If it doesn't, ask to be let out of the
cab. The meters have a flag that switches the meter rate;
this should be in the number one position (20% less expensive), except on Sundays, holidays, between 10 pm and 6
am, when driving outside the zona sul and during December as a Christmas bonus for the drivers (no joke!).

Make sure meters are cleared before you start (find
out the current starting number). Make sure the tabela
is original, not a photocopy. The taxi drivers that hang
out near the hotels are sharks. It's worth walking a block
to avoid them. Most people don't tip taxi drivers,
although it's common to round off the fare to the higher
number.

The meters are weighted towards distance not time. This gives the drivers an incentive to drive quickly (for a head rush tell your driver that you are in a bit of a hurry) and travel by roundabout routes. Taxis don't always run during thunderstorms because alcohol-powered cars stall easily in the wet, but buses usually plough on ahead. It's illegal for cabs to take more than four passengers. This is, of course, irrelevant except for the fact that most cabs won't do it because of conventions of the trade.

The white Coopertramo radio-dispatched taxis (☎ 260-2022) are 30% more expensive than the yellow-and-blue cabs, but they will come to you and they are safer.

BICYCLE

Cycling is popular with Cariocas. There's a bike path around Lagoa Rodrigo de Freitas, one in Barra da Tijuca, and one on the oceanfront from Ipanema to Leme. The *ciclóvia* (bike path) is currently being extended into the city to Praça 15 de Novembro. If you have a bit of road sense and don't mind mixing it with the traffic, a bike is a fun way to get around the zona sul.

Bicycle Rental

Stop Bike (☎ 275-7345), in the small arcade at Rua Barata Ribeiro 181, has a few mountain bikes to rent for US$15 a day, and it gives good deals if you rent for longer. The lady who runs the shop speaks English. If you just want to cruise the beachfront at Copacabana and Ipanema, bikes can be rented on Sundays and holidays on Avenida Atlântica in front of Rua República do Peru, at a cost of US$3 per hour.

WALKING

For God's sake be careful! Drivers run red lights, run up on sidewalks and stop for no-one and nothing.

BOAT

Ferries and hydrofoils to Niterói and Ilha da Paquetá leave from the ferry terminal near Praça 15 de Novembro. For information, see the Centro section of the Things to See & Do chapter.

JOHN MAIER, JR.

Cycling is popular in Rio

ORGANISED TOURS

Most of the larger tour companies operate sightseeing tours of Rio. They include Gray Line (☎ 294-1444; fax 259-5847), Expeditours (☎ 287-9697; fax 521-4388) and Kontik-Franstur (☎ 255-2442). Their brochures are sitting on the reception desks of many hotels. Tours cover the usual tourist destinations. Prices are quite reasonable. A four-hour tour to Corcovado and Tijuca costs around US$25.

For a more personalised tour, Rio Custom Tours (☎ 274-3217), run by Maria Lúcia Yolen, is recommended. Maria Lúcia is an excellent guide who likes to show that Rio is not all samba, beaches and Corcovado. Some of her tours include the Sunday Mass at São Bento, complete with Gregorian chants, a trip to the Casa do Pontal and its excellent folk-art collection, and a tour through Santa Teresa. She will pick you up and drop you off at your hotel.

Historic Rio Tour

Run by art historian Professor Carlos Roquette (☎ 322-4872), who speaks English and French as well as Portuguese, these tours bring old Rio to life. Itineraries include a night at the Teatro Municipal, Colonial Rio, Baroque Rio, Imperial Rio and a walking tour of Centro. Professor Roquette really knows his Rio, and if you have an obscure question, I'm sure he would welcome it.

Favela Tour

If you want to visit a favela, you'd be crazy to do it on your own. Since large amounts of cocaine are trafficked through them each week, there are lots of young, heavily armed characters around. Don't get the idea, though, that favelas are complete slums. The ones I've seen reminded me more of some poor country village. But unless you go with a local, there will be a lot of suspicious eyes on you. The safest alternative is to take one of the favela tours that now operate in Rio. Marcelo Armstrong (☎ 322-2727, mobile 989-0074) is the pioneer of favela tourism. He takes individuals and small groups to visit Rocinha, the largest favela in Rio, and Vila Canoas, near São Conrado. The tour takes in a school, medical centre and private houses, and you come away with a good idea how a favela operates. Some of the climbs are steep, so you need to be reasonably fit. You can take a camera, but ask permission before taking anybody's picture and don't take photos of suspicious or armed characters. Avoid going after heavy rain, because mudslides are common.

Villa Riso Colonial Tour

Villa Riso in São Conrado, next to the Gávea Golf Club, re-creates a colonial *fazenda* (farm), complete with employees wearing colonial gear. The house and gardens actually date from the early 18th century. A three-hour tour includes a buffet lunch, normally a *feijoada* or *churrasco* (see the Places to Eat chapter), and a medley of Brazilian theatrical music. You must make reservations (☎ 322-1444; fax 322-5196). Cost is US$40 and this includes pick-up and return to your hotel.

Things to See & Do

HIGHLIGHTS

Pão de Açúcar (Sugar Loaf)

Pão de Açúcar, God's gift to the picture postcard industry, is dazzling. From its peak, Rio is undoubtedly the most beautiful city in the world. There are many good times to make the ascent, but sunset on a clear day is the most spectacular. As day becomes night and the city lights start to sparkle down below, the sensation is delightful.

Everyone must go to Pão de Açúcar, but if you can, avoid going from about 10 to 11 am and 2 to 3 pm, which is when most tourist buses are arriving. Avoid cloudy days as well.

To reach the summit, 395 metres above Rio and the Baía de Guanabara, you have to take two cable cars. The first takes you up 220 metres to Morro da Urca. From here, you can see Baía de Guanabara and further up the winding coastline. On the ocean side of the mountain is Praia Vermelha, in a small, calm bay. Morro da Urca has its own restaurant, souvenir shops, a playground, a helipad and an outdoor theatre. The Beija Flor samba school puts on a show on Monday from 9 pm to 1 am. Less touristy shows are the Friday and Saturday carioca nights, at which some excellent musicians perform; check the local papers for listings.

A unique souvenir of your trip is the photo plate for US$10. As you go up the mountain, roving photographers will take your picture. Then while you're on Pão de Açúcar, they will develop the film and stick your face on a plate. You're under no pressure to buy here. If you don't want it they'll just stick another photo on top of yours. Make sure to treasure it, because after a couple of years the photo will fade away. Hopefully your memory of the trip up will stay fresh.

The second cable car goes up to Pão de Açúcar. At the top, you have a wonderful view of the city, Rio's Corcovado mountain with the statue of Christ with his arms outstretched, and the famous long curve of Praia de Copacabana. There's a fast-food place and souvenir shops, but the view's the attraction. Don't rush it – you can stay up for as long as you want. Take some time to wander the pathways below.

JOHN MAIER, JR

The cable car up Pão de Açúcar

The two-stage cable cars (☎ 541-3737) leave about every 30 minutes from Praça General Tibúrcio at Praia Vermelha in Urca. They operate daily from 8 am to 10 pm and cost US$8. Take a bus marked 'Urca' from Centro or Flamengo (No 107) or a No 500, 511 or 512 from the zona sul. The open-air bus that runs along the Ipanema and Copacabana beaches also goes to Pão de Açúcar. For information about climbing Pão de Açúcar, see the Climbing section in this chapter.

Corcovado & Cristo Redentor

Corcovado (Hunchback) is the mountain and Cristo Redentor (Christ the Redeemer) is the statue. The mountain rises straight up from the city to 709 metres. The statue, with its welcoming outstretched arms, stands another 30 metres high and weighs over 1000 tonnes. At night, the brightly lit figure of Christ is visible from all over the city.

The statue was originally conceived as a national monument to celebrate Brazil's 100 years of independence from Portugal. The 100 years came and went in 1922 without the money to start construction, but in 1931 the statue was completed by French sculptor Paul Landowski, thanks to some financial assistance from the Vatican.

The view from the top is a spectacular panorama of Rio and its surroundings. Christ's left arm points toward the zona norte, and Maracanã, the largest soccer stadium in the world, is easily visible in the foreground. You can see the international airport just beyond and the Serra dos Órgãos mountain range in the far distance. In front of Christ is Pão de Açúcar, in its classic postcard pose. To the right you can see the Lagoa Rodrigo de Freitas, the race-track, Jardim Botânico, and over to Ipanema and Leblon.

Corcovado lies within the Parque Nacional da Tijuca. You can get there by car or by taxi, but the best way is to go up in the cog train – sit on the right-hand side going up for the view. The round trip costs US$11 and leaves from Rua Cosme Velho 513 (Cosme Velho). You can get a taxi there or a bus marked 'Rua Cosme Velho' – a No 184 or 180 bus from Centro and Glória, a No 583 from Largo do Machado, Copacabana and Ipanema, or a No 584 from Leblon. Taxi drivers are quite open to making

CHRIS BEALL

Cristo Redentor (Christ the Redeemer)

a deal about return trips with waiting time. The cost (around US$20) for two or more people would work out cheaper than the train fares.

During the high season, the trains, which only leave every 30 minutes, can be slow going. Corcovado and the train are open from 8 am to 6.30 pm. A word of warning. Choose a clear day to come up to the top, otherwise you'll be disappointed. It may be clear at sea level and cloudy up high, so check the mountains before you make a move. For information about climbing Corcovado, see the Climbing section in this chapter.

Largo do Boticário If you have some time before the train leaves, walk up Rua Cosme Velho towards the tunnel. The first road on your right is the Largo do Boticário, a picturesque colonial-looking square featured in many postcards of the city.

CENTRO

Rio's centre is all business and bustle during the day and absolutely deserted at night and on weekends. It's a working city – the centre of finance and commerce. The numerous high-rise office buildings are filled with workers who pour onto the daytime streets to eat at the many restaurants and shop at the small stores. Lots of essential services for the traveller are in the centre. The main airline offices are here, as are foreign consulates, Brazilian government agencies, money exchange houses, banks and travel agencies.

The centre is the site of the original settlement. Most of the city's important museums and colonial buildings are here. Small enough to explore on foot, the city centre is lively and interesting, and occasionally beautiful, despite the many modern, Bauhaus-inspired buildings.

Two wide avenues cross the centre: Avenida Rio Branco, where buses leave for the zona sul, and Avenida Presidente Vargas, which heads out to the sambódromo and the zona norte. Rio's modern subway follows these two avenues as it burrows under the city. Most banks and airline offices have their headquarters on Avenida Rio Branco.

Sightseeing is safer here during the week, because there are lots of people around. On weekends, you stand out much more.

Walking Tour

There's more to Rio than beaches. Don't miss exploring some of the city's museums, colonial buildings, churches (of course) and traditional meeting places –

restaurants, bars, shops and street corners. The centre of Rio, now a potpourri of the new and old, still has character and life. Here's our suggested walking tour. Many of the places mentioned are described in more detail in the appropriate sections.

Take a bus or the metro to **Cinelândia** and find the main square along Avenida Rio Branco; called **Praça Floriano**, it's the heart of Rio today. Towards the bay is the **Praça Mahatma Gandhi**. The monument was a gift from India in 1964. Behind the praça and across the road, the large aeroplane hangar is the **Museu de Arte Moderna**.

Praça Floriano comes to life at lunch time and after work when the outdoor cafés are filled with beer drinkers, samba musicians and political debate. The square is Rio's political marketplace. There's daily speechmaking, literature sales and street theatre. Most city marches and rallies culminate here on the steps of the old **Câmara Municipal**.

Across Avenida Rio Branco is the **Biblioteca Nacional**. Built in 1910 in the neoclassic style, it's open to visitors and usually has an exhibition. The most impressive building on the square is the **Teatro Municipal**, home of Rio's opera, orchestra and gargoyles. The theatre was built in 1905 and revised in 1934 under the influence of the Paris Opéra. The front doors are rarely open, but you can visit the ostentatious Assyrian Room Restaurant & Bar downstairs (entrance in Avenida Rio Branco). Built in the 1920s and 30s, it's completely covered in tiles, with beautiful mosaics. In Avenida Rio Branco you'll also find the **Museu Nacional de Belas Artes**, housing some of Brazil's best paintings.

Now do an about-face and head back to the other side of the Teatro Municipal and walk down the pedestrian-only Avenida 13 de Maio (on your left are some of Rio's best *suco* (juice) bars). Cross a street and you're in the Largo da Carioca. Up on the hill is the recently restored **Convento de Santo Antônio**. The original church here was started in 1608, making it one of Rio's oldest. The church's Santo Antônio is an object of great devotion to many Cariocas in search of husbands. The church's sacristy, which dates from 1745, has some beautiful jacaranda-wood carving and Portuguese blue tiles.

Gazing at the skyline from the convent, you'll notice the Rubik's-cube-like **Petrobras building**. Behind it is the ultramodern **Catedral Metropolitana** (the inside is cavernous with huge stained-glass windows). If you have time for a side trip, consider heading over to the nearby *bondinho* (little tram) that goes up to **Santa Teresa**.

Next find the shops along 19th-century Rua da Carioca. The old wine and cheese shop has some of

JOHN MAIER, JR.

JOHN MAIER, JR.

Top & Bottom: Downtown Rio

JOHN MAIER, JR.

ANDREW DRAFFEN

Top: Teatro Municipal
Bottom: Chafariz da Piramide

Brazil's best cheese from the Canastra mountains in Minas Gerais. It also has bargains in Portuguese and Spanish wines. Two shops sell fine Brazilian-made instruments, including all the Carnaval rhythm-makers, which make great gifts. There are several good jewellery shops off Rua da Carioca, on Rua Ramalho Ortigão.

Whenever we're near Rua da Carioca 39 we stop at the **Bar Luis** for a draft beer and lunch or snack. Rio's longest-running restaurant, it was opened in 1887 and named Bar Adolf until WW II. For decades, many of Rio's intellectuals have chewed the fat while eating Rio's best German food here.

At the end of the block you'll pass the **Cinema Iris**, which used to be Rio's most elegant theatre (sadly, it's now a porno-movie and strip joint), and emerge into the hustle of Praça Tiradentes. It's easy to see that this was once a fabulous part of the city. On opposite sides of the square are the **Teatro João Caetano** and the **Teatro Carlos Gomez**, which show plays and dance performances. The narrow streets in this part of town house many old, mostly dilapidated, small buildings. It's worth exploring along Rua Buenos Aires as far as **Campo de Santana** and then returning along Rua da Alfândega. Campo de Santana is a pleasant park, once the scene – re-enacted in every Brazilian classroom – of Emperor Dom Pedro I, King of Portugal, proclaiming Brazil's independence from Portugal. Wander around the park and try to spot some of the agoutis that run wild there.

Back near Avenida Rio Branco, at Rua Gonçalves Dias 30, hit the **Confeitaria Colombo** for coffee and turn-of-the-century Vienna. Offering succour to shopping-weary matrons since 1894, the Colombo is best for coffee (very strong) and desserts.

From here, cross Avenida Rio Branco, go down Rua da Assembléia, stop at Riotur and TurisRio if you want tourist information, then continue on to **Praça 15 de Novembro**. In the square is the **Chafariz da Piramide** (Pyramid Fountain), built in 1789, and a **craft market**. Facing the bay, on your right is the **Paço Imperial**, which was the royal palace and the seat of government. With independence it was ingloriously relegated to the Department of Telegraphs, but it has been restored.

On the opposite side of the square is the historic **Arco de Teles**, running between two buildings. Walking through the arch you'll see, immediately on your left, the elegant and very British **English Bar** – a good place for a quiet, expensive lunch or drink. The shops along the stone streets here have a waterfront character. There are several seafood restaurants, fishing-supply shops and a couple of simple colonial churches. It's a colourful area.

Facing the square is the Igreja de NS do Carmo do Antiga Sé, which was the metropolitan cathedral until 1976. It held the most important religious services during imperial times.

Back at Praça 15 de Novembro, take the overpass to the **waterfront**, where ferries leave to **Niterói** and **Ilha de Paquetá**. The ferry to Niterói takes only 15 minutes and you never have to wait long. Consider crossing the bay and walking around central Niterói if you have some time (the feel is different from Rio – much more like the rest of Brazil). Even if you return immediately the trip is worth it just for the view.

When you're facing the bay, the **Restaurante Alba Mar** is a few hundred metres to your right. It's in a green gazebo overlooking the bay. The food is good and the atmosphere just right. On Saturdays the building is surrounded by the tents of the **Feira de Antiguidades**, a strange and fun hodgepodge of antiques, clothes, foods and other odds and ends. If you want to extend your walking tour, go back through Arco de Teles and follow the street around toward Rua Primeiro de Março. Walk up along the right-hand side and you'll come to the **Centro Cultural do Banco do Brasil (CCBB)**. Go in and have a look at the building and any of the current exhibitions. Most are free. Then have a look behind the CCBB at the **Casa França-Brasil**. From there, you'll be able to see the **Igreja NS de Candelária**. Have a look inside and then keep going up Rua Primeiro de Março, through the naval area, to Rua Dom Gerardo, the last street before a hill. **Mosteiro de São Bento** is on top of the hill. To get there, go to Rua Dom Gerardo 40 and take the lift to the 5th floor. From Rua Dom Gerardo, head back toward Avenida Rio Branco, and try to imagine that in 1910 it was a tree-lined boulevard, with sidewalk cafés – the Champs Elysées of Rio.

Biblioteca Nacional

Inaugurated in 1910, the library is the largest in Latin America, with over eight million volumes. Designed by Francisco Marcelino de Souza Aguiar, the building is neoclassic, surrounded by Corinthian columns. On the ground floor to the left is the periodical section, and to the right are general works. On the 2nd floor are many rare books and manuscripts, including two copies of the rare Mainz Psalter Bible printed in 1492. Most of these rare books can only be viewed on microfilm.

The library sits at Avenida Rio Branco 219/239 and is open Monday to Friday from 9 am to 8 pm and on Saturdays from 9 am until 3 pm. The rare-books section is only open during the week from 9 am to 6 pm.

Centro Cultural do Banco do Brasil

In a beautiful restored building dating from 1906, the Centro Cultural do Banco do Brasil (CCBB) was reopened in 1989 and is now the best cultural centre in the country, with more than 120,000 visitors per month. Its facilities are world-class and include a cinema, two theatres and lots of exposition space. There's always something going on there, so before you go, have a look at the entertainment listings. We dropped in one afternoon to see an interesting exhibition of swimsuits and beach paraphernalia, aptly called 'The Museu Vai a Praia' (The museum goes to the beach). While there we managed to catch an excellent lunch-time concert featuring some fine *choro* music. The CCBB also has a permanent exhibition showing the history of money in Brazil. Don't miss this place, even if you just include a trip through the lobby on a walking tour.

At Rua Primeiro de Março 66, it's open from Tuesday to Sunday from 10 am to 10 pm. Entry is free, although some of the events have a small charge.

Casa França-Brasil

Next to the CCBB, the Casa França-Brasil is another cultural centre that has diverse exhibitions. During our last visit it was displaying pictures and prints of old Rio. It's in an old customs house dating from 1820 and is considered the most important classical revival building in Brazil, even though the columns are wooden. The

ANDREW DRAFFEN

Interior of Centro Cultural do Banco do Brasil

centre opened in 1990 and aims to expand cultural relations between France and Brazil.

Churches

Note that in this book, we use the abbreviation NS for Nossa Senhora (Our Lady) or Nosso Senhor (Our Lord).

Mosteiro de São Bento This is one of the finest examples of colonial church architecture in Brazil. Built between 1617 and 1641 on Morro de São Bento, one of the four hills that once marked colonial Rio, the monastery has a fine view over the city. The simple facade hides

ANDREW DRAFFEN

JOHN MAIER, JR.

Top: Mosteiro de São Bento
Bottom: Nossa Senhora de Candelária

a baroque interior richly decorated in gold. On Sundays, the Benedictine High Mass is accompanied by a choir of monks singing Gregorian chants.

The monastery is open every day (except Saturday) from 7 to 11.15 am and 2.30 to 6 pm.

The Sunday Mass with chanting starts at 10 am, but get there early as it gets crowded. Entry is free. Shorts may not be worn to the Mass by either men or women.

To reach the monastery from Rua Dom Gerardo, go to No 40 and take the lift to the 5th floor.

Catedral Metropolitana Work on the cone-shaped Cathedral began in 1964, and it was inaugurated in 1976, but it still isn't finished. Some day, they say, it will have a sacred-art museum. It's worth a look inside to see the four huge stained-glass windows. With a capacity for 20,000 worshippers, the Cathedral is open weekdays from 8 am to noon and 1 to 6 pm and on weekends from 8 am to noon. No shorts are allowed.

Nossa Senhora de Candelária Built between 1775 and 1894, NS da Candelária is the largest and richest church of Imperial Brazil. The interior is a spectacular combination of baroque and Renaissance revival styles. The painted cupola is superb.

The church is open from Monday to Friday from 7.30 am to noon and 1 to 4 pm and on weekends from 7.30 am to noon. Sunday Mass is at 9, 10 and 11 am. Entry is free. Watch out for the traffic as you cross to the church.

Convento Santo Antônio & Igreja São Francisco da Penitência Overlooking the Largo da Carioca, the convent was built between 1608 and 1615. It contains the chapel of NS das Dores da Imaculada Conceição. The miracle-working priest Fabiano de Cristo, who died in 1947, is entombed here. The convent is open weekdays from 2 to 5 pm. Next door is the baroque Igreja São Francisco da Penitência, dating from 1736. It has an elaborately carved wooden altar and a roof panel by José Oliveira Rosa depicting the stigmatisation of St Francis. It's open weekdays from 1 to 5 pm.

Museums

Museu da Imagem e do Som Contains an archive of records, tapes, film and photographs that chronicles Brazil's social history. Its music archive is outstanding. The Sound and Image museum is open Monday to Friday from 1 to 6 pm. It's at Praça Rui Barbosa 1.

Museu Histórico Nacional Restored in 1985, this former colonial arsenal is filled with historic relics and interesting displays, one of the best being the re-creation of a colonial pharmacy. The building is near the bay at Praça Marechal Âncora.

Museu Histórico e Diplomático Housed in the restored Palácio Itamaraty (☎ 253-7961), which was home to Brazil's presidents from 1889 until 1897, the museum has an impressive collection of art and antiques. Located at Rua Marechal Floriano 196 (a short walk from Presidente Vargas metro station), the museum has guided tours on Monday, Wednesday and Friday from 1 to 4 pm. To guarantee a tour in English or French, call the palace before you visit.

Museu de Arte Moderna At the northern end of Parque do Flamengo, looking a bit like an airport hangar, is the Museu de Arte Moderna. Construction began in 1954, but for much of the past few years all that one has been able to see of the museum are its grounds, done by Brazil's most famous landscape architect, Burle Marx (who landscaped Brasília).

The museum was devastated in 1978 by a fire that consumed 90% of its collection. The museum has worked hard to rebuild its collection, and today it's the most important centre of contemporary art in Rio, with a permanent display of over 4000 works by Brazilian artists. It's open Tuesday to Sunday from noon to 6 pm.

Museu Naval Behind the Museu de Arte Moderna, the Museu Naval is open Tuesday to Friday from 11.30 am to 5.30 pm, and Saturdays and Sundays from 9 am to 5.30 pm. It documents the Brazilian navy's role in WW II and has ship models.

Monumento Nacional dos Mortos da II Guerra Mundial This monument to the soldiers who fought in WW II contains a museum, mausoleum and the Tomb of the Unknown Soldier. The museum exhibits uniforms, medals and documents from Brazil's Italian campaign. There's also a small lake, and works by Ceschiatti and Anísio Araújo de Medeiros. It's open from Tuesday to Sunday from 10 am to 5 pm.

Museu Nacional de Belas Artes At Avenida Rio Branco 199 is Museu Nacional de Belas Artes (☎ 240-0068), Rio's premier fine-art museum. There are over 800 original paintings and sculptures in the collection. The most important gallery is the Galeria de Arte Brasileira, with 20th-century classics such as Cândido Portinari's Café. There are also galleries with foreign art (not terribly good) and contemporary exhibits.

The museum is open Tuesday to Friday from 10 am to 6 pm; and Saturday, Sunday and holidays from 2 to 6 pm. Photography is prohibited. Take any of the city-bound buses and get off near Avenida Rio Branco, or take the metro to Carioca station.

If you'd like a guided tour in English, phone first to make a booking.

Museu Naval e Oceanográfico This museum chronicles the history of the Brazilian navy from the 16th century to the present. It includes an exhibition of miniature warships, maps and ships' instruments. Close to Praça 15 de Novembro at Rua Dom Manuel 15, the museum is open every day from noon to 4.30 pm.

Sambódromo & Museu do Carnaval Designed by Oscar Niemeyer and completed in 1984, the Sambódromo (see separate map) also houses the Museu do Carnaval. It contains lots of material relating to the history of Rio's samba schools. It's open Tuesday to Sunday from 11 am to 5 pm. Enter through Rua Frei Caneca. Empty sambadromes are like empty stadiums – there's not a lot happening.

Paço Imperial On one side of Praça 15 de Novembro, the former imperial palace was built in 1743 as a governor's residence, but was later the home of Dom João and his family. In 1888, Princesa Isabel proclaimed the freedom from slavery act on the steps. The building was neglected for many years, but has now been restored and is used for temporary exhibitions and concerts.

Cinelândia

At the southern edge of the business district, Cinelândia's shops, bars, restaurants and movie theatres are popular day and night. There are also several decent, reasonably priced, hotels. The bars and restaurants get crowded at lunch and after work, when there's often samba in the streets. There's a greater mix of Cariocas here than in any other section of the city. Several gay and mixed bars stay open until late.

JOHN MAIER, JR.

JOHN MAIER, JR.

Top: Sambódromo Stadium
Bottom: Ilha Fiscal

Lapa

By the old aqueduct that connects the Santa Teresa trolley and the city centre is Lapa, the scene of many a Brazilian novel. This is where boys used to become men and men became infected. Prostitution still exists here but there are also several music clubs, like the Circo Voador and Asa Branca, and some very cheap hotels. Lapa goes to sleep very late on Fridays and Saturdays.

Ilha de Paquetá

This island in the Baía de Guanabara was once a very popular tourist spot and is now frequented mostly by families from the zona norte. There are no cars on the island. Transport is by foot, bicycle (there are literally hundreds for rent) or horse-drawn carts. There's a certain dirty, decadent charm to the colonial buildings, unassuming beaches and businesses catering to local tourism. Sadly, the bay is too polluted to swim in safely and the place gets very crowded.

Go to Paquetá for the boat ride through the bay and to see Cariocas at play – especially during the Festa de São Roque, which is celebrated over five days in August. Boats (☎ 231-0396) leave from near the Praça 15 de Novembro in Centro. The regular ferry takes one hour and costs 50c. The hydrofoil is worth taking, at least one way. It gets to the island in 25 minutes and costs US$7. The ferry service goes from 5.30 am to 10.30 pm, leaving every two to three hours. The hydrofoil leaves every hour on the hour from Rio (8 am to 5 pm) and returns every hour from Paquetá (8 am to 5.30 pm).

Ilha Fiscal

The lime-green neo-Gothic palace sitting in the Baía de Guanabara that looks like something out of a fairytale was designed by engineer Adolfo del Vecchio and completed in 1889. Originally used to supervise port operations, the palace is famous as the location of the last Imperial Ball on 9 November 1889. It's now used by the navy ministry, so visits must be arranged in advance.

Ponte Rio Niterói

The Ponte Rio Niterói is 15.5 km long, 60 metres high and 26.6 metres wide, with two three-lane roads. There's a toll booth three km from the Niterói city centre.

Ferry to Niterói

This is the poor person's bay cruise. It costs about 30c and the views are great, particularly returning to Rio around sunset. Over at Niterói you can walk around a bit to see Rio's poor relation or catch a local bus to Niterói's beaches. Leaving from Praça 15 de Novembro (in Centro), the ferry goes every 20 minutes and is always full of commuters. Buses to Praça 15 de Novembro include: from Flamengo, No 119; from Copacabana, No 119, 413, 415, 154, 455 or 474; and from Ipanema, No 474 or 154.

SÃO CRISTÓVÃO

Maracanã

This stadium, Brazil's temple of soccer and a colossus among colosseums, easily accommodates over 100,000 people and on occasion – the World Cup game of 1950 or Pelé's last game – has squeezed in close to 200,000 crazed fans (although it's difficult to see how). If you like sports, if you want to understand Brazil, or if you just want an intense, quasi-psychedelic experience, then by all means go see a game of *futebol*, preferably a championship game or one between rivals Flamengo (Fla) and Fluminense (Flu). There's a sports museum inside the stadium. It has photographs, posters, cups and uniforms of Brazilian sporting greats, including Pelé's famous No 10 shirt. The museum is open weekdays from 11 am to 5 pm. Enter through gate No 18 on Rua Professor Eurico Rabelo.

Quinta da Boa Vista

Quinta da Boa Vista was the residence of the imperial family until the republic was proclaimed. Today it's a large and busy park with gardens and lakes that's crowded on weekends with football games and families from the zona norte. It is open from 8 am to 7 pm. The former imperial mansion houses the Museu Nacional and Museu da Fauna. The Jardim Zoológico, Rio's zoo, is 200 metres away.

To get to Quinta da Boa Vista, from Centro take the metro to São Cristóvão or bus No 472 or 474; from the zona sul take bus No 472 or 474 as well.

Museu Nacional This museum and its grand imperial entrance are still stately and imposing, and the view from the balcony to the royal palms is majestic.

However, the graffitied buildings and unkempt grounds have suffered since the fall of the monarchy.

There are many interesting exhibits: dinosaur fossils, sabre tooth tiger skeletons, beautiful pieces of pre-Columbian ceramics from the littoral and planalto of Peru, a huge meteorite, hundreds of stuffed birds, mammals and fish, gory displays of tropical diseases and exhibits on the peoples of Brazil.

The latter are most interesting. Rubber-gatherers and Indians of the Amazon, lace workers and *jangadeiro* fishers of the Northeast, candomblistas of Bahia, *gaúchos* of Rio Grande do Sul and *vaqueiros* (cowboys) of the sertão are all given their due. What's interesting about these exhibits is that with a little bit of effort and a lot of travelling you can see all of these peoples in the flesh. The Indian exhibit is particularly good – better than that of the FUNAI Museu do Índio.

The museum is open Tuesday to Sunday from 10 am to 5 pm, and admission costs about US$1 (free on Thursdays).

Jardim Zoológico

The zoo (☎ 254-2024), at Quinta da Boa Vista behind the Natural History Museum, is worth a look. There are lots of Brazilian animals, but the star of the place is an ape called Tião, who gets a birthday party every year on 16 January. It's open from Tuesday to Sunday from 9 am to 4.30 pm. Entry is US$2, but children under one metre get in for free.

Museu do Primeiro Reinado

Housed in the mansion of the former Marquesa de Santos, this museum depicts the history of the First Reign. The collection includes documents, furniture and paintings. Close to the Quinta da Boa Vista at Avenida Dom Pedro II 293, it's open from Tuesday to Friday from 11.30 am to 5 pm. Entry is free.

SANTA TERESA

This is one of Rio's most unusual and charming neighbourhoods. Situated along the ridge of the hill that rises from the city centre, Santa Teresa has many of Rio's finest colonial homes. In the 19th century Rio's upper crust lived here and rode the *bonde* (tram) to work in the city.

During the '60s and '70s many artists and hippies moved into Santa Teresa's mansions. Just a few metres below them the favelas spread on the hillsides. Great train robber Ronnie Biggs now lives up here. It's necessary to be cautious here, especially at night.

Santa Teresa Bondinho

The bondinho (little tram) goes over the Arcos da Lapa – the old aqueduct – to Santa Teresa from Avenida República do Chile and Senador Dantas in Centro. Santa Teresa is a beautiful neighbourhood of cobbled streets, hills and old homes. Favelas down the hillsides have made this a high-crime area. Young thieves jump on and off the tram very quickly. Go, but don't take valuables.

JOHN MAIER, JR.

Bicycle racing the bondinho in Santa Teresa

Public transport stops at midnight, so you'll need a car if you are going anywhere after that time.

There's a small **Museu do Bonde** at the central tram station with a history of Rio's tramways since 1865 for bonde buffs. You may wonder why people choose to hang onto the side of the tram even when there are spare seats. It's so they don't have to pay.

The **Museu Chácara do Céu** (☎ 224-8981), Rua Murtinho Nobre 93, Santa Teresa, is a delightful museum that occupies part of the old mansion of wealthy industrialist and arts patron Raymundo Ottoni de Castro Maya. It contains art and antiques from his private collection, which he bequeathed to the nation, including works by Monet, Vlaminck, Portinari and Picasso to name a few. The house is surrounded by beautiful gardens and has a great view of Baía de Guanabara.

It's open from Wednesday to Saturday from noon to 5 pm and on Sundays and holidays from 1 to 5 pm. Entry is US$4 (free on Sundays). To get there by bus, take the No 206 or 214 from the Menezes Cortes bus terminal in Centro to the 'Curvelo' stop.

GLÓRIA

Igreja de Nossa Senhora da Glória do Outeiro

Looking over the bairro (suburb) that bears its name, this baroque beauty was the favourite of Dom Pedro II. He was married and his daughter, Princesa Isabel, was baptised here. The church, built in 1714, had its altar carved by Mestre Valentim. On 15 August, worshippers celebrate the Festa de NS da Glória do Outeiro (see Festivals & Cultural events in the Facts for the Visitor chapter).

The church is open Monday to Friday from 8 am to noon and 1 to 5 pm. On weekends it's open from 8 am to noon. Sunday Mass is at 8 am and noon. To get there, take the metro to Glória and climb up the Largo da Glória.

CATETE

Museu da República

The Museu da República, housed in the Palácio do Catete, has been wonderfully restored. Built between 1858 and 1866 and easily distinguished by the bronze condors on the eaves, the palace was occupied by the president of Brazil from 1896 until 1954, when Getúlio Vargas killed himself here. His bedroom, where the suicide took place, is on display. The museum has a good collection of art and artefacts from the republican period. It's open Tuesday to Friday from noon to 5 pm. Admission is US$1.

Museu Folclorico Edson Carneiro

This small museum should not be missed – especially if you're staying nearby in the Catete/Flamengo area. It has excellent displays of folk art – probably Brazil's richest artistic tradition – a folklore library, and a small craft shop with some wonderful crafts, books and folk records at very cheap prices.

The museum is next to the grounds of the Palácio do Catete. The address is Rua do Catete 181, Catete, and it's open Tuesday to Friday from 11 am to 6 pm, and Saturdays, Sundays and holidays from 3 to 6 pm.

FLAMENGO

Catete and Flamengo have the bulk of inexpensive hotels in Rio. Flamengo was once Rio's finest residential district and the Palácio do Catete housed Brazil's president until 1954, but with the new tunnel to Copacabana the upper classes began moving out in the 1940s. Flamengo is still mostly residential. The apartments are often big and graceful, although a few high-rise offices have recently been built amongst them. With the exception of the classy waterfront buildings, Flamengo is mostly a middle-class area. There is less nightlife and fewer restaurants here than in nearby Botafogo or Cinelândia.

Museu Carmen Miranda

The small Museu Carmen Miranda at the southern end of Parque do Flamengo, across the street from Avenida Rui Barbosa 560, is open Tuesday to Friday from 1 to 4 pm. Carmen, of course, was Hollywood's Brazilian bombshell, although she was actually born in Portugal. She made it to Hollywood in the 1940s and has become a cult figure in Rio. During Carnaval hundreds of men dress up as Carmen Miranda lookalikes. The museum is filled with Carmen memorabilia and paraphernalia, including costumes, posters, postcards, T-shirts, records and a small exhibit.

Museu do Telefone

For telephone enthusiasts, this museum has a lot of antique phones and traces the evolution of the telephone in Brazil. Dom Pedro II was a telephone enthusiast. The museum is at Rua 2 de Dezembro 63 and is open Tuesday to Sunday from 9 am to 5 pm. Entry is free.

BOTAFOGO

Botafogo's early development was spurred by the construction of a tram that ran up to the botanical garden linking the bay and the lake. This artery still plays a vital role in Rio's traffic flow and Botafogo's streets are extremely congested. There are several palatial mansions here that housed foreign consulates when Rio was the capital of Brazil. This area has fewer high-rise buildings than much of the rest of Rio.

There are not many hotels in Botafogo but there are lots of good bars and restaurants where the locals go to avoid the tourist glitz and high cost of Copacabana.

Museu do Índio

At Rua das Palmeiras 55, the Museu do Índio (☎ 286-8899) has a good library with over 25,000 titles, a map and photo collection and a quiet garden. The displays concentrate on the economic, religious and social life of Brazil's indigenous people. There's also a small craft shop. It's open weekdays from 10 am to 5 pm. Entry is free.

Museu Villa-Lobos

This museum is in a century-old building and is dedicated to the memory of Heitor Villa-Lobos. This great Brazilian composer, regarded as the father of modern Brazilian music, was the first to combine folkloric themes with classical forms. As well as personal items, there's an extensive sound archive. Located at Rua Sorocaba 200 in Botafogo, it's open from Monday to Friday from 10 am to 5.30 pm.

Museu Casa Rui Barbosa

The former mansion of famous Brazilian jurist Rui Barbosa is now a museum containing an impressive archive of 77 million volumes, including manuscripts and first editions of many Brazilian authors, like Machado de Assis and José de Alencar. One of the museum's precious treasures is a rare 1481 edition of Dante's *Divine Comedy*, with illustrations by Botticelli. The museum, at Rua São Clemente 134, is open Tuesday to Friday from 1 to 4 pm. Entry is US$1.

COPACABANA

The famous curved beach you know about. What's surprising about Copacabana is all the people who live there. Fronted by beach and backed by steep hills, Copacabana is for the greater part no more than four blocks wide. Crammed into this narrow strip of land are 25,000 people per sq km, one of the highest population densities in the world.

Only three parallel streets traverse the length of Copacabana. Avenida Atlântica runs along the ocean. Avenida NS de Copacabana, two blocks inland, is one-way, running in the direction of the business district. One block further inland, Rua Barata Ribeiro is also one-way, in the direction of Ipanema and Leblon. These streets change their names when they reach Ipanema.

Copacabana is the capital of Brazilian tourism. It's possible to spend an entire Brazilian vacation without leaving it, and some people do just that. The majority of Rio's medium and expensive hotels are here and they are accompanied by plenty of restaurants, shops and bars. For pure city excitement, Copacabana is Rio's liveliest theatre. It is also the heart of Rio's recreational sex industry. There are many *boîtes* (bars with strip shows) and prostitutes; anything and everyone is for sale.

From Christmas to Carnaval, prices here are exorbitant, hotels are full and restaurants get overcrowded. The streets are noisy and hot.

Museu Histórico do Exército e Forte de Copacabana

Built in 1914, the fort preserves its original characteristics, with walls up to 12 metres thick, fortified with Krupp canons. The museum displays weapons, but one of the best reasons to visit is the fantastic view of Copacabana. The fort is open from Tuesday to Sunday between 10 am and 4 pm. Entry is free.

IPANEMA

Ipanema and Leblon are two of Rio's most desirable districts. They face the same stretch of beach and are separated by the Jardim de Alah, a canal and adjacent park. It's a residential area, mostly upper class and becoming more so as rents continue to rise. Most of Rio's better restaurants, bars and nightclubs are here.

Museu H Stern

The headquarters of the famous jeweller H Stern, at Rua Garcia D'Avila 113, contains a museum. You may find the 12-minute guided jewellery tour interesting if you're in the neighbourhood. There is a permanent exhibition of fine jewellery, some rare mineral specimens and a large collection of tourmalines. There is no pressure to buy jewellery, though you may not be able to resist the temptation. With a coupon you can get a free cab ride to and from the shop and anywhere in the zona sul. Hours are 8 am to 6 pm on weekdays and 8.30 am to 12.30 pm Saturday mornings.

Museu Amsterdam Sauer

Next door to H Stern at Rua Garcia D'Avila 105, this museum also has a precious stone collection. It's open from Monday to Friday from 10 am to 5 pm and Saturdays from 9.30 am to 1 pm.

RECREIO DOS BANDEIRANTES

Museu Casa do Pontal

Owned by Frenchman Jaques Van de Beuque, this impressive collection of over 4500 pieces is one of the best folk-art exhibitions in Brazil. Works are grouped according to themes, including music, Carnaval, religion and folklore.

The museum is just past Barra at the Estrada do Pontal 3295. It's open on weekends from 2 to 5.30 pm.

MARECHAL HERMES

Museu Aerospacial

This museum maintains expositions on Santos Dumont (the Brazilian father of aviation), Air Marshal Eduardo Gomes, the history of Brazilian air mail and the role of Brazil's air force in WW II. There are lots of old planes, motors and flying instruments. Highlights are replicas of Santos Dumont's planes, the *14 Bis* and the *Demoiselle*. The museum is at Avenida Marechal Fontenele 2000 in Campo dos Afonsos. It's open weekdays from 9 am to 3 pm and weekends from 10 am to 4 pm. Entry is free. The museum is in the western zone of the city. Take bus No 701, 702 or 703 from Centro.

PARKS & GARDENS

The first parks and gardens in the city were laid out near the end of the 18th century, but it was not until the arrival of the Portuguese royal family in 1808 that attention was given to the aesthetics of the city. Parks were created in a European style, like the Passeio Público, remodelled in 1860 by French botanist Auguste Glaziou. Burle Marx is Brazil's most famous landscaper. He designed the Parque do Flamengo, and later went on to design the gardens of Brasília.

Parque Nacional & Floresta da Tijuca

Tijuca is all that's left of the tropical jungle that once surrounded Rio de Janeiro. In 15 minutes you can go from the concrete jungle of Copacabana to the 120-sq-km tropical jungle of Parque Nacional da Tijuca. A more rapid and drastic contrast is hard to imagine. The forest is an exuberant green, with beautiful trees, creeks and waterfalls, mountainous terrain and high peaks. It has an excellent trail system. Candomblistas leave offerings by the roadside, families have picnics, and serious hikers climb the summit of Pico da Tijuca (1012 metres).

The heart of the forest is the **Alto da Boa Vista** area in the Floresta da Tijuca (the forest), with several waterfalls (including the 35-metre Cascatinha de Taunay), peaks and restaurants. It's a beautiful spot. It is also home to different species of birds and animals including iguanas and monkeys. This area has several good day hikes. Maps of the forest are obtained at the small artisan shop just inside the park entrance, which is open from 7 am to 9 pm daily.

The entire park closes at sunset and is rather heavily policed. Kids have been known to wander off and get lost in the forest – it's that big. It's best to go by car, but if you can't, catch a No 221, 233 or 234 bus.

The best route by car is to take Rua Jardim Botânico two blocks past the botanical garden (heading away from Gávea). Turn left on Rua Lopes Quintas and then follow the Tijuca or Corcovado signs for two quick left turns until you reach the back of the botanical garden, where you go right. Then follow the signs for a quick ascent into the forest and past the Vista Chinesa (get out for a view) and the Mesa do Imperador. Go right when you seem to come out of the forest on the main road and you'll see the stone columns to the entrance of Alto da Boa Vista on your left in a couple of km.

You can also drive up to Alto da Boa Vista by heading out to São Conrado and turning right up the hill at the Parque Nacional da Tijuca signs.

Jardim Botânico

Open daily from 8.30 am to 5.30 pm, the garden was first planted by order of the prince-regent Dom João in 1808. There are over 5000 varieties of plants on 141 hectares. Quiet and serene on weekdays, the botanical garden blossoms with families and music on weekends. The row of palms, planted when the garden first opened, the Amazonas section and the lake containing the huge Vitória Régia water lilies, are some of the highlights. It's not a bad idea to take insect repellent.

The garden is on Rua Jardim Botânico 920 (see the Ipanema & Leblon map and the separate Jardim Botânico map). To get there take a 'Jardim Botânico' bus: from Centro, No 170; from the zona sul, No 571, 572, or 594.

After the garden walk, go a few blocks down Rua Jardim Botânico, away from the beach, to Alfaces at Rua Visconde da Graça 51 for an excellent light lunch with an assortment of salads and good desserts at outdoor tables.

JOHN MAIER, JR.

Squirrel eating a mango in the Jardim Botânico

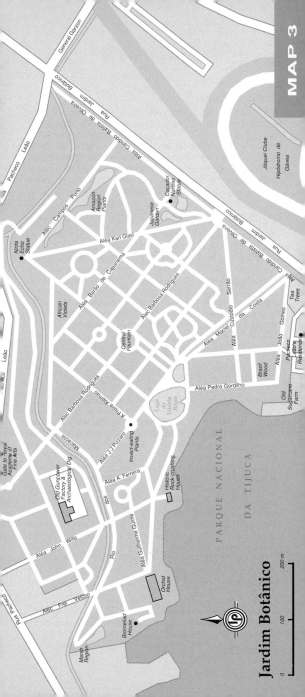

MAP 3

Jóquei Clube
Hipódromo de
Gávea

General Garzon

Rua Jardim Botânico

Aléia Cândido Batista de Oliveira

Rua Pacheco Leão

Aléia Campos Porto

Caçador Narciso Statue

Amazon Region Plants

Japanese Garden

Aléia Karl Glasi

Ninfa Echo Statue

Aléia Barão de Capanema

African Violets

Aléia Barbosa Rodrigues

Rua Jardim Botânico

Aléia Cândido Batista de Oliveira

Serrão

Tea Trees

Aléia Maciel Custódio

Aléia da Costa

Aléia João Gomes

Central Fountain

Pacheco Leitão Residence

Aléia Barbosa Rodrigues

A. Freira Atenão

Lago da Vitória Régia

Aléia Pedro Gordilho

Brazil Wood

Old Sugarcane Farm

Leão

Macacos

Aléia J J Pizzaro

Insect-eating Plants

Gate to Royal Academy of Fine Arts

Old Gunpowder Factory & Archaeological Dig

Aléia A. Ferreira

Historic Rock-crushing House

PARQUE NACIONAL

DA TIJUCA

Aléia John Wills

Rio

Aléia Guilherme Guinle

Rua Pacheco

Aléia Frei Veloso

Orchid House

Bromeliad House

Marsh Region

0   100   200 m

Jardim Botânico

Parque Lage

Just a few blocks down from the Jardim Botânico at Rua Jardim Botânico 414, this is a beautiful park at the base of Parque Nacional da Tijuca. There are gardens, little lakes and a mansion which now houses the Escola de Artes Visuais – there are often art shows and sometimes performances there. It's a tranquil place, with no sports allowed and a favourite of families with small children. It's open from 9 am to 5 pm. Take a 'Jardim Botânico' bus.

Passeio Público

The oldest park in Rio, the Passeio Público was built in 1783 by Mestre Valentim, a famous Brazilian sculptor, who planned it to look like Lisbon's botanical garden. In 1860 it was remodelled by French landscaper Glaziou. It features some large trees, a pond with islands and an interesting crocodile-like fountain. The entrance gate was built by Valentim. Before the Flamengo park landfill, the sea came up to the edge of the park. It's open daily from 8 am to 6 pm. The closest metro stop is Cinelândia.

Parque do Flamengo

The result of a landfill project that levelled the São Antônio hill in 1965, the park spreads out over 1,200,000 sq metres of shoreline. It runs all the way from downtown Rio through Glória, Catete, Flamengo itself and on around to Botafogo. Designed by famous Brazilian landscaper Burle Marx, Flamengo is a park with loads of fields and a bay for activities and sports. During the week it hosts round-the-clock football games (joining a few hundred spectators at a 3 am game is one of Rio's stranger experiences), but the park really comes to life on weekends. It features some 170,000 trees of 300 different species. There are three museums – Museu Carmen Miranda, the Monumento Nacional dos Mortos da II Guerra Mundial and Museu de Arte Moderna. At the south end is Rio's, a big outdoor restaurant that's ideal for people and bay watching. The park is not considered safe at night.

To get there take buses marked 'Via Parque do Flamengo': from Centro No 125 or 132, and from the zona sul No 413 or 455.

Parque da Catacumba

With high-rise buildings on both sides, Catacumba is on the Morro dos Cabritos, which rises from the Lagoa Rodrigo de Freitas. It was the site of a favela that was destroyed to make the park. A shaded park for walkers only, it's a good place to escape the heat and see some excellent outdoor sculptures. At the top of the hill there is a great view. Catacumba also has free Sunday afternoon concerts during the summer in its outdoor amphitheatre, featuring some of Rio's best musicians. Check the Sunday newspaper for details. The park is open daily from 7 am to 5 pm.

Parque do Catete

The grounds of the Palácio do Catete (the old presidential palace) are now the Parque do Catete, a quiet refuge from the city with monkeys hanging from the giant trees.

Special performances in the park include concerts, plays and other popular events.

Morro do Leme

Morro do Leme, behind Praia do Leme, east of Avenida Princesa Isabel in Copacabana, is an environmental protection area. Its 11 hectares of Atlantic rainforest are home to numerous bird species, such as the saddle and bishop tanagers, thrushes and the East Brazilian house wren, with its notable trill. The area is open on weekends between 8 am and 4 pm, but it's necessary to book (☎ 275-7696).

Bosque da Barra

This park covers 500,000 sq metres of salt-marsh vegetation and provides a refuge and breeding area for many small birds and animals. The woods also contain a jogging track and bicycle path. It's on Avenida das Américas at the corner of Avenida Alvorada in Barra da Tijuca, and is a short walk from the urban bus terminal. It's open daily from 7 am to 5 pm.

Parque do Cantagalo

Also known as Parque Brigadeiro Faria Lima, the park is used mainly for sports. Carioca families like to cruise the lake in paddle boats, or hire bikes and hit the bike path around the lake. It's on Avenida Epitácio Pessoa in Lagoa (see the Copacabana map). Entry is free.

Parque da Chacrinha

This is a peaceful park in the middle of Copacabana where it's possible to spot capuchin monkeys in the large trees. It's at the end of Rua Guimarães Natal. From the zona sul, hop on any bus going down Avenida NS de Copacabana, get off at Rua Rodolfo Dantas and head towards Rua Barata Ribeiro where it meets Praça Cardeal Arco Verde. Rua Guimarães Natal begins at the praça. The park is open daily from 8 am to 5 pm.

Parque Ecológico Municipal Chico Mendes

Created in 1989 and named after the slain Brazilian ecological activist, this park protects the remaining sandspit vegetation from real estate speculators. Animals found in the park include butterflies, lizards and the broad-nosed cayman. The park is at km 17.5 of Avenida das Américas. To get there by bus, take a 387 'Castelo-Marambaia' bus (it goes through Copacabana, Ipanema and Leblon) and get off in Recreio dos Bandeirantes. The park is open daily from 8 am to 5 pm.

Parque Garota de Ipanema

A small park next to Arpoador rock, it features a skating rink and small playground, as well as a lookout with a good view of Praia de Ipanema. On weekends, concerts are often held in the park. It's open daily from 7 am to 7 pm.

Parque Guinle

Designed by French landscaper Gochet, the park has a European flavour, with a small lake, lanes and lawns. Overlooking the park is the Palácio da Laranjeiras, the official residence of the President when in Rio. The park is in Rua Gago Coutinho, Laranjeiras.

Parque do Marapendi

At the end of Avenida Sernambetiba in Recreio dos Bandeirantes, this biological reserve preserves 700,000 sq m for study and has a small area for leisure, with workout stations and games areas. It's open daily from 8 am to 5 pm.

BEACHES

The beach, a ritual and way of life for the Carioca, is Rio's common denominator. People of all walks of life, in all shapes and sizes, congregate on the sand. It is their backyard. To the casual observer one stretch of sand is the same as any other. Not so. The beach is complex.

Different times bring different people. Different places attract different crowds. Before and after work, exercise is the name of the game. Tanning is heaviest before 2 pm. On prime beach days, the fashionable pass the morning out at Barra and the afternoon back at their spot in Ipanema.

Every 20 metres of coastline is populated by a different group of regulars. For example, Arpoador has more surfers and people from the zona norte. In front of the luxury hotels you'll always find tourists and a security force watching over them. Wherever you do go, don't take valuables.

Twenty-two lifesaving *postos* (posts) dot the beaches of the zona sul. They're decorated with pictures illustrating the sporting life of Rio. For a small fee (about 50c), you can have a shower and get changed inside the posto.

GUY MOBERLY

Beach bums on Copacabana Beach

Signs along the waterfront every couple of hundred metres advise swimmers if the conditions are *própria* or *imprópria* with regard to pollution. Unfortunately, it doesn't inspire much confidence when you see one that says imprópria next to one that says própria, on the same stretch of beach.

Swimming isn't recommended at any of the bay beaches because of the sewage and industrial waste that pollutes the water. Work on the long-awaited treatment plants is just beginning.

Kiosks along the promenade are good places to rehydrate. They sell coconut milk straight from the nut, which is a great thirst quencher. On the beach, you can buy just about anything you need without moving, and the vendors are colourful characters who must be the fittest people on the beach.

Flamengo

This popular beach is a thin strip of sand on the bay, with a great view. The park and beach were a landfill project. Within an easy walk of most of the budget hotels in Catete/Flamengo, there's a different class of Carioca here than on the luxurious beaches to the south, and it's fun to watch them play. Swimming here, though, is definitely suspect. There always seems to be a lot of rubbish in the water.

Botafogo

This small beach is on a calm bay inlet looking out at Pão de Açúcar. The Rio Yacht Club and Bâteau Mouche are next door.

Urca

A small beach only 100 metres long, Praia da Urca is used mostly by military personnel and their families. It's right next to the Fortaleza de São João.

Vermelha

Praia Vermelha sits below Morro da Urca, facing the sea. Its thick sand, unlike any other beach in Rio, gave the beach its name *vermelha* (red). The water is usually calm, as the beach is protected by the headland. There's a nice jogging track behind the beach (see Walking & Jogging later in this chapter).

Copacabana/Leme

The world's most famous beach runs 4.5 km in front of one of the world's most densely populated residential areas. From the scalloped beach you can see the granite slabs that surround the entrance to the bay – a magnificent meeting of land and sea. The last km to the east, from Avenida Princesa Isabel to Morro do Leme, is called Praia do Leme. When you go to Copacabana, which you must, do as the locals do: take only the essentials with you. The area is now heavily policed and lit at night, so it's OK to walk around during the evening. Avenida NS de Copacabana is more dangerous; watch out at weekends when the shops are closed and there are few locals around.

There's always something happening on the beach during the day and on the sidewalks at night: drinking, singing, eating and all kinds of people checking out the scene; tourists watching Brazilians, Brazilians watching tourists; the poor, from nearby favelas, eyeing the rich, the rich avoiding the poor; prostitutes looking for tricks; johns looking for treats.

The gay section of the beach, known as the Stock or Stock Market, runs between the Copacabana Palace Hotel and Rua Fernando Mendes.

Arpoador

This small beach is wedged between Copacabana and Ipanema. There's good surfing here, even at night (when the beach is lit), and a giant rock that juts out into the ocean with a great view. A lot of people from the zona norte come down here on weekends.

Ipanema/Leblon

These two beaches are really one, although the beach narrows on the Leblon side, separated by the canal at Jardim de Alah. Ipanema, like the suburb, is Rio's richest and most chic beach. There isn't quite the frenzy of Copacabana, and the beach is a bit safer and cleaner. There are only two sidewalk cafés facing the ocean in Ipanema – Barril 1800 and Albericos – and one in Leblon – Canecão.

The word *ipanema* is Indian for 'dangerous, bad waters'. The waves can get big and the undertow is often strong. Be careful, and swim only where the locals are swimming.

Different parts of the beach attract different crowds. The beach at Posto 9 is Garota de Ipanema, right off Rua

JOHN MAIER, JR.

JOHN MAIER, JR.

Top: Fitness station on Copacabana Beach
Bottom: Copacabana Beach

JOHN MAIER, JR.

JOHN MAIER, JR.

Top: Ipanema Beach
Bottom: Pepino Beach

Vinícius de Morais. Today it's also known as the Cemetério dos Elefantes because of the old leftists, hippies and artists who hang out there, but it's also popular with the young and beautiful who like to go down there around sunset and smoke a joint. The beach in front of Rua Farme de Amoedo, also called Land of Marlboro and the Crystal Palace, is the gay beach. Ipanema is now lit up in the evenings, and many family groups come down with their barbecues and cook on the beach. It's the safest the beach has been at night for many years.

Vidigal

Under the Sheraton Hotel and the Morro Dois Irmãos, this beach is a mix of the hotel and favela dwellers who were pushed further up the hill to make way for the Sheraton. Security is good here, as the only entrance is under surveillance by hotel staff. It's a quiet beach, with few vendors.

Pepino/São Conrado

After the Sheraton there is no beach along the coast for a few km until Praia do Pepino in São Conrado. You can also take Avenida Niemeyer to the tunnel leading to Barra da Tijuca.

Pepino is a beautiful beach, less crowded than Ipanema. It's where the hang-gliders hang out when they're not hanging up there. Along the beach are two big resort hotels, the Hotel InterContinental and Hotel Nacional. Behind them, nestled into the hillside, is Brazil's biggest favela, Rocinha.

Bus No 591 or 592 goes to Pepino. Don't take valuables, as these buses are frequent targets of robbers. There is also an executive bus (No 2016 'São Conrado') that goes along Copacabana and Ipanema beaches to Pepino.

Barra da Tijuca

The next beach out is Barra. It's 12 km long, with clean, green water. The first few km are filled with bars and seafood restaurants. The young and hip hang out in front of *barraca* (stall) No 1 – also known as the barraca do Pepê, after the famous Carioca hang-gliding champion who died during a competition in Japan. The further out you go the more deserted it gets, and the barracas become trailers. It's calm on weekdays and crazy on hot summer weekends.

Barra's population has doubled in the past 10 years and it's currently the most fashionable place to live in Rio. There are more than a hundred closed condominiums, and the area is now known as the 'California Carioca'.

Recreio dos Bandeirantes

At the southern tip of Barra, Recreio is being built up fast. Crowded on weekends, the beach is almost deserted during the week. The large rock acts as a natural breakwater, creating the effect of a calm bay.

Prainha

Prainha, the next beach past Recreio, is one of the best surfing beaches in Rio, so it's always full of *surfistas*. There's also a controversial nude beach between Prainha and Grumari.

Grumari

The most isolated and unspoiled beach close to the city, Grumari is quiet during the week and packed on weekends by Cariocas looking to get away from city beaches. It is a beautiful setting, with mountains and natural vegetation. Four km have been set aside as an Environmental Protection Area, which should stop it becoming more cheesecake for the rich. Scenes from the movie *Blame it on Rio* were filmed here.

From Grumari, a narrow road climbs over a jungle-covered hillside toward **Guaratiba**. There's a good view of the Restinga de Marambaia, closed off to the public by a naval base. Cariocas enjoy eating a seafood lunch at one of the restaurants in the area. Point da Grumari is at a bend in the road just up from Grumari. In Pedra da Guaratiba, the fishing village at the bottom of the hill, are the restaurants Candido's, Tia Palmira and Quatro Sete Meia.

LOOKOUTS

At the end of Leblon at the start of Avenida Niemeyer, the **Mirante do Leblon** lookout has a fine view of Leblon and Ipanema. It has a 24-hour kiosk and is popular during the evening with Cariocas heading to or leaving the motels a bit further along the road. It's a good place to watch the sea on stormy days.

On the Estrada das Paineiras halfway to Corcovado, it's worth a stopover at the **Mirante Dona Marta** lookout to have a look at the view of Baía de Guanabara and Botafogo. It has a helipad.

On a small hill between Botafogo and Urca, the **Mirante do Pasmado** lookout offers fine views of Pão de Açúcar and Corcovado. It's at Rua General Severiano in Botafogo.

On the Estrada das Canoas, one of the access roads to Floresta da Tijuca, the **Mirante das Canoas** lookout offers a good view of São Conrado, Morro Dios Irmãos, Pedra Bonita and Pedra da Gávea.

ACTIVITIES

Ballooning

The most popular flight is the one between the Autódromo de Jacarepaguá and Barra da Tijuca. The flights (☎ 221-8441), in balloons which can hold four people, last about 30 minutes and climb between 150 and 1500 metres. Children must be over five years old.

Climbing

Climbing in Brazil is best during the cooler months of the year – April to October. During the summer, the tropical sun heats the rock up to oven temperatures and turns the jungles into saunas. Climbing during the summer is still pursued, although only primarily in the early morning or late afternoon when the sun's rays are not so harsh.

The best thing about rock climbing in Brazil is that one hour you can be on the beach and the next on a world-class rock climb 300 metres above a city. Brazil has lots of fantastic rock climbs, ranging from the beginner level to still unconquered routes. In Rio de Janeiro, the centre of rock climbing in Brazil, there are 350 documented climbs within 40 minutes of the city centre.

Climbing Pão de Açúcar (Sugar Loaf) On Pão de Açúcar (395 metres), there are 32 established climbing routes. Climbers are often seen scaling the western face below the cable cars. One of the best hikes is up the back side of Pão de Açúcar. Besides the breathtaking view of the ocean below, one is also compensated by not having to pay for the cable-car ride. The hike takes 1½ hours and doesn't require equipment or a lot of climbing experience, but does have two 10 to 15-metre exposed parts that require agility and common sense.

The hike begins on the left-hand side of Praça General Tibúrcio (the same praça where the cable cars are boarded), where a paved jogging track runs for 1200 metres along the base of Morro de Tijuca and Pão de Açúcar. At the end of the track pick up the trail on the other side of the cement tank in the tall grass. Follow this trail (always taking the uphill forks) for 100 metres. At the old foundations, some 30 metres above the water, the trail ascends steeply for 60 metres until levelling off on the narrow ridge. From the ridge, the broad eastern flank of Pão de Açúcar is seen. The trail to follow is up the far left-hand side ridge.

At the base of the rock the trail deviates slightly to the right for the next 40 metres until coming to two iron bolts on the smooth exposed rock. This is the first exposed area, which, while crossed easily without ropes, requires agility and alertness. There is nothing to break a fall except the rocks in the ocean, 120 metres below.

From the second bolt stay next to the rock slab for the following six metres. In the gap between the first rock slab and the next slab it is safer to step up on to the second rock slab rather than continuing along the exposed face. Twenty metres higher up there is a third iron bolt, which is a good place to take in the view before tackling the crux of the climb – above the clearly defined path. At the fourth bolt, the hike becomes a climb for the next 10 metres. This section is best climbed by finding the holds behind the rock slabs and pulling yourself up. After the sixth and final bolt, the climbing is over. Follow the well-defined path up 200 metres to the small children's park at the top.

Climbing Corcovado Corcovado (709 metres) offers technically difficult climbs with fantastic views of Pão de Açúcar and Lagoa Rodrigo de Freitas. Private guides and the clubs are the best means for unravelling its many diverse routes. Well-equipped and experienced climbers can easily climb its eastern face on the route K-2 (rated 5.9).

The climb begins 200 metres below the summit. To get to the base of the climb, take the train to the top and instead of ascending the stairs to the left, follow the road out of the parking lot for 15 minutes. After the first rocky outcrop, on the northern side, descend two more turns in the road. At the second turn there is a cement railing, behind which is a poorly maintained trail.

Follow this trail as it hugs the base of the rock for 200 metres around to the eastern face of the mountain. Don't be discouraged by the tall grass that obstructs the trail; just keep to the base of the rock. On the eastern face the start of the climb is at the 20-metre crack in the whitened rock. From there the climb is clearly marked with well-

---

Climbing Vocabulary
Although most Brazilians in the clubs know a little English, not everyone does. It helps to know a little Portuguese to smooth the way.

equipment	*equipamento*
bolt	*grampo*
rope	*corda*
carabiner	*mosquetão*
harness	*baudrie*
backpack	*mochila*
webbing	*fita*
chalk powder	*pó de magnésio*
rock	*rocha*
summit	*topo/cume*
crack	*fenda*
route	*via/rota*
a fall	*queda*
to be secured	*estar preso*
a hold	*uma agarra*
to belay	*dar segurança*
to make a stupid mistake and fall	*tomar uma vaca*

---

placed bolts to the top, just underneath the statue of Christ.

It's a good idea to contact some of the climbing clubs listed in this chapter, which have details of further trekking options.

Climbing Clubs For anyone interested in climbing and hiking, Rio's clubs are the single best source of information as well as the best meeting place for like-minded people. The clubs meet regularly and welcome visitors. All of the following clubs are well-organised and have notice boards listing excursions on the weekends.

Centro Excursionista Brasileiro
Avenida Almirante Barroso 2-8 Andar, Centro, Rio de Janeiro, RJ CEP 20031. CEB has a membership of 900, meets on Wednesday and Friday evenings and is geared toward trekking and day hikes. CEB also runs a small restaurant which is open from 6 pm, Monday to Friday, where people meet informally to plan excursions.

Centro Excursionista Rio de Janeiro
Avenida Rio Branco 277/805, Centro, Rio de Janeiro, RJ CEP 20040. CERJ, with an active membership of 50, meets on Tuesday and Thursday evenings. CERJ offers the

greatest diversity of activities ranging from hikes to technical climbing.

Clube Excursionista Carioca

Rua Hilário de Gouveia 71/206, Copacabana, Rio de Janeiro, RJ CEP 22040 (☎ Marcelo Ramos (021) 227-8398). Meeting on Wednesday and Friday evenings at 10.30 pm, this club specialises in difficult technical climbing.

Cycling

Cycling is popular with Cariocas. There's a bike path around Lagoa Rodrigo de Freitas, one in Barra da Tijuca, and one on the oceanfront from Ipanema to Leme. The *ciclóvia* (bike path) is currently being extended into the city to Praça 15. If you have a bit of road sense and don't mind mixing it with the traffic, a bike is a fun way to get around the zona sul. On Tuesday nights, Riobikers take to the streets. Riobikers started out as a group of cyclists who enjoyed riding in a group. The idea caught on and now every Tuesday night, thousands of bikers take to the road from Leblon to the Museu de Arte Moderna in Aterro do Flamengo. It's the thing to do on a Tuesday night. The streets are closed to other traffic after 9 pm and bikers move off at around 9.30 pm from Leblon.

Stop Bike (☎ 275-7345), in the small arcade at Rua Barata Ribeiro 181, has a few mountain bikes to rent for US$15 a day, and it gives good deals if you rent for longer. The woman who runs the shop speaks English. If you just want to cruise the beachfront at Copacabana and Ipanema, bikes can be rented on Sundays and holidays on Avenida Atlântica in front of Rua República do Peru, at a cost of US$3 per hour.

Clube Kraft Point (☎ 205-6155) organises groups who want to do some night riding during the week. On weekends it organises group trail-riding in the Floresta da Tijuca. As long as you have a bike, you can join in.

Fishing

Fishing boats are available for rent at the Marina da Glória (☎ 205-6447). Price depends on what you're after. During the marlin season from November to January, a charter for five people costs around US$1000.

Golf

Rio has two 18-hole golf courses close to the city: Gávea Golf Club (☎ 322-4141) at Estrada da Gávea 800, and Itanhangá Golf Club (☎ 429-2507) at Estrada da Barra 2005. The clubs welcome visitors from 7 am to sunset, but the Gávea Golf Club only accepts visitors from the major hotels like the InterContinental (which is next door) and the Sheraton.

Green fees are around US$70 a round, plus club hire of US$15. On weekends, you need to be invited by a member.

A cheaper option is Golden Green (☎ 433-3950), which has six tricky par-three holes. It's open daily from 7 am to 6 pm. It charges US$18 for six holes and US$28 for 12 holes. Club and cart rental are an extra US$10. It's near Praia Barra da Tijuca at Posto 7.

Hang-Gliding, Para-Gliding & Ultra-Leve

If you weigh less than 80 kg (about 180 lb) and have US$80 you can do the fantastic hang-glide off 510-metre Pedra Bonita onto Praia do Pepino in São Conrado. This is one of the giant granite slabs that towers above Rio. No experience is necessary. To arrange a *voo duplo* (double flight) go out to Pepino and the pilots will be waiting on the beach. We're told that the winds are very safe here and the pilots know what they are doing. Guest riders get their bodies put in a kind of pouch that is secured to the kite.

Flight Information Know your exact weight in kg in advance. Ideally your pilot should be heavier than you. If you're heavier than the pilot, he will have to use a weight belt and switch to a larger glider. If you're over 80 kg, you're out of luck. You don't need any experience or special training – anyone from seven to 70 years can do it.

Cautious flights depend on atmospheric conditions. You can usually fly on all but three or four days per month, and conditions during winter are even better. In an emergency, like a sudden change in weather, a hang-glider pilot can fly down to the beach in less than 90 seconds. Pilots also carry a parachute which is designed to support the weight of two passengers and the glider itself, which is supposed to fall first and cushion the blow.

Most tandem pilots can mount a camera with flash, wide-angle lens, motor drive and a long cable release on a wing tip to take pictures of you in flight. Other flyers too provide this service. If you want to take pictures yourself you must realise that take-off and landing pictures are impossible since you can't be encumbered with equipment. Your camera must fit into the velcro pouch in the front of your flight suit. It's a good idea to have

JOHN MAIER, JR.

JOHN MAIER, JR.

Top: There are two golf courses close to Rio
Bottom: Hang-gliding off Pedra Bonita

the camera strap around your neck and a lens cover strapped to the lens or you will risk beaning a Carioca on the head and losing equipment. Flights are usually extremely smooth so it's possible to take stable shots. Hang-gliders themselves are dramatic shots, especially when taken from above.

Flying Over Rio

The climb up to the take-off point was awesome. Pedra Bonita looms over São Conrado's Pepino beach. The road winds up through the lush green Tijuca forest. We were waved on through the private entrance to the hang-gliding area and the engine whined as we climbed the extremely steep hill.

When we reached the top, our pilot assembled the glider, untangled the cables, tightened the wing nuts and slipped elastic bands over the wing struts. Up close the glider looked flimsy. We put on our flight suits and practised a few take-off sprints near the platform, literally a five-metre-long runway of wooden boards inclined 15° downhill. We were 550 metres above sea level and a few km inland from the beach. If I were a rock and Rio were a vacuum, it would take me over 10 seconds to kiss the dirt.

I wore old sneakers for traction and two good-luck charms to amuse the ambulance crew I anticipated would be piecing through the tangled ball of crumpled metal, torn nylon and mangled flesh down below.

With the glider resting at the top of the runway, we clipped ourselves onto it and checked the balance of the craft as we hung side by side. The pilot adjusted his weight belt, all the straps, the velcro leg cuffs and helmet and gave me very brief instructions: hold on to the cuff of his shorts, keep my hands to myself, resist the temptation to hold the control bar or cables (this can throw the glider), and when he gave the count 'um, dois, tres, ja!', go very fast.

We checked the windsocks on either side of the platform, the surface of the sea and the rippling of the leaves to ascertain the direction, speed and flow of the wind. A smooth wind coming inland from a flat sea is best. 'Um, dois, tres, ja!' Four bounding steps and we were flying. It's not the free-fall sinking feeling you get from elevators, but a perfect calm. I closed my eyes and felt as if I was still – the only movement, a soft wind caressing my face. Miraculously, it seemed I was suspended between earth and sky. To our left was Rocinha, the most famous of the zona sul's favelas, to the right Pedra Bonita, and below us the fabulous homes of Rio's rich and famous. We floated over skyscrapers and Pepino beach, made a few lazy circles over the water, and before I knew it, it was time for the descent. To land we stood upright, pointed the nose up, the glider stalled and we touched down on the sand gentle as a feather. ■

For the experience of a lifetime, it's not that expensive: US$80 for anywhere from 10 to 25 minutes of extreme pleasure. The price includes being picked up and dropped off at your hotel. Arrive early and allow for plenty of time to get things assembled, move things around etc. If you fly early in the day, you have more flexibility with delays.

The best way to arrange a flight is to go right to the far end of Praia do Pepino on Avenida Prefeito Mendes de Morais, where the fly-boys hang out at the Voo Livre club. Recommended flyers include Alonso Cunha, who can be reached on his beeper (☎ 266-4545, code 8LB). Ruy Marra is another excellent tandem glider pilot and widely regarded as one of the best pilots in Rio. He runs Super Fly Agency (☎ 322-2286) in Lagoa at Avenida Epitácio Pessoa 3624, room 201. (Ruy is also the person to see if you're interested in para-gliding.) Rejane Reis (☎ 322-6972) also does tandem flights. She's highly recommended by readers. For more information call the Associação Brasileiro de Voo Livre (☎ 322-0266), which also offers classes.

Ultra-leve (Ultralight) flights are more comfortable than hang-glider flights, but then you have to listen to the motor. Trips last around 30 minutes and leave from the Aeroporto do Jacarepaguá in Barra. The Clube Esportivo de Ultra-Leve (☎ 342-8025) has long-range ultralights that can stay up for over two hours. Flights cost around US$20.

Helicopter Flights

Joy flights over the city can be arranged by Helisight (☎ 511-2141; 259-6995 on weekends). It has three helipads at strategic scenic locations: Mirante Dona Marta, just below Cristo Redentor; Lagoa Rodrigo de Freitas; and Morro da Urca, the first cable-car stop as you go up to Pão de Açúcar. Helisight has 10 different flights to choose from. Five-minute flights cost US$30, while 30-minute flights cost US$500 for four people. They're a definite 'video opportunity'.

Hiking

Rio's always been good for hiking and offers some outstanding nature walks. Visitors can hike one of the many trails through Floresta da Tijuca or head to one of the three national parks within a few hours of the city.

Since Eco 92, there's been a boom in organised hiking around the city. Expeditours (☎ 287-9697; fax 521-4388), one of the premier ecotourism agencies in Brazil, can provide many options. Grupo Ar Livre (☎ 208-3029) also offers some good hikes in groups of up to 20 people. Its trip around the five deserted beaches hidden in the mountains at Barra de Guaratiba is excellent.

Sailing

Out in Barra, you can get into sailing Hobie Cat 16s. Bix Sportsmix (☎ & fax 439-4552) at Avenida Sernambetiba 3500, Bloco B, Apt 302, rents these catamarans for US$40 for two hours, not including preparation time. It does include pick-up and drop-off at your hotel. A 10-hour course is US$175. The instructors are highly experienced and speak several languages, such as English, Dutch, German and French.

Scuba Diving

Diving is very popular in Angra dos Reis, a few hours south of Rio. Conditions are ideal and there are lots of shipwrecks and deserted islands. In Rio, Aquamaster (☎ 205-7070, Angra 65-2146) organises trips for all levels. It's at counter 7 in the Marina da Glória. In Angra, its address is Estrada do Contorno 100, Praia da Enseada. If you have snorkelling gear, try going off the point at Arpoador on a calm morning. You'll see some nice fish.

Surfing

Surfing is very popular in Rio, with the locals ripping the fast, hollow beach breaks. When the surf is good, it gets crowded. Arpoador, between Copacabana and Ipanema, is where most surfers congregate in the city. It's lit up at night. There are some fun beach breaks further out in Barra, Grumari and Recreio. Prainha, between Recreio and Grumari, has the best waves close to the city. For more information, see the Beaches section earlier in this chapter. Boards can be rented in Rio, but they're so cheap to buy that you'd be crazy not to buy one, especially if you've planned a surfing expedition down the coast. A brand-new board is a steal at US$150 to US$200, and we saw some decent second-hand ones for as little as US$50. Galeria River at Rua Francisco Otaviano 67 in Arpoador, is an arcade full of surf shops.

Surfing School Escolinha do Rico at Praia Barra da Tijuca, opposite Avenida Sernambetiba 3100, is run by the Brazilian ex-champion and former professional surfer. Young surfers five and over are supervised by a team of life-savers. It's open every day.

JOHN MAIER, JR.

Surf's up on Ipanema

Tai Chi Chuan

Enthusiasts might like to join in one of the daily sessions held at Praça NS da Paz in Ipanema. They're at sunrise and 5 pm.

Tennis

The climate's not ideal for tennis, but if you fancy a game, book a court at the InterContinental (☎ 322-2200) or Sheraton (☎ 274-1122). Courts are available to non-guests. Lob Tênis (☎ 205-9997) at Rua Stefan Zweig 290 in Laranjeiras, rents courts for US$25 an hour and opens until midnight. In Barra, there are many tennis centres, including Akxe Sportside Club (☎ 325-3232) at Avenida Professor Dulcídio Cardoso 100, Clube Canaveral (☎ 399-2192) at Avenida das Américas 487, and Rio Sport Center (☎ 325-6644) at Avenida Ayrton Senna 2541.

Walking & Jogging

There are some good walking and jogging paths in the zona sul. If you're staying in the Catete/Flamengo area, Parque do Flamengo has plenty of space and lots of workout stations. Around Lagoa Rodrigo de Freitas is 9.5 km of cycling, jogging and walking track. At the Parque do Cantalago there, you can rent bicycles, tricycles or quadricycles. Along the seaside, from Leme to Barra da Tijuca, there's a bike path and footpath. On Sundays the road itself is closed to traffic and is full of cyclists, joggers, rollerbladers and prams.

Closed to bikes but not to walkers and joggers is the Pista Cládio Coutinho, between the mountains and the sea at Praia Vermelha in Urca. It's open daily from 7 am to 6 pm and is very secure because the army maintains guard posts. People in bathing suits aren't allowed in (unless they're running). It's a nice place to be around sunset.

Language Courses

IBEU (☎ 255-8332) has a variety of Portuguese language classes that start every month or two. The cost for a four-week course that meets three times a week is about US$150. For information stop by the 5th floor of Avenida NS de Copacabana 690. Next door to IBEU is a Casa Matos shop which sells the language books for the IBEU courses. It's a good place to pick up books or dictionaries to study Portuguese on your own. Other places that offer courses include Britannia (☎ 511-0143), with branches in Botafogo, Leblon and Barra; Berlitz (☎ 240-6606) in Centro and Ipanema; and Feedback (☎ 221-1863), in Centro, Copacabana, Ipanema, Botafogo and Barra.

Places to Stay

Hotels in Rio are ranked from one star for the cheapest to five for the most luxurious. A five-star hotel has a pool or two, at least two very good restaurants, a nightclub and bar, gym, sauna and a beauty salon. A four-star hotel has a good restaurant, a sauna and a bar. A three-star hotel may have everything a four-star hotel has, but there's something that downgrades it; the furnishings may be a bit shabby, cheaper or sparser. There's a big gap between three-star and two-star establishments. A two-star hotel is usually clean and comfortable, but that's about all. All hotels with a star rating have air-con in the rooms, though some of the older models sound like you're in a B-52 bomber! Breakfast is usually included in the room rate.

Despite the rating system, there are still plenty of decent places without stars that you can stay in if you're travelling on a tight budget and need a safe place to sleep. Air-con is usually optional (if available), but mostly the rooms in such hotels have fans. Staff at hotels not regulated by Embratur may try to slip in additional charges or commit other assorted petty crimes against the tourist. Threaten to call Sunab price regulation if this happens, discuss a price before accepting a room, and also ask if a 10% service charge is included.

Making a reservation is a good idea in Rio, especially if you plan to stay in a mid-range or top-end hotel. It can save you up to 30% on the room rate. If you want to make sure you have an ocean view, request it when you make your reservation. Such a room will cost around 20% more. At Carnaval time hotel prices go up and it's not a good time to arrive without a reservation.

Prices we've quoted here in the mid-range and top-end hotels are the rate for a standard room if you walk in off the street, so you should be able to get the price down a bit by making a reservation.

PLACES TO STAY – BOTTOM END

Camping

In Barra, the Camping Clube do Brasil has a camp site, *CCB RJ-9* (☎ 493-0628), at Avenida Sernambetiba 3200. It has good facilities and is opposite the beach. It charges US$8 per person. The club also has another site, *CCB RJ-10* (☎ 437-8400), further out at Recreio dos

Bandeirantes, also opposite the beach. It charges the same price as CCB RJ-9. There are two other camp sites in Recreio. *Novo Rio* (☎ 437-8213) at Avenida das Américas, km 18, is in a grassy area with plenty of shade and charges US$12 per person. *Ostal* (☎ 437-8213) at Avenida Sernambetiba 18790 is opposite the beach and charges US$8 per person. It also rents small chalets for US$12 a head.

Hostels

Youth hostels in Brazil are called albergues da juventude, and in the last few years the Brazilian organisers have been getting their act together. There are now more than 90 hostels and more are planned. Most state capitals and popular tourist areas have at least one. Although quality varies widely, the cost is very reasonable and is regulated by the federation in Brazil. A night in a hostel will cost around US$8 per person, depending on inflation. It's not always necessary to be a member to stay in one, but it'll cost you more if you're not. International Youth Hostel cards are accepted, but if you arrive in Brazil without one you can buy guest membership cards for about US$20 from the head office in each state. Booklets listing the hostels and describing how to get there (in Portuguese) are available at these offices and most travel agents.

The head office of the Federação Brasileira dos Albergues da Juventude (FBAJ; ☎ (021) 2524829) is at Rua da Assembléia 10, room 1211, Centro, Rio de Janeiro, CEP 20011, RJ. The FBAJ publishes a useful directory of Brazilian hostels, and it's available from most news-stands for US$6.

The Rio youth hostels are quite good. *Chave do Rio de Janeiro* (☎ 286-0303; fax 246-5553), in Botafogo, is a model youth hostel. You'll meet lots of young Brazilians here from all over the country. It gets busy, so you need to make reservations during peak holiday times. The only problem with this place is its location, but if you get the hang of the buses quickly, it shouldn't hamper you too much. From the rodoviária, catch a 170, 171 or 172 bus and get off after the Largo dos Leões. Go up Rua Voluntários da Pátria until Rua General Dionísio, then turn left. The hostel is at No 63.

A good place for budget travellers to stay in Copacabana is the *Copacabana Praia* youth hostel (☎ 236-6472) at Rua Tenente Marones de Gusmão 85. Although it's a few blocks from the beach it's still excellent value. A relaxed and friendly place, it charges US$8 for members, US$10 for nonmembers and US$25 for double apartments with a stove and a refrigerator. It will also rent you sheets if you don't have any.

Hotels

The best area for budget hotels is Glória/Catete/Flamengo. This used to be a desirable part of the city and is still quite nice. Many of the places used to be better hotels, so you can get some pleasant rooms at very reasonable prices. Quartos (rooms without bathrooms) are always a few dollars cheaper than apartamentos (rooms with bathrooms). These hotels are often full from December to February, so reservations are not a bad idea. At other times, you can usually find a place quite easily.

From Glória to Lapa, near the aqueduct, on the edge of the business district, there are several more budget hotels. Generally, these are hardly any cheaper than the hotels further from the city in Catete, yet they are run down and the area is less safe at night. If, however, everything else is booked up you'll see several hotels if you walk along Rua Joaquim Silva (near the Passeio Público), then over to Avenida Mem de Sá, turn up Avenida Gomes Freire and then turn right to Praça Tiradentes. The *Hotel Marajó* at Avenida Joaquim Silva 99 is recommended.

Glória The *Hotel Turístico* (☎ 225-9388), Ladeira da Glória 30, is one of Rio's most popular budget hotels, even though its prices are getting a bit high for what it offers. There are always plenty of gringos staying here and the staff are friendly. It's across from the Glória metro station, 30 metres up the street that emerges between two sidewalk restaurants. The rooms are clean

JOHN MAIER, JR.

The Sheraton Hotel in Vidigal

and safe, with small balconies. The hotel is often full but it does take reservations. Singles/doubles start at US$15/25 for quartos and US$20/30 for apartamentos.

Right near the Glória metro station, the *Hotel Benjamin Constant*, Rua Benjamin Constant 10, is one of the cheapest places around. The rooms are small and dingy but they cost only US$4.50 per person.

Catete/Flamengo The *Hotel Ferreira Viana* (☎ 205-7396) at Rua Ferreira Viana 58 has cramped but cheap singles/doubles at US$8/12 (US$15 with air-con) and an electric shower down the hall.

On busy Rua do Catete are four budget hotels worthy of note. The *Hotel Monte Blanco* (☎ 225-0121) at Rua do Catete 160, a few steps from the Catete metro stop, is very clean and has air-con. Its singles/doubles are US$14/16. Ask for a quiet room in the back. It has round beds and sparkling wall paint.

Up the stairs at Rua do Catete 172, the *Hotel Vitória* (☎ 205-5397) has clean apartamentos for US$11/16 for singles/doubles.

The *Hotel Imperial* (☎ 205-0212) at Rua do Catete 186 is a funky hotel with parking. The quality and prices of the rooms vary from US$25/35 for singles/doubles with bathrooms. Some of the rooms have air-con. The *Hotel Rio Claro* (☎ 225-5180), a few blocks down at Rua do Catete 233, has musty singles for US$12 and doubles with air-con, TVs and hot showers for US$16.

The *Hotel Hispánico Brasileiro* (☎ 225-7537) at Rua Silveira Martins 135 has big, clean apartamentos. Singles/doubles are US$14/16.

Turn off Rua Bento Lisboa down the quiet Rua Arturo Bernardes for a couple more budget hotels: the *Monterrey* (☎ 265-9899) and *Hotel Rio Lisboa* (☎ 265-9599) are at Nos 39 and 29 respectively. The first is cheaper and friendlier. Single/double quartos go for US$7/10 and apartamentos cost US$15. At the Rio Lisboa, single quartos cost US$7 and apartamentos are US$9/15 for singles/doubles. These two are the cheapest places in Catete.

Cinelândia The *Nelba Hotel* (☎ 210-3235) at Rua Senador Dantas 46 is in a good central location in the heart of Cinelândia. A two-room, three-bed suite with a high-pressure hot shower, air-con, phone and TV is US$18/28 for singles/doubles. The *Itajuba Hotel* (☎ 210-3163; fax 240-7461) at Rua Álvaro Alvim 23 has better rooms (with refrigerators) than the Nelba Hotel and is quieter. Singles/doubles are US$22/30.

Santa Teresa The *Hotel Santa Teresa* (☎ 242-0007) is attractive and has a small pool, car parking and rates that include three meals. Singles/doubles with a bath are US$20/25; without a bath, US$14/20. Santa Teresa is a beautiful neighbourhood, but somewhat dangerous, and after midnight there is no public transport. The hotel is at Rua Almirante Alexandrino 660. To get there, take a taxi if you're carrying valuables. If not, take the bondinho to Vista Alegre and then follow the tracks downhill to the old mission-style building.

Copacabana If you want to stay where the sun always shines and the lights never go out, you can probably find a cheap Copacabana hotel room.

As far as budget hotels go, the *Hotel Angrense* (☎ 255-3875) is one of Copacabana's cheapest. It has clean and dreary singles/doubles for US$17/25 with a bath and US$14/19 without. It's at Travessa Angrense 25. The road isn't on most maps but it intersects Avenida NS de Copacabana just past Rua Santa Clara. A few blocks away, the *Hotel Copa Linda* (☎ 267-3399) is almost as cheap. The small and basic rooms cost US$19 a single and US$26 a double. It's at Avenida NS de Copacabana 956 on the 2nd floor.

Near the youth hostel, at Rua Décio Vilares 316, is a small, delightful hotel, the *Santa Clara* (☎ 256-2650), with singles/doubles starting at US$22/25.

PLACES TO STAY – MIDDLE

If you want to be near the beach, there are several reasonably priced hotels in Copacabana, a couple in Ipanema and even some in Leblon. They all get busy in the high season, so it might pay to book. For the same price you can get a cheerier room in Flamengo or in the centre near Cinelândia (the Cinelândia hotels are also convenient if you're heading to the airport or rodoviária soon). There are a few places in Barra da Tijuca, but it's a long way out from the action, and you'll be spending a lot of money on taxis or time on buses.

Hotels

Catete/Flamengo The *Hotel Flórida* (☎ 285-5242; fax 285-5777), one of Rio's best mid-range hotels, is at Rua Ferreira Viana 81, near the Catete metro station. Popular with package tour groups, the Flórida has only three faults: it's not in Ipanema, it always seems to be booked up, and it's jacked up its prices since a recent renovation.

Rooms have private baths with good, hot showers and polished parquet wood floors. Singles/doubles cost US$50/73. There's a cheap restaurant and a safe for valuables. Make your reservations well in advance for stays during the high season.

Down the block at Rua Ferreira Viana 29, the *Regina Hotel* (☎ 225-7280; fax 285-2999) is a respectable mid-range hotel with a snazzy lobby, clean rooms and hot showers; singles/doubles start at US$24/29.

At Rua Silveira Martins 20 is the *Hotel Inglês* (☎ 265-9052), a good two-star hotel where singles/doubles cost US$22/29.

Further into Flamengo, near the Largo do Machado metro station, the elegant palm-tree-lined Rua Paiçandú has two excellent mid-range hotels. The *Hotel Venezuela* (☎ 205-2098) at No 34 is clean and cosy. All the rooms have double beds, air-con, TV and hot water; it costs US$25 a double. The *Hotel Paysandú* (☎ 225-7270) at No 23 is a two-star Embratur hotel with singles/doubles for US$24/32. Both are good value for money.

Leme In a pleasant neighbourhood, the *Acapulco* (☎ 275-0022; fax 275-3396) at Rua Gustavo Sampaio 854, is a three-star Embratur hotel costing US$40/50 for singles/doubles with bath. It's one block from the beach, behind the Meridien Hotel. It's good value and doesn't charge the 10% service fee.

On the oceanfront at Avenida Atlântica 866, the *Hotel Praia Leme* (☎ 275-3322) is a small, clean place that always seems to be full. Breakfast is served in the room. Children under six stay free and there's a sofa-bed in each room. Oceanfront rooms cost US$60 a double; others are a bit cheaper.

Copacabana The *Grande Hotel Canada* (☎ 257-1864; fax 255-3705), Avenida NS de Copacabana 687, has singles for US$27 and doubles for US$35 (there is no elevator for the cheapest rooms). The rooms are modern, with air-con and TV. It's two blocks from the beach in a busy area.

The *Hotel Martinique* (☎ 521-4552; fax 287-7640) combines a perfect location with good rooms at a moderate price. It's on the quiet Rua Sá Ferreira at No 30, one block from the beach at the far end of Copacabana. Clean, comfortable rooms with air-con start as low as US$28/40 for singles/doubles; it also has a few tiny singles for US$19.

Also one block from the beach, the *Hotel Toledo* (☎ 257-1990; fax 287-7640) is at Rua Domingos Ferreira 71. It's the best value two-star hotel in Copacabana. The rooms are as fine as many higher priced hotels. Good-sized singles/doubles start at US$35/43; it also has some tiny singles for US$20. The *Biarritz Hotel* (☎ 521-6542; fax 287-7640) is a small place at Rua Aires Saldanha 54, close to the beach behind the Rio Othon Palace. Singles/doubles start at US$22/35 and all rooms have air-con and TV. Also try the *Apa Hotel* (☎ 255-8112; fax 256-3628), three blocks from the beach at Rua República do Peru 305. Singles/doubles are US$37/46.

If you want to spend more money and stay on the beachfront, there are lots of hotels along the strand. Remember, rooms with ocean views cost about 20% more than internal rooms or those that face away from

JOHN MAIER, JR.

Soaking up the sun at the Nacional Rio Hotel

the beach. Most of the cheaper hotels don't have a pool either, but then the beach is across the road.

The *Hotel Trocadero Othon* (☎ 257-1834; fax 263-4564), Avenida Atlântica 2064, has smallish three-star singles/doubles for US$75/90. Service is good and its restaurant, the Moenda, serves very good Brazilian food.

The old *Excelsior* (☎ 257-1950; fax 256-2037), a member of the Horsa group, at Avenida Atlântica 1800 near the Copacabana Palace, has been refurbished. Spacious singles/doubles are US$65/70. It offers good service and discount rates.

The *Riviera* (☎ 247-6060; fax 247-0242), Avenida Atlântica 4122, has basic singles/doubles for US$65/80. The *Hotel Debret* (☎ 521-3332; fax 521-0899) at Avenida Atlântica 3564 is a traditional hotel in a converted apartment building. It has attractive colonial-style furnishings and rooms for US$70/100 a single/double. The entrance is on Rua Almirante Gonçalves.

The *Lancaster Othon* (☎ & fax 541-1887) at Avenida Atlântica 1470, is a small, charming hotel. In a converted luxury Art-Deco apartment house with an impressive marble staircase, it has spacious rooms, and the ones at the front have a terrace. Singles/doubles start at US$75/90. Children under eight stay free and babysitting is available.

You can get an oceanfront apartment at the *Arpoador Inn* (☎ 247-6090; fax 511-5094), Rua Francisco Otaviano. This six-floor hotel is the only hotel in Ipanema or Copacabana that doesn't have a busy street between your room and the beach. The musty beachfront rooms are more expensive than those facing the street but the view and the roar of the surf make it all worthwhile. If you want a beachfront room, make a reservation. Singles/doubles start at US$50/80 but there are discounts.

Ipanema There are three relatively inexpensive hotels in Ipanema. The *Hotel São Marco* (☎ 239-5032; fax 259-3147) is a couple of blocks from the beach at Rua Visconde de Pirajá 524. Rooms are small but have aircon, TV and fridge. Singles/doubles start at US$45/48. The *Hotel Vermont* (☎ 521-0057; fax 267-7046), Rua Visconde de Pirajá 254, also has very simple rooms at US$35/40. Call for reservations at both these hotels.

The *Ipanema Inn* (☎ 287-6092), around the corner from the Caesar Park at Rua Maria Quitéria 27, is a modern place which should appeal to both beach-loving and budget-conscious travellers. TV is an optional extra and the hotel provides umbrellas and towels for the beach. Singles/doubles cost US$40/60.

Leblon The *Hotel Carlton* (☎ 259-1932), Rua João Lira 68, is on a very quiet street, one block from the beach in Leblon. It's a small, worn but friendly hotel, away from the tourist scene. It's a good place for families on a budget, as two-room suites with sitting room are available. Singles/doubles are US$40/45.

Barra da Tijuca *Praia Linda* (☎ 494-2201; fax 494-2201) is well located at Avenida Sernambetiba 1430. There are a few restaurants close by and the beach is just over the road. Modern, functional rooms start at US$35/40 a single/double. A touch more expensive is the three-star *Tropical Barra* (☎ 399-0660; fax 287-7640) at Avenida Sernambetiba 500. It has a decent restaurant and bar, and comfortable, basic rooms. Singles/doubles go for US$40/50. A couple of other decent three-star hotels include the *Entremares* (☎ 494-3887; fax 493-1868) at Avenida Erico Verissimo 846, with single/double rooms for US$45/55, and the *Atlântico Sul* (☎ 437-8411; fax 437-8777), further out at Avenida Sernambetiba in Recreio dos Bandeirantes, opposite the beach. Singles/doubles here are US$50/60.

PLACES TO STAY – TOP END

Hotels

Glória/Flamengo Behind a beautiful white facade is the five-star *Glória* (☎ 205-7272; fax 245-1660) at Rua do Russel 632. Once a grand '20s beachfront hotel, the Glória fell off the pace when the tunnel went through to Copacabana and Ipanema. It even lost its beach when the big landfill of 1965 was landscaped into Parque do Flamengo. That didn't stop it from maintaining its status as a fine hotel. It was upgraded and renovated in 1990 and it's easily the best hotel close to the city centre. Favoured by business travellers, package tour groups and politicians, the Glória is a classy place. Singles/doubles start at US$80/100. Close by is the other top hotel in the area, the *Novo Mundo* (☎ 225-7366; fax 265-2369) at Praia do Flamengo 20. Once a luxury hotel, the Novo Mundo has slipped a bit, but it provides good service and a great view of Pão de Açúcar for US$60/70 a standard single/double.

Leme The *Leme Othon Palace* (☎ & fax 275-8080; see the Copacabana map) at Avenida Atlântica 656 is a decent five-star hotel with a good restaurant, Le Cordon Bleu, and a good bar, the Leme Pub, which has live music on weekends. Standard singles/doubles start at US$100/110; a beachfront room will cost a bit more.

JOHN MAIER, JR.

JOHN MAIER, JR.

Top: The Sheraton
Bottom: The Rio Palace Hotel

ANDREW DRAFFEN

JOHN MAIER, JR.

Top: The Copacabana Palace
Bottom: The Nacional Rio

Copacabana The *Rio Atlântica Suite Hotel* (☎ 255-6332; fax 255-6410) at Avenida Atlântica 2964 is a modern hotel, less than 10 years old, right in the middle of the Copacabana strand. As the name suggests, it has a lot of suites good for families of two adults and two kids. Amenities include rooms for the handicapped, nonsmoking floors, gym and a 24-hour deli. Suites start at US$150, but there are some cheaper rooms. Kids under 12 years old stay for free (only if accompanied by adults, that is).

The *Luxor Copacabana* (☎ 257-1940; fax 255-1858) at Avenida Atlântica 2554 has a good, central location. The jacaranda-wood furnishings add an earthy touch. Singles/doubles start at US$100/120. The *Luxor Regent* (☎ 287-4212; fax 267-7963) at Avenida Atlântica 3716 – the Ipanema end of Copacabana – provides good service at reasonable prices. Rooms start at US$90/100, and there's a good restaurant, the Forno e Fogão.

The *Ouro Verde* (☎ 542-1887; fax 542-4597) is a Swiss-owned place that's ideal for travellers of all kinds, but particularly business travellers. It has a business centre, an excellent restaurant and a classy reading room. Singles/doubles start at US$70/80. The *California Othon* (☎ & fax 257-1900) at Avenida Atlântica 2616 is reasonable, with singles/doubles for US$100/130, though the singles are a bit small. It supplies towels and umbrellas for the beach.

The *Miramar Palace* (☎ 247-6070; fax 521-3294) at Avenida Atlântica 3668 is a friendly place, with a good view out to the fort at Copacabana. Comfortable rooms start at US$100/120, but there are low-season discounts.

Ipanema The *Everest Rio Hotel* (☎ 287-8282; fax 521-3198) is a modern five-star place a block from the beach at Rua Prudente de Morais 1117. The floor-to-ceiling windows are a nice touch. Its suites are good for families and there's a small playground. Singles/doubles are US$90/110, but there are discounts. Popular with business travellers, its corporate rate is US$70 a double.

On the beachfront, the *Sol Ipanema* (☎ 267-0095; fax 247-1685) is a quiet hotel opposite Posto 9 where the beautiful people go. It supplies towels, chairs and umbrellas. Rooms start at US$100, but the view is worth an extra US$25. The *Praia Ipanema* (☎ 239-9932; fax 239-6889) at Viera Souto 706 is in a great location right on the border with Leblon. Rooms with small balconies start at US$100/120. There's a good restaurant, La Mouette.

Leblon The *Leblon Palace* (☎ 511-2000; fax 274-5741) is a good-value four-star hotel two blocks from the beach at Avenida Ataulfo de Paiva 204. It has a business centre with secretarial services, computer and fax. Singles/doubles with covered balconies go for US$70/80.

On the beach, the *Marina Palace* (☎ 259-5212; fax 259-0941) and the *Marina Rio* (☎ 239-8844; fax 259-0941) are both run by the same group. They are only a block apart, at Avenida Delfim Moreira 630 and 696 respectively. The five-star Marina Palace has fine restaurants – the Gula Gula and the Guilhermina Café. It's a sedate place, with good service and rooms starting at US$150/200. It's a pity the windows don't open. The four-star Marina Rio is a bit cheaper, with large rooms for US$130/170. Guests may use the facilities at the Marina Palace, which has a pleasant pool area.

São Conrado Next to the InterContinental, the *Nacional Rio* (☎ 322-1000; fax 322-0058) is another in the Horsa group. Designed by Brasília architect Oscar Niemeyer to make the most of the view, the hotel is popular with convention groups. Guests can also use the nearby Gávea Golf Club (for about US$85 a round including club rental). Singles/doubles start at US$110/130.

Barra da Tijuca The *Rio Hotel Residência* (☎ 385-5000), at Avenida Sernambetiba 6250, is an aparthotel in Barra with rooms starting at around US$100 a double. Sporting facilities are good, and include a pool and tennis and squash courts. The restaurant La Petit Paris serves very good French food.

PLACES TO STAY – OVER THE TOP

Rio is a good place to spoil yourself, and there are a handful of places that fall into the deluxe category. If you have the money, or a business expense account, try one of these.

Hotels

Leme The *Meridien* (☎ 275-9922; fax 541-6447) at Avenida Atlântica 1020 is modern, luxurious and chic. Popular with Europeans, the Meridien is home to some fine restaurants and bars. For French food, Café de la Paix is down below, and one of Rio's best, the Paul Bocuse supervised St Honoré, with its great food and spectacular view, is at the top. Le Rond Point Bar is cosy and the Rio Jazz Club is open to guests and members. On New Year's Eve, the hotel turns into a fireworks cascade. Rooms start at US$180/200 a single/double.

Copacabana Of the many top hotels in Rio, the twenties-style *Copacabana Palace* (☎ 255-7070; fax 235-7330), at Avenida Atlântica 1702, is the one favoured by royalty and rock stars. It is truly a symbol of the city. After a massive facelift, it is a modern luxury hotel as well. With a great pool and excellent restaurants, the formal Bife D'Ouro and the Pergula, the Copacabana Palace is a wonderful splurge. Standard apartments cost US$140/160 a single/double, or you might like to try the presidential suite for only US$1500 a night.

At Avenida Atlântica 3264, the *Rio Othon Palace* (☎ 255-8812; fax 263-4564) is another one of Copacabana's landmarks. A favourite with package tourists, there is a good *churrascaria* (barbecue house), and the Skylab Bar on the roof is popular with locals. Rooms start at US$150/180. Its suites are very good.

The *Rio Palace* (☎ 521-3232; fax 227-1454) at Avenida Atlântica 4240 has excellent views and luxurious public areas. It's very popular with US tourists and has a long list of stars who've stayed there. Frank Sinatra sang in the auditorium. The Cassino Atlântico shopping centre is right there and its restaurant, La Pré Catalan, is very good. The pool area is nice, but why are the pools covered at 4 pm? Singles/doubles start at US$170/200.

Ipanema In Ipanema, the *Caesar Park* (☎ 287-3122; fax 521-6000) at Avenida Vieira Souto 460 is favoured by ex-dictators, and business people with large expense accounts. Service is impeccable. The restaurants – Tiberius, on the 23rd floor, and Petronius, specialising in seafood – are both excellent, and the sushi bar, Mariko, is good but expensive. The feijoada (see the Places to Eat chapter) on Saturdays at the Caesar is legendary. The spectacular breakfast views are also a good start to the day. Security is tight on the beach in front, too. Singles/doubles begin at US$220/270. The imperial suite is a steal at US$3000 a night.

Vidigal The *Sheraton* (☎ 274-1122; fax 239-5643) at Avenida Niemeyer 121 is a true resort hotel, one of the few in Rio with large grounds. The beach is almost private and sporting facilities are excellent, including tennis, lovely pools and a good health club. Amenities include a tour desk, airline offices, a nonsmoking floor, a business centre and two very good restaurants – Casarão, a churrascaria, and Valentinos, serving Italian and international fare. The Casa da Cachaça is a fine place to relax. Singles/doubles start at US$160/180.

São Conrado The *InterContinental* (☎ 322-2200; fax 322-5500) in São Conrado is luxurious. It's the place to stay if you never want to leave the hotel. All rooms have a balcony, the restaurants are good and the pools are a treat. It's close to the São Conrado shopping mall, but apart from that there's not much walking to be done unless it's to the beach. The hotel runs a complimentary bus shuttle to Copacabana and Ipanema. The large grounds and top facilities make this ideal for kids. Singles/doubles start at US$180/200.

LONG-TERM ACCOMMODATION

A relatively inexpensive option in Copacabana, Ipanema and Leblon is to rent an apartment by the week or the month. There are loads of agencies. You could try Brasleme Imóveis (☎ 542-1347), Rua Barata Ribeiro 92-A, Copacabana. They rent apartments for a minimum of three days starting from US$75. Apartur Imóveis (☎ 287-5757), Rua Visconde de Pirajá 371 S/204, Ipanema, offers similar deals. Fantastic Rio (☎ 541-0615; fax 237-4774), Avenida Atlântica 974, apartment 501, in Leme rents luxury apartments, from one-bedroom flats to four-bedroom beachfront places. Prices range according to length of stay, but they're definitely good value. Also recommended is Yvonne Reimann (☎ 227-0281), who rents self-contained flats to visitors for a week or more. Prices are around US$40 a night for a two-room flat.

If you are interested in renting an apartment, you could look under *temporada* or *apartamentos para aluguel* in any daily newspaper. If you just want a room in someone's house or apartment, look under *vaga* or *quarto*.

Aparthotels

There are also residential hotels, or aparthotels, that are often more spacious and less expensive than normal hotels. This has been the fastest growing sector in the hotel industry in the past few years, so there are lots of small, modern apartments available. Prices vary from the mid-range to the top end, and during the low season, large discounts are usually available.

The *Rio Flat Service* (☎ 274-7222; fax 239-8792) has three residential hotels that are more like apartments. All apartments have a living room and a kitchen. Without the frills of fancy hotels, they still have a swimming pool, breakfast and room service. Apartments start at US$50. The *Copacabana Hotel Residência* (☎ 256-2610), Rua Barata Riveiro 222, is similar to the Rio Flat Service. The guide given out by Riotur has a full listing of aparthotels in the various suburbs.

Places to Eat

Vou matar quem 'tá me matando.
I'm going to kill what's killing me.
(A popular saying when sitting down to eat)

Cariocas love to eat out, so you can look forward to everything from top-quality French cuisine to something more traditional, like a meal in a churrascaria (barbecue house) or a spicy feijoada.

Serious restaurant-goers would be wise to buy *Guia Rio/ São Paulo Restaurantes* or *Guia dos Restaurantes do Rio* at a newsstand. Concierges at nicer hotels may have a copy.

In Rio, Cariocas dine late. Restaurants don't get busy until 10 pm on weekends.

Most places in Rio will bring you a *couvert*, whether you ask or not. This is optional, so you are perfectly within your rights to send it back. The typical couvert is a ridiculously overpriced and tedious basket of bread, crackers, pheasant eggs and a couple of carrot and celery sticks. Most restaurants will still bring free bread with soup.

A 10% tip is generally included in the bill. If not it's customary to leave at least 10%. Standard operating procedure in most Rio restaurants is to overcharge the customer. Some places don't even itemise their bills. Don't hesitate to look at the bill and ask the waiter: *pode discriminar?* (can you itemise?). Also, take your time and count your change – short-changing is very common in Brazil. It's all part of the game.

Many of the top restaurants won't accept credit cards, which is not surprising considering the instability in the economy in the past 10 years. If the real maintains its strength, more places are likely to accept cards in future.

BRAZILIAN FOOD

Feijoada

As Carioca as Pão de Açúcar or Cristo Redentor, *feijoada completa* constitutes an entire menu. With a *caipirinha* aperitif (see the following Drinks section), the properly prepared feijoada is made up of black beans slowly cooked with a great variety of meat – dried tongue, pork offcuts – all well-seasoned with salt, garlic, onion and oil. It must be accompanied by white rice and kale cut into fine strips, then tossed with croutons, fried manioc flour and pieces of orange.

Feijoada has its origins in Portuguese cooking, which uses a large variety of meats and vegetables; fried manioc flour and the kale are also Portuguese favourites. Farofa (manioc flour) is a legacy of the Indians, for whom it is an essential dietary ingredient. Africans added the spice and the tradition of using pork offcuts, which were the only part of the pig given to the slaves. Cariocas eat feijoada at least once a week, usually on Saturdays for lunch.

Churrascarias

Meat lovers will adore churrascarias – Rio's traditional barbecue houses. A *rodízio* is an all-you-can-eat affair, with dozens of waiters circling the tables with skewers of meat. Expect everything from filet mignon, steak, pork ribs, ham and even chicken livers. Salads come with all this and usually contain a good variety of ingredients. One thing is guaranteed – you won't feel like doing the samba soon afterwards! Prices vary, but you should be able to find a rodízio for around US$10.

Brazilian Dishes

Acarajé – a speciality of Bahia, Acarajé is made from peeled brown beans mashed in salt and onions and then fried in dendê oil. Inside these delicious fried balls is *vatapá* (see this list), dried shrimps, pepper and tomato sauce. Dendê oil is strong stuff. Many stomachs can't handle it.

Angú – a cake made with very thin cornflour called *fubá* and mixed with water and salt.

Bobó de camarão – manioc paste cooked and flavoured with dried shrimps, coconut milk and cashew nut.

Camarão á paulista – unshelled fresh shrimps fried in olive oil with lots of garlic and salt.

Canja – a big soup with chicken broth. More often than not a meal in itself.

Carangueijada – a kind of crab cooked whole and seasoned with water.

Carne de sol – a tasty salted meat grilled and served with beans, rice and vegetables.

Caruru – one of the most popular Brazilian dishes brought from Africa, made with okra or other vegetables cooked in water. The water is then drained, and onions, salt, shrimps and malagueta peppers are added, mixed and grated together with the okra paste and dendê oil. Traditionally, a sea fish such as garoupa is then added.

Casquinha de carangueijo or Siri – stuffed crab. The meat is prepared with manioc flour.

Cozido – any kind of stew, usually with more vegetables than other stew-like Brazilian dishes (eg potatoes, sweet potatoes, carrots and manioc).

Dourado – found in fresh water throughout Brazil; a scrumptious fish.

Feijoada – the national dish of Brazil. This meat stew, served with rice and a bowl of beans, is eaten throughout the country. There are many variations, depending on what animal happens to be walking through the kitchen while the chefs are at work. All kinds of meats go into feijoada, and it is accompanied by orange peels, peppers and farinha.

Frango ao molho pardo – chicken pieces stewed with vegetables and then covered with a seasoned sauce made from the blood of the bird.

Moqueca – a kind of sauce or stew and a style of cooking from Bahia. There are many kinds of moqueca: fish, shrimp, oyster, crab or a combination. The moqueca sauce is defined by its heavy use of dendê oil and coconut milk, and often contains peppers and onions. A moqueca must be cooked in a covered clay pot.

Moqueca capixaba – a moqueca from Espírito Santo that uses lighter *urucum* oil from the Indians instead of dendê oil.

Pato no tucupi – roast duck flavoured with garlic and cooked in the *tucupi* sauce made from the juice of the manioc plant and *jambu*, a local vegetable. A very popular dish in Pará.

Peixada – fish cooked in broth with vegetables and eggs.

Peixe a delícia – broiled or grilled fish usually made with bananas and coconut milk. Delicious in Fortaleza.

Prato de verão – translates literally as summer plate and is served at many suco stands in Rio. Basically, it's a fruit salad.

Pirarucu ao forno – pirarucu, the most famous fish from the rivers of Amazônia, oven-cooked with lemon and other seasonings.

Tacacá – an Indian dish of dried shrimps cooked with pepper, jambu, manioc and much more.

Tutu á mineira – a bean paste with toasted bacon and manioc flour, often served with cooked cabbage.

Vatapá – a seafood dish with a thick sauce made from manioc paste, coconut and dendê oil. Perhaps the most famous Brazilian dish of African origin.

Xinxim de galinha – pieces of chicken flavoured with garlic, salt and lemon. Shrimps and dendê oil are often added. ■

Vegetarian Food

Vegetarians have a good range of options in health-conscious Rio. There are juice bars on nearly every corner and lots of healthy lunch and dinner spots. The salad bars are good at the churrascarias, too, if you don't mind looking at large skewers of meat floating around the room.

DRINKS

Fruit Juice

Sucos in Brazil are divine. They vary by region and season (the Amazon has fruits you won't believe). Request them *sem açúcar e gelo* or *natural* if you don't want sugar and ice.

Often you'll get some water mixed into a suco; if you're worried about getting sick ask for a *vitamina*, which is juice with milk. Banana and avocado are great with milk.

Another way to avoid water is to drink orange juice, which is rarely adulterated and mixes well with papaya, carrot and several other fruits and vegetables. An orange juice, beet and carrot combo is popular in Rio.

Caldo de cana is a tasty juice extracted directly from lengths of sugar cane, usually while you wait.

ANDREW DRAFFEN

ANDREW DRAFFEN

Top & Bottom: Juice bars

Fruit

Expand your experience of fruit juices and ice creams beyond pineapple and orange to play blind man's bluff in Rio with your taste buds. From the savoury nirvana of *graviola* to the confusingly clinical taste of *cupuaçú*, fruits and juices are a major Brazilian highlight.

This is a partial list of the more unusual Brazilian fruits, particularly those found in Rio. Many of the fruits of the Northeast and Amazon have no English equivalent, so there's no sense in attempting to translate their names: you'll just have to try the exotic tastes of *ingá, abiu, mari-mari, pitanga, taperebá, sorva, pitamba, uxí, pupunha, seriguela, bacuri* and *jambo*. The following taste descriptions are unashamedly subjective: be bold with your choices and enjoy!

açaí – gritty, forest berry taste and deep purple colour; fruit of the açaí palm tree, also used in wines and syrups

acerola – wonderful cherry flavour; a megasource of vitamin C

bacaba – Amazonian fruit used in wines and syrups

biribá – Amazonian fruit eaten plain

buriti – palm-tree fruit with a mealy flavour and a hint of peach followed by an odd aftertaste; also used in ice cream and for wine

cacau – pulp from cocoa pod; tastes wonderfully sweet and creamy – nothing like cocoa, which is extracted from the bean

caja – pear-like taste

cajú – fruit of cashew (the nut is enclosed in an appendage of the fruit); has a tart taste like a cross between lemon and pear

carambola – starfruit; has a tangy, citrus flavour

cupuaçú – cool taste, strangely clinical; best with milk and sugar

fruto-do-conde – green, sugar-apple fruit; very popular

genipapo – what could be imagined as curdled cow's piss – not everyone's favourite; better as a liqueur

goiaba – guava

graviola – custard apple; aromatic, with an exquisite taste

jaca – large fruit of the jackfruit tree

mangaba – tart flavour; similar to a pear

murici – mealy fruit with vague caramel taste

pupunha – fatty, vitamin-rich Amazonian fruit taken with coffee

sapotí – gritty, semi-sweet like Worcestershire sauce; Brits may even recognise a hint of Marmite – rather confusing for a fruit!

tamarindo – pleasantly acidic, plum-like

tapereba – gritty texture; flavour resembles cross between acerola and sweet potato ∎

Coffee & Tea

Cariocas take their coffee as strong as the devil, as hot as hell, and as sweet as love. They call it cafezinho and drink it as an espresso-sized coffee without milk. The cafezinho is taken often and at all times. *Café com leite* is coffee with hot milk, usually drunk for breakfast.

Chá, or tea, is not nearly as important a drink as coffee, except in the state of Rio Grande do Sul, where the gaúchos like *maté*, a strong tea drunk through a silver straw from a hollow gourd.

Soft Drinks

Refrigerantes (soft drinks) are found everywhere and are cheaper than bottled water. Coke is number one, guaraná number two. Made from the berry of an Amazonian plant, guaraná has a delicious, distinctive taste.

Alcohol

Beer Brazilians, like most civilised people, enjoy their beer served icy cold – *(estupidamente gelada)*. A cerveja is a 600-ml bottled beer. Of the common brands, Antártica is the best followed by Brahma (although Cariocas argue that Brahma is better in Rio), Skol, Kaiser and Malt 90. The best beers are the regional ones, like Bohemia from Petrópolis, Cerpa and Original from Pará, Cerma from Maranhão and the tasty Serramalte from Rio Grande do Sul. Bavaria is a tasty beer which only comes in 300-ml bottles and is found in the more up-market bars. Caracu is a stout-like beer, also only available in 300-ml bottles. Very popular now is Xingu, a sweet, black beer from Santa Catarina.

Chopp (pronounced 'shoppee') is a pale blond Pilsner draught, lighter and far superior to canned or bottled beer. In some bars you may even find *chopp escuro* – a dark beer. Rio is the place to find the perfect Brazilian chopp, preferably while watching the sun set over the Cidade Maravilhosa, or the mist-covered shoreline of Praia de Ipanema as the sun sinks behind the Dois Irmãos. About all the Portuguese you should need to know on such occasions is *'Moço, mais um chopp!'* ('waiter, one more "shoppee"!').

Wine Jorge Amado wrote a satire about nationalist generals running Brazil who drink Brazilian wine in public and avoid the stuff like the plague in private. Well, Brazilian wine is improving but it's not great.

Forrestier is at the top of a very low heap of vintages. The whites are better than the reds and the Argentine wines are much better than both.

Cachaça Cachaça, *pinga* or *aguardente* is a high-proof, dirt-cheap sugar-cane alcohol produced and drunk throughout the country. Cachaça literally means booze. Pinga (which literally means drop) is considered more polite, but by any name it's cheaper than spit and far more toxic. The production of cachaça is as old as slavery in Brazil. The distilleries grew up with the sugar plantations, first to supply local consumption and then to export to Africa to exchange for slaves.

There are well over 100 brands of cachaça, with differences in taste and quality. A cheap cachaça can cut a hole in the strongest stomach lining. Velho Barreiro, Ypioca, Pitú, Carangueijo, and São Francisco are some of the better labels. Many distilleries will allow you to take a tour and watch the process from raw sugar to rot gut and then sample some of the goodies. The smaller distilleries usually make a much smoother cachaça than the commercial brands. The *Academía da Cachaça*, Rua Conde Bernadotte 26 in Leblon, is the appropriate place to sample some of the good stuff.

Other Alcoholic Drinks Caipirinha is the Brazilian national drink and Cariocas usually drink at least two. The ingredients are simple: cachaça, lime, sugar and crushed ice, but a well-made caipirinha is a work of art. *Caipirosca* is a caipirinha with vodka replacing cachaça. *Caipirissima* is still another variation, with Bacardi rum instead of cachaça. *Batidas* are wonderful mixes of cachaça, sugar and assorted fruit juices.

PLACES TO EAT – BOTTOM END

There's lots of fast food in Rio: you'll see the 'golden arches' all over the place and a local version called *Bobs*. There are other chains around the city, like *La Mole*, which has cheap, decent Italian food. Pizzas are a popular Brazilian fast food, and you'll see plenty of pizzerias. Pizzas are standard menu items in most restaurants. They're a good option for solo travellers.

Traditional Brazilian fast food can be found at the juice bars and the *botecos*. Botecos (often called *botequims)* are Cariocas' local bars. Patrons drop in for a cafezinho and a shot of cachaça before work, and a snack, a caipirinha or a chopp later in the day. Botecos are not known for their cleanliness, but nobody seems to mind

JOHN MAIER, JR.

Fried shrimp cooked on the beach

– not the Cariocas anyway. The quality of food served by botecos varies but can be good. Try such delights as a coxina de galinha (a savoury chicken wrapped in dough) or a pastel de palmito (a small pastry with palm heart inside).

The plates at the many botecos are big enough to feed two and the price is only US$4 to US$5. For something lighter, and probably healthier, you can eat at a suco bar. Most have sandwiches and fruit salads. Make a habit of asking for an *embalagem* (doggie bag) when you don't finish your food. Wrap it and hand it to a street person.

Galetos are small restaurants serving barbecued chicken and steak. It's grilled over the open flame as you sit behind the counter watching it, and Cariocas of all kinds sidle up to the counter and hop into a galeto with the couvert of chopped onions, tomato and bread rolls. The whole thing costs around US$3. You'll do plenty of finger lickin'.

Babushka's and *Alex* are the two best ice-cream chains in town.

PLACES TO EAT – MIDDLE

The next step up is to go to one of the traditional places. Brazilians love to eat well and cheaply, and there are lots of establishments – each with its own speciality and quirks – where the waiters all wear ill-fitting white jackets and the menus are many pages long.

Centro

There are lots of restaurants in Centro, most catering to the lunch-time working crowd. We've mentioned some of the traditional ones in the walking tour of Centro (see the Things to See & Do chapter).

Cinelândia

Associação Macrobiótica (☎ 220-7585) is one floor up at Rua Embaixador Regis de Oliveira 7. Macrobiotics is pretty popular in Brazil's cities and the food here is inexpensive and simple. Try the soup and rice dishes. It is open Monday to Friday from 11 am to 3 pm.

Lanchonete Bariloche is at Rua Alcindo Guanabara 24-D, across from Rua Senador Dantas. This cheap little counter joint has wood-grilled steaks for US$5 and is open until 2 am. *Churrascolândia Restaurante* (☎ 220-9534) at Rua Senador Dantas 31 is a steakhouse which also has tasty steaks cooked on a wood grill for US$6.

Lapa

Restaurante Ernesto, on the corner of Rua da Lapa and Rua Teotônio Regatas, is close to the arch of the viaduct that the trolley crosses to head up to Santa Teresa. It's a good place to eat if you're going to a show in the city. *Semente* at Rua Joaquim Silva 138 attracts a big lunch crowd, attracted by the mix of natural and oriental cuisine. It's inexpensive and open from 11 am to 11 pm on weekdays. *Bar Brasil* and *Nova Capela*, at Avenida Mem de Sá 90 and 96 respectively, are two traditional places in Lapa, both dating from the beginning of this century. Bar Brasil has German food with a Brazilian touch, and one of its plates will feed two easily. Nova

Capela has cheap, traditional Portuguese food. Its bad-tempered waiters are legendary.

Santa Teresa

In Santa Teresa, at Rua Almirante Alexandrino 316-B, *Bar do Arnaudo* has some of the best Northeastern food in the city. Try the excellent carne do sol. It is open from noon to 11 pm Tuesday to Saturday and Sundays from 11 am to 6 pm. It's closed Mondays. *La Cave de Paris* at Rua Oriente 437 has live music and some of the best crepes in the city for around US$3.

Catete & Largo do Machado

There are lots of options in the Largo do Machado area. Some Cariocas feel that this is the best part of Rio for food fans. On Largo do Machado, *Estacão Largo do Machado* has good fish, while *Casa dos Galetos*, on Rua do Catete, is good for chicken and steak, and has reasonable salad. Also on Catete, *Pizzaria Machado* has a pasta rodízio for lunch weekdays. *Adega Portugália* at Largo do Machado 30-A is an Iberian-style bar and restaurant, with garlic and meat hanging from the ceiling and wine bulging off the shelves. It serves a variety of fish and meat dishes that vary from the usual Rio fare. Try the bolinhos de bacalhau (cod fish balls) for 50c each with a Portuguese wine. For a feast try the roast cabrito (kid – the four-legged kind with little horns growing out of its head) for US$7. *O Cortiço* has a good lunch buffet for US$3.

Restaurant Amazónia (☎ 225-4622) at Rua do Catete 234 has good steak and a tasty broiled chicken with creamed corn sauce, both for about US$6.

La Bonelle, at Rua Conde de Baependi 62, has high-quality food, and just around the corner, *Luigis* at Senador Correa 10 has a good reputation. The *Museum* restaurant in the Palácio do Catete offers a good menu in pleasant surroundings. Its main courses are around US$10. A couple of more up-market places in the area are *Alho e Óleo* at Rua Barque de Machado 13 and *Alcaparra* at Praia do Flamengo 150.

Botafogo & Flamengo

While it doesn't have many hotels, Botafogo has stacks of corner bars and botecos. Most are nothing special, but there are some good restaurants scattered around the area.

David, the owner of *Rajmahal* (☎ 541-6999) at General Polidoro 29, Botafogo, is British, but the food is all Indian and quite good. Meals cost about US$10 and the place is a bit off the beaten path. The restaurant is spacious and refreshingly calm for Rio. It's open in the evenings from Tuesday to Sunday.

The popular *Churrascaria Majórica* (☎ 245-8947), Rua Senador Vergueiro 11/15, Flamengo, has good meat, reasonable prices and an interior done in gaúcho kitsch. It's open for lunch and dinner.

Cafe Lamas (☎ 205-0198), at Rua Marques de Abrantes 18-A, Flamengo, has been operating since 1874 and is one of Rio's most renowned eateries. It has a lively and loyal clientele and is open for lunch and dinner with a typical meaty menu and standard prices; try the grilled linguiça or the filet mignon.

There are also a few decent restaurants in the Rio Sul shopping centre, like the *Fun Club* and *Guilhermina* both with a varied menu, and the *T-Bone* barbecue house.

Leme

Máriu's (☎ 542-2393) at Avenida Atlântica 290, Leme, has an all-you-can-eat deal for US$10. Many people think this is Rio's best churrascaria and they may be right. Be prepared to wait during prime time as it gets a big tourist crowd. It's open from 11.30 to 1.30 am.

Restaurante Shirley at Rua Gustavo Sampaio 610-A has delicious seafood plates from US$7 to US$12. Try the mussel vinaigrette appetiser or the octopus and squid in ink for US$10.

Copacabana

Copacabana is a great place for the budget-conscious tourist to eat. There are botecos and small restaurants on almost every corner.

For cheap grilled chicken, there are lots of galetos in Copacabana. They include *O Crack dos Galetos* at Avenida Prado Junior 63, one block from the beach, and *Quick Galetos* at Rua Duvivier 284, near the Hotel Internacional Rio. *Lope's Confeiteria* at Avenida NS de Copacabana 1334, off Júlio de Castilhos, is an excellent lanchonete (a stand-up lunch counter) with big portions and little prices for typical Brazilian food.

Restaurante Lucas at Avenida Atlântica 3744 is across from Rua Souza Lima and has reasonably priced German dishes starting at US$6. *Churrascaria Jardim* at República do Peru 225 has a rodízio, á la carte and a self-serve per-kilo option. At Siqueira Campos 138, *Adega Perola* has quite a few items not usually found in Rio. Try its chicken in red wine.

JOHN MAIER, JR.

ANDREW DRAFFEN

Top: Street-side café in Copacabana
Bottom: The Lord Jim Pub in Ipanema

Arataca at Rua Domingues Ferreira 41 (near the American Express office) is one of several Arataca restaurants in Rio which feature the exotic cuisine of the Amazon. This place is actually a counter-lunch stand and deli, around the corner from one of its regular restaurants, with the same food as at the restaurants but for only half the price. In addition to the regional dishes such as vatapá for US$4 and pato (duck) for US$5, it serves real guaraná juice (try it) and delicious sorbets made from Amazonian fruits.

Mab's, on Avenida Atlântica (the Copacabana side of Princesa Isabel, across from the Meridien), has excellent seafood soup in a crock, chock full of piping hot creepy-crawlies for US$6.

The traditional *Cervantes* is Rio's best sandwich joint and is also a late-night hang-out for a strange and colourful crew. It's on the infamous Avenida Prado Junior, where everyone and everything goes at night. Meat sandwiches come with pineapple (US$3). The steaks and fries are excellent too.

Macro Nature, down the Travessa Cristiano Lacorte, is the best vegetarian restaurant/health-food shop in Copacabana. The menu is brief and very organic; the soup is excellent. It has sucos, sandwiches, yoghurt and health foods to go and everything is cheap. The *ponto de encontro de pessoas saudáveis* (the meeting point for healthy people), as it calls itself, is open Monday to Friday from 9 am to 10.30 pm and Saturdays and Sundays from 9 am to 6 pm.

Il Veronese, Rua Visconde de Pirajá 29A, is off Gomes Carneiro. For an inexpensive meal, Veronese has takeaway Italian pastas (the best in Rio according to local sources), pizzas and pastries.

Le Bon Jus at the corner of Teixeira de Melo and Visconde de Pirajá is a good juice and sandwich bar.

Ipanema

If you can't afford to stay at the *Caesar Park* hotel, go down there one Wednesday or Saturday from noon to 4 pm and sample its famous Brazilian feijoada. Ex-President Collor considers it the best around, and for US$15 it's excellent value for money.

Via Farme (☎ 227-0743) at Rua Farme de Amoedo 47 offers a good plate of pasta at a reasonable price – something which is usually hard to find. The four-cheese pasta and the seafood pasta dishes are excellent and portions are large enough for two to share. Most dishes are less than US$8. It is open from noon to 2 am.

Barril, at both 1800 Avenida Vieira Souto and Avenida Rainha Elizabete at the beach, is open late into the night. This trendy beach cafe, below Jazzmania (see the Entertainment chapter), is for people meeting and watching. After a day at Praia de Ipanema, you can stroll over to the *Shell Station* across the street from Barril 1800 for Babushka's terrific ice cream.

Boni's, Rua Visconde de Pirajá 595, is a favourite for fast food. It has excellent pastries and fresh coffee with enough force to turn Bambi into Godzilla.

Porcão (☎ 521-0999), Rua Barão da Torre 218, has steadily been moving up in the churrasco ratings game. Again, it's all you can eat for about US$8 a person. It opens at 11 am and closes at 2 am.

Bar Lagoa, on the lake, is Rio's oldest bar/restaurant. It doesn't open till 7.30 pm but only closes at 3 am. There's always a good crowd and you can just drink beer, or you can eat a full meal for US$7 to US$10. The food is excellent, the menu typical, and the atmosphere great.

Natural (☎ 267-7799) at Rua Barão da Torre 171 is a very natural health-food restaurant which has an inexpensive lunch special with soup, rice, vegies and beans for less than US$4. Other good dishes are pancakes with chicken or vegetables.

Esquina, a 24-hour bar/restaurant at the corner of Vinícius de Morais and Prudente de Morais, has a splendid mural, good atmosphere and huge lunch portions for around US$4 – very cheap by Ipanema standards.

Delicats, at Avenida Henrique Dumont near Rua Visconde de Pirajá, is Rio's only deli and has lots of homemade food. They make the best potato knish (dumplings) south of New York. They also have pastrami, herring, rye bread and other treasures from the old country, but sadly no bagels.

Lino's, at the corner of Farme de Amoedo and Visconde de Pirajá is a good juice and sandwich bar. Readers recommend its 'heavenly' sucos.

Banana Café, at Rua Barão da Torre 368, is a trendy (overpriced) bar/restaurant. It has 19 different types of pizza and eight types of sandwich. If you're drinking, try a black velvet (dark chopp with champagne). It's open till 6 am.

Chez Michou, Rua Paul Redfern 44, is a popular creperie with a young crowd. It opens till 4 am but closes on Tuesdays.

Fans of Japanese food should hit the *Kabuki Japanese Buffet*, Rua Visconde de Pirajá 365. It's reasonably priced and open Monday to Saturday from 10 am to 7 pm.

Leblon

Sabor Saúde, Avenida Ataulfo de Paiva 630, is Rio's best health-food emporium and is open daily from 8.30 am to 10.30 pm. It has two natural food restaurants: downstairs has good meals for US$4 while upstairs is more

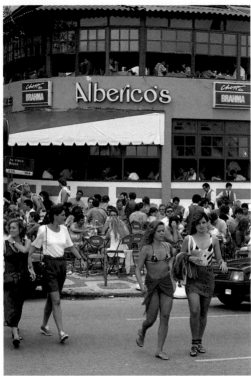

JOHN MAIER, JR.

Corner bar/restaurant in Ipanema

expensive (it has great buffet feasts for US$6). There's also a small grocery shop and takeaway food counter.

Celeiro, at Rua Dias Ferreira 199, has a fantastic salad bar. It's open from 11.30 am to 5 pm every day except Sunday. Don't let the silly name put you off at *Restaurante Bozó* (☎ 274-0147), Rua Dias Ferreira 50 – these people are very serious about their food. Try the scrumptious and filling medallions of filet mignon wrapped in bacon and smothered in pepper sauce.

Gávea

Guimas (☎ 259-7996), Jose Roberto Macedo Soares 5, is one of our favourite restaurants. It's not cheap, but the prices (US$20 to $US30 per person) are fair for the out-standing cuisine you're served.

Guimas offers what most restaurants in Rio lack: cre-ative cooking. Try the pernil de carneiro (lamb with onions) or the Oriental shrimp curry and a Rio salad. The small but comfortable open-air restaurant opens at 8 pm and gets very crowded later in the evening. If you order one of their boa lembrança specials, you'll receive an attractive ceramic plate. They don't accept credit cards.

Floresta da Tijuca

Os Esquilos is a beautiful colonial restaurant in Alto da Boa Vista in the national park. It has a typical menu which is not expensive. It is open Tuesday to Sunday from noon to 7 pm. *A Floresta* is the other restaurant in the forest, with reasonable food in a rustic setting.

PLACES TO EAT – TOP END

Rio is loaded with fancy restaurants which are not that expensive for the visitor. In most you can spend less than US$20 per person – especially if you decline the couvert, which is usually a rip-off – and the most expensive are often less than US$30. Here are of some of the best.

Centro

The French Restaurant *Les Champs Elysees* (☎ 220-4713) at Avenida Presidente Antonio Carlos 58 is open from noon to 4 pm weekdays. It is on the top floor of the French consulate building and offers an elegant busi-ness-lunch option.

The Japanese *Miako* (☎ 222-2397) is on the 1st floor of Rua do Ouvidor 45. It is open from 11.30 am to 3 pm and 6 to 10 pm weekdays and 11.30 am to 3 pm Saturdays. A lunch-time favourite, it uses very fresh ingredients.

Botafogo

Café Brasil (☎ 266-6483) at Rua Capitão Salomão 35 is a Brazilian restaurant open from 11.30 am to 1 pm (2 pm on Fridays and Saturdays). Its speciality is comida mineira (food from Minas Gerais), eaten for lunch, not dinner.

Club Gourmet (☎ 295-1097), a French restaurant at Rua General Polidoro 186, is a must for serious gourmets. The food is first class.

Zen (☎ 552-7097) at Praia de Botafogo 228 is open from noon to 2.30 pm and from 7 pm to midnight (closed

Sundays). Its extensive menu includes Chinese, Japanese and Korean dishes.

Adega do Valentim (☎ 541-1166) is a Portuguese restaurant at Rua da Passagem 176 open from noon till 2 am daily. The baked rabbit with spicy rice is excellent.

Sol e Mar (☎ 295-1896) at Avenida Repórter Nestor Moreira 11 is a seafood restaurant open daily from 11 am to 3 am. Somewhat pricey and stuffy, it comes complete with serenading violinists. It's one of the few places in the city that's right on the bay, and the outdoor tables provide a spectacular view. It's a favourite with wealthy tourists.

Flamengo

Alcaparra (☎ 225-3937) at Rua Praia do Flamengo 150 is open from noon to 1 am every day. It serves home-made pasta and good fish dishes.

Alho e O'leo (☎ 205-2541) at Rua Buarque de Macedo 13 is open from noon to 1 am daily and has an excellent seafood pasta.

Rios (☎ 551-1131) at Parque Brig Eduardo Gomes has a great view of the bay and Pão de Açúcar. It has a large lunch buffet from 11.30 am to 4 pm. In the evenings it's a quiet piano bar.

Leme

The French restaurant *Le Saint Honoré* (☎ 546-0880) is on the 37th floor of the Meridien Hotel on Avenida Atlântica 1020. It has a great view and great food supervised by Paul Bocuse. This is one of the best. It's open from 8 pm to 1 am (closed Sundays).

Another French restaurant in the Meridien Hotel is *Café de la Paix* (☎ 546-0881). It's open for lunch and dinner daily, and has an excellent lunch buffet and Saturday feijoada.

For superb seafood pasta, head for the Italian *Da Brambini* (☎ 275-4346) at Avenida Atlântica 514-B. It's open from noon to 1 am.

Copacabana

Copacabana has a large selection of French restaurants.

One of the specialities at *Le Bec Fin* (☎ 542-4097) is flaming garlic shrimp. The restaurant, at Avenida NS de Copacabana 178-A, is open from 7 pm until 2 am.

Ouro Verde (☎ 542-1887) at Avenida Atlântica 1456 is open from noon to midnight. Try the filé a moscovita (beef flambéd in vodka with condensed milk and caviar).

Le Pré Catalan (☎ 521-3232) has a traditional French menu with a touch of the tropics. The food is spicy. The restaurant is on level E of Avenida Atlântica 4240 and is open from 7.30 pm to midnight (closed Sundays).

At *Traiteurs de France* (☎ 235-6440) the coq au vin is delicious and the sweets are irresistible. It's at Avenida NS de Copacabana 386 and is open from noon to 6.30 pm (closed Sundays).

Finally, when you've had enough of French food, try *Cipriani* (☎ 255-7070) at the Copacabana Palace Hotel, where fine northern Italian cuisine is served in a marvellous setting overlooking the pool. It's open from noon to 3 pm and from 8 pm to midnight.

Ipanema

Siri Mole & Cia (☎ 267-0894) serves good Bahian food, such as moqueca de siri mole – spicy crab stew. It's at Rua Francisco Otaviano 50 and is open from noon to midnight daily.

At *Casa da Feijoada* (☎ 267-4994), Rua Prudente de Morais 10, Loja 10, you can eat feijoada any day of the week between noon and 1 am.

The *Esplanada Grill* (☎ 239-6028) at Rua Barão da Torre 600 is a churrascaria that serves high-quality meat. It's open from noon to 4 pm and from 7 pm to 2 am (Friday to Sunday from noon to 2 am).

Madame Butterfly (☎ 267-4347) is a Japanese restaurant serving excellent sukiyaki. It's at Rua Barão da Torre 472 and is open from noon to 2 am.

The Portuguese *Mercearia do Barão* (☎ 287-4842) has the same owners as Antiquarius in Leblon. It is less formal and less expensive but still very good. It's at Rua Barão da Torre 348 and is open from 7 pm to 3 am (noon to midnight on Sundays; closed on Mondays).

Grottamare (☎ 287-1596) at Rua Gomes Carneiro 132 is open from 7 pm to 1 am weekdays and from noon to 1 am on weekends. It serves fresh, well-prepared seafood – try the massa ao frutos do mar.

Also in Ipanema, and highly recommended, is *Petronius* (☎ 287-3122), at the Caesar Park Hotel. Its bandeja imperial is a seafood platter that serves two. It's open from 7.30 pm to 1 am.

Leblon

Mr Zee (☎ 294-0591) is a Chinese restaurant at Rua General San Martin 1219 open from 7.30 pm to 12.30 am (closed Sundays). Try the spiced shrimp.

Plataforma (☎ 274-4022) at Rua Adalberto Ferreira 32 is a big, noisy churrascaria frequented by artists, politicians and tourists alike. It's open from 11 am to 2 am.

Antiquarius (☎ 294-1049) is an elegant Portuguese restaurant that's good for a splurge. It's at Rua Aristides Espinola 19 and is open from noon to 2 am.

Lagoa & Jardim Botânico

Mistura Fina (☎ 266-5844) at Avenida Borges de Medeiros 3207, Lagoa, is open from noon to 3 am. Try the filé ao funghi e pimenta verde (steak with mushroom and green pepper sauce).

One of the top French restaurants in Rio is *Troisgras* (☎ 226-4542). It's at Rua Custódio Serrão 62, Jardim Botânico, and is open from 7.30 pm to 12.30 am (closed Sundays).

In the same area is the charming, Italian *Quadrifoglio* (☎ 226-1799). It's at Rua Maria Angélica 43, Jardim Botânico, and is open from 12.30 to 3.30 pm and 7.30 pm to 1 am. One of its specialities is ravioli de maça ao creme e semente de papoula (apple ravioli with cream and poppy seed sauce).

Other Areas

Tia Palmira (☎ 410-8169) serves traditional Brazilian food in a great outdoor setting and can be very crowded at weekend lunch times. It's at Caminho do Souza 18, Barra de Guaratiba, and is open from 11 am to 5 pm (closed Mondays).

Lokau (☎ 982-0549) is a seafood restaurant in a lovely location overlooking a lagoon. It's at Avenida Sernambetiba 13500, Barra da Tijuca, and is open from noon to 1 am (from noon to 8 pm on Sundays). It can be crowded on weekends.

Cândidos (☎ 395-1630) at Rua Barros de Alarcão 352, Pedra de Guaratiba, is a traditional seafood place adored by Cariocas. Try a seafood moqueca. It's open from noon to 9 pm (from noon to 11 pm Saturdays).

Entertainment

Any night of the week is a good one for going out and joining Cariocas at what they love: singing or dancing. Cariocas love to go out in the evening, and I haven't met a gringo yet who's complained about Rio's nightlife.

To find out what's going on, pick up the *Jornal do Brasil* at any newsstand and turn to the entertainment section. On Fridays the publication includes an entertainment magazine called *Programa* which lists the week's events. *O Globo* also includes its *Rio Show* magazine on Fridays. For even more listings, check the *Veja Rio* lift-out in the weekly *Veja* magazine. The entertainment sections are easy to figure out, even if you don't speak Portuguese.

Nightlife varies widely by the neighbourhood. Leblon and Ipanema have up-market, trendy clubs with excellent jazz. Botafogo has cheaper, popular clubs with more dancing and samba. Cinelândia and Lapa in the centre have a lot of samba and pagode and are also the heart of gay Rio. Try some of the bars around Sala Cecília Mendes. Copacabana is a mixed bag, with some good local hang-outs but also a strong tourist influence with a lot of sex for sale.

MUSIC

Samba

If you want to see and hear samba, you can go to one of the big tourist productions, head to one of the samba school rehearsals, or go to one of the escolas de samba (samba clubs).

The big tourist shows are glitzy, lavish, Vegas-style performances, with plenty of beautiful, topless mulatas who make samba look easy. The most popular ones are Scala (239-4448) at Avenida Afrânio de Mello Franco in Leblon, and Plataforma (☎ 274-4022) at Rua Adalberto Ferreira 32 in Leblon. Shows start around 10 pm.

Pão de Açúcar has a regular performance of the samba school Beija Flor on Mondays from 9 pm to 1 am. It's expensive and touristy, but it's samba.

Samba Schools In the samba schools, thing's start to heat up in October. That's when, after intense lobbying, they finally choose the samba do enredo that their members will defend with blood, sweat and beer in the

Sambódromo. Rehearsals are generally open to the public for watching and joining in the samba. It costs only a few dollars to get in, and you can really make a night of it. Check with Riotur or the newspaper to get the schedules and locations. In order of distance away from the zona sul, the major school addresses are:

São Clemente
    Rua Assunção 63, Botafogo
Estácio de Sá
    Rua Miguel de Frias 35, Cidade Nova (☎ 293-8994)
Salgueiro
    Rua Silva Teles – Andaraí
Unidos de Vila Isabel
    Boulevard 28 de Setembro 355, Vila Isabel
Unidos da Tijuca
    Avenida Francisco Bicalho 47, Centro
Mangueira
    Rua Visconde de Nitcrói 1072, Mangueira (☎ 234-4129)
Imperatriz Leopoldinense
    Rua Professor Lacê 235, Ramos (☎ 270-8037)
Império Serrano
    Avenida Ministro Edgard Romero 114, Madureira (☎ 450-1285)
Portela
    Rua Clara Nunes 81, Oswaldo Cruz (☎ 390-0471)
Beija Flor
    Rua Praçinha Wallace Paes Leme 1025, Nilópolis (☎ 791-2866)
Mocidade Independente de Padre Miguel
    Rua Coronel Tamarindo 38, Padre Miguel (%y332-5823)

Samba Clubs Cordão Bola Preta (☎ 240-8049) is a big dance house with different types of popular music played each night. It has serestas, roda de samba and pagode. The club is right in the centre, on the 3rd floor of Avenida 13 de Maio. Another good place to samba, but out in the suburbs, is Pagode Domingo Maior (☎ 288-7297) at Rua Gonzaga Bastos 268, Vila Isabel. It's probably a good idea to go with a Brazilian if you don't speak Portuguese. In the zona sul, Nega Fulô (☎ 266-6294) at Rua Conde de Irajá 132 in Botafogo and the Olímpico Clube (☎ 235-2909) at Rua Pompeu Loureiro 116 are the spots to head for. You're unlikely to find any other tourists there. If you want to hear some of the best pagode around, the group that plays next to the Rio Palace Hotel every Sunday afternoon is dynamite.

Forró

Forró is the popular dance music of Brazil's Northeast and there are plenty of Northeasterners in Rio going out dancing every weekend. We actually like the accordion-laced forró more than most of the current samba. The dancing is a blast and the orchestras really cook. The dance halls are called *gafieiras*, and the two most famous ones are both in Centro: Estudantina (☎ 232-1149), on the 1st floor of Praça Tiradentes 79, and Elite (☎ 232-3217), on the 1st floor of Rua Frei Caneca 4. They go Thursday, Friday and Saturday nights until about 4 am. The cover charge is US$4. Other gafieiras are Night & Day (☎ 220-7299), at Avenida Rio Branco 277, and Domingueira Voadora, the popular Sunday dance programme at the Circo Voador in Lapa (see the Big Venues section later in this chapter). If you don't fancy going into the city, Carinhoso (☎ 287-3579) at Rua Viscondé de Pirajá 22 in Ipanema is the zona sul alternative.

Jazz

In September or October every year, Rio hosts the Free Jazz Festival, which brings together some of the top international jazz greats and their skilful Brazilian counterparts. It's held at the Hotel Nacional in São Conrado, but many of the musicians can be found at other jazz spots later in the evening, jamming the night away. Big names to attend in recent years include George Benson, Ray Charles, Dizzy Gillespie, Stephane Grapelli, Etta James and The Count Basie Orchestra, to name but a few.

At any other time in Rio, fans can hit one of the many jazz venues in the zona sul. The music ranges from hot jazz to the cool bossa nova sounds of popular Brazilian music. Jazzmania (☎ 227-2447), Avenida Rainha Elizabete 769, Copacabana, is Rio's most serious jazz venue. It has more international stars than any other club, but also the best of Brazilian jazz. The club is expensive at around US$15 cover on weekends and a little less on weekdays. The music starts about 11 pm and goes late. People's (☎ 294-0547), at Avenida Bartolomeu Mitre 370 in Leblon, is a posh club with some of the best names in jazz. To hear the great music you have to endure a US$10 cover charge and incessant smoking and talking from a snobby crowd. When it gets crowded the Yves St Laurent crowd seems to get in and seated, while the Levis crowd gets left at the door.

Other important venues include Mistura Fina (☎ 286-0195) at Avenida Borges de Medeiros 3207 in Lagoa and Vinícius (☎ 267-5757) at Rua Vinícius de Moraes 39. There are plenty of other places to hear jazz and bossa nova. Have a look at the newspapers mentioned in the introduction to this section.

Discos

There are many discos with bright lights and loud music in the big city, but the hip venues change regularly – check out a copy of *Programa*. Interestingly, many of the discos have stiff dress codes and admission charges, designed in part to deter the many prostitutes who come to meet tourists. Some are even called private clubs and require you to pay US$20 through a concierge at your five-star hotel in order to enter.

The current favourites are Resumo da Ópera, Avenida Borges de Medeiros 1426 in Lagoa; Dr Smith, Rua da Passagem 169 in Botafogo; and the Fun Club, on the 4th floor of the Rio Sul shopping mall. There are many, many more.

Help deserves a special mention here. It calls itself the biggest disco in Latin America and no-one seems to doubt it. It's at Avenida Atlântica 3432 in Copacabana. It's full of 'professional' ladies, and lots of drunken gringos seem to get robbed just outside. That doesn't mean you shouldn't go there – it's definitely an interesting place – but keep the above-mentioned warning in mind.

BARS

Centro & Lapa

Getting a taxi late at night in Lapa or Cinelândia isn't a problem; there is also limited bus service all night long. You can catch buses to the zona sul along the Praça Mahatma Gandhi on Avenida Luis de Vasconcelos.

Suburban Dreams at Pedro Lessa 41, Centro, behind the Biblioteca Nacional, is a bar, open until very late, and right in the centre. It's the only thing open on the block. The bar is frequented by many gays, Blacks and zona norte people. It's a good change from the zona sul club scene but don't bring too much money to this part of town late at night. There's no cover charge. Chopp da Lapa, at Mem de Sá 17, is a lively spot. Bar Brasil in Lapa is an old bohemian hang-out and is always lively. Some Cariocas who live in the zona sul only come into the centre to go to Bar Brasil. Lapa, along Avenida Mem de Sá, is generally an interesting area to explore at night.

Botafogo

Some decent bars in the bairro include Das Schoppen at Rua Real Grandeza 129, Big Ben at Rua Muniz Barreto 374, and Soho and Village, both on Rua Visconde da Silva at Nos 22 and 10 respectively.

JOHN MAIER, JR.

JOHN MAIER, JR.

Top & Bottom: Help, Latin America's biggest disco

Copacabana

The beachfront bars are a good place to have a couple of chopps in the early evening, but as the night wears on things get a little seedier, and it might be time to move on. The Sindicato do Chopp has two branches in Copacabana (Avenida Atlântica and Rua Santa Clara 18) and one in Ipanema on Rua Farme de Amoedo. They're popular with locals and get pretty noisy. Galeria Alaska on Avenida NS de Copacabana has a transvestite show and dancing and is a centre of gay Rio.

Ipanema, Leblon & Lagoa

There are several expensive restaurants/clubs/bars in Ipanema, Leblon and Lagoa which have good music but look like a scene right out of Los Angeles or New York. Chiko's Bar, Avenida Epitácio Pessoa 560 on the lake, goes late and has no cover charge. Mistura Up at Rua Garcia d'Avila 15 and Un Deux Trois (☎ 239-0198) at Rua Bartolomeu Mitre 123 are also popular.

Lord Jim's British pub is the place to go if you want to play darts. It's at Rua Paul Redfern 63 in Ipanema. The Garota de Ipanema is at Rua Vinícius de Morais 49 and has lively open-air dining. There are always a few foreigners checking out the place where Tom Jobim and Vinícius de Moraes were sitting when they wrote 'The Girl from Ipanema'. A recent Brazilian Playboy survey rated their chopp as the best in Rio – a bold claim indeed, but who could resist a sample after a rap like that? Their petiscos are delicious.

The Zeppelin Bar, behind the Sheraton Hotel on Avenida Niemeyer, is a quaint bar/restaurant overlooking the ocean. It's medium priced, with great live folk and pop music from Thursday to Sunday night. A very relaxed atmosphere.

Bar Lagoa is our favourite bar and is also one of Rio's oldest. Attempts have been made to close it down to build a high-rise, high-tech condo complex, but opposition has been too strong. It's open from about 7.30 pm to 3 or 4 am. Food and drink are available, and the Carioca crowd is loud.

BIG VENUES

Rio plays host every week to a different set of national and international stars, as well as holding large rock and jazz festivals each year. There's no central booking system, so tickets to the shows need to be purchased from the box office at the venue. Use the concierge at your hotel to get hold of tickets. It's much easier.

The Metropolitan (☎ 385-0515), in Via Parque Shopping in Barra da Tijuca, opened in 1994 and is now the major venue for top international and Brazilian acts, as well as opera, ballet, Broadway musicals and Carnaval balls. For visitors staying in the zona sul, this is a disadvantage for all but the well-heeled, because a taxi from, say, the Meridien to the Metropolitan costs around US$40 one way.

Other more accessible venues include Canecão (☎ 295-3044), which still gets the big stars of music, both national and international. It's right next to the giant Rio Sul shopping mall at the entrance to the Copacabana tunnel.

Maracanã (☎ 264-9962) is the venue for the biggest shows in Rio. It has played host to Frank Sinatra, Sting, Madonna, Paul McCartney and the Rolling Stones.

Maracanãzinho is the smaller stadium next to Maracanã in São Cristóvão. Big shows used to play there, but there hasn't been one since the Midnight Oil concert in 1993 when two fans were killed in a freak accident.

Circo Voador (☎ 221-0406) under the Arcos da Lapa is a big tent with reggae, samba and trio elétrico music. Its Sunday night dances can be really crowded. They start at 11 pm and go till late. The cover charge is US$4. Down the block is Asa Branca (☎ 224-9358) at Avenida Mem de Sá. It has samba and pagode shows that aren't staged for tourists, though they are staged shows.

CINEMAS

Most movies in the cinemas are screened in their original language with Portuguese subtitles; consequently there are plenty of films in English. Brazil gets most of the hits from the USA, including many of the violent Rambo-type films. Brazilians also adore comedians like Woody Allen and the Marx Brothers.

For a complete listing of cinemas and current films, look in the daily newspaper. If the titles are written in Portuguese, the English translation is usually underneath. The latest French releases are also popular in Rio.

THEATRE

There's not much point going to the theatre if you don't understand Portuguese, which is a pity, because there are many fine Brazilian actors and playwrights. If you fancy a look anyway, there's a full listing available in the

JOHN MAIER, JR.

Cinema in downtown Rio

entertainment sections of the newspapers mentioned in the introduction to this chapter.

GAY RIO

Rio is the gay capital of Latin America. There are lots of gay clubs in Cinelândia and Copacabana. Amarelinho at Praça Floriano 55 in Cinelândia and Club Rio (☎ 521-6740) at Travessa Cristiano Lacorte 46 in Copacabana are popular gay bars. For shows, the Galería Alaska in Copacabana is the place to go. The House of Boys (☎ 257-1670) is a gay bar/disco complete with steam rooms and cabins. It's at Rua Siqueira Campos 43, in the basement. There are also plenty of gay saunas, advertised in the press as *termas*.

GAMBLING

Casinos in Brazil were closed in 1946 after a presidential decree outlawed gambling. That hasn't stopped Cariocas, who love to have a flutter on their favourite numbers in the illegal *jogo do bicho*, the thriving numbers game that's been around for more than a century. If you've ever wondered what all those guys with note pads and little tables are doing sitting around all over Rio, now you know. Legal gambling takes the form of lotteries, *raspadinhas* (scratch 'n' win tickets) and betting on sporting events such as football and horse racing. Lately, other types of gambling have also been tolerated – notably, bingo. It may be a sign that in the not-too-distant future casinos will make a comeback.

Anyone who thinks bingo is only played by little old ladies in church halls will get a surprise in Rio. The large, luxurious bingo houses are just like casinos, except the only thing that gets played is bingo! And there's no Brazilian equivalent of bingo chatter of the 'two fat ladies 88' variety either. This is serious gambling and the games are quite quick. Playing bingo is fashionable among Cariocas but we can't seriously advise anyone going to Rio to try it. What would you tell your friends back home? If you do get curious, the two most popular bingo palaces are Bingo Arpoador, Rua Francisco Otaviano 35 in Copacabana, and Scala Bingo, Avenida Afrânio de Mello Franco 292 in Leblon.

MOTELS

Motels are a Rio institution and should never be confused with hotels. They have names like Sinless, Escort and Holiday. Rented by the hour, for short stays only, the motel is the Brazilian solution to the lack of privacy caused by overcrowded living conditions. Used by adults who still live with their parents, kids who want to get away from their parents, parents who want to get away from their kids and couples who want to get away from their spouses, they are an integral part of the nation's social fabric. They are a bedrock of Brazilian morality, and are treated by Brazilians with what most outsiders consider to be incredible nonchalance.

The quality of motels varies, reflecting their popularity with all social classes. Most are out on the approach roads to the city, like Avenida Brasil in the zona norte and Avenida Niemeyer between Leblon and São Conrado. With walled-in garages for anonymity, a three-storey suite usually has a hot tub on the top floor with skylights that open, and a sauna and bathroom on the

2nd floor. The suites often have circular vibra-beds with mirrors overhead, a video recorder with adult movies piped over loudspeakers, and room service with a menu full of foods and sex toys (with instructions). The more expensive suites have touches like Roman fountains gushing away. For the best suites, expect to pay around US$100 for 12 hours – more on weekends. Standard rooms cost quite a bit less, and are a lot of fun too.

Motels are a unique cultural experience and can be a lot of fun. Some of the more popular are Sinless (☎ 322-3944), Avenida Niemeyer 214, and Shalimar (☎ 322-3392), next door. Holiday (☎ 494-2650) is at Estrada de Furnas 3700 in Barra da Tijuca.

RED LIGHT

The two main red-light areas in Rio are in Lapa, along Rua Mem de Sá, and in Copacabana. Lapa is much seedier than Copacabana, although you need to be wary in both. In Copacabana, Praça do Lido is the centre of the red-light area. There are lots of erotic shows/strip joints on Rua Duvivier (New Munich and Don Juan), Rua Belfort Roxo (Pussy Cat Bar), Rua Ronaldo de Carvalho (Lido and Golden Club) and Avenida Princesa Isabel (Barbarela Boite, New Scotch Boite and La Cicciolina). The erotic shows often include live sex acts. Cover charge is between US$20 and whatever they think they can squeeze out of you. It usually includes a two-drink minimum. If you decide to have more than two drinks, make sure you find out the price beforehand or you're in for a shock. If you offer to buy one of the girls a drink, don't be surprised if she orders the most expensive one.

The price of sex varies. Hookers on the street charge around US$40 – more if you want to use a condom! In the clubs, prices range from US$100.

Escort services are also widely available in Rio, and advertise freely in the daily and tourist press under *Termas e Serviços de Massagem*.

Sport

FOOTBALL

Soccer was introduced to Brazil after a young student from São Paulo, Charles Miller, returned from his studies in England with two footballs and a rule book and began to organise the first league. It quickly became the national passion, and Brazil has since won four World Cups. Brazilians are crazy about the game.

When the team beat Italy in the 1994 World Cup, millions danced in the streets and a mass hysteria gripped the country for weeks.

Brazilians play the world's most creative and artistic style of football, with moves like the overhead backward

JOHN MAIER, JR.

Football is the national passion

bicycle kick, the back-of-the-heels flip-on and the banana kick, could only come from Brazil. You'll see tiny kids playing skilled, rough matches in the streets, on the beaches, just about anywhere.

Complementing the action on the field are the fanatical fans in the stands, chanting, waving banners and streamers, pounding huge samba drums, exploding firecrackers, Roman candles and smoke bombs (in the team colours); launching incendiary balloons; throwing toilet paper, beer and even dead chickens – the scene, in short, is sheer lunacy. Football is a religion in Brazil, and its cathedral is Maracanã – the largest stadium in the world.

For the sports fan, a trip to the football in Rio is essential. If you happen to be in town when arch rivals Flamengo and Fluminense play off, don't miss it.

You have to be very careful if you go to Maracanã. Don't wear a watch or jewellery. Don't bring more money than you need for tickets, transport and refreshments. The big question is how to get to and from the game safely.

The big games are held on Sundays at 5 pm year round. Tourist buses leave from major hotels at 2.30 pm (they often run a bit late) for 5 pm Sunday games. They cost about US$25, which is a rip-off, but they are the safest and easiest way to get to the game. They drop you off and pick you up right in front of the gate and escort you to lower-level seats. Unfortunately this is not the best perspective for watching the game, but it is the safest because of the overhead covering which protects you from descending objects (like cups full of bodily fluids).

However you get to the stadium, it's a good idea to buy these lower-level seats, called *cadeira*, instead of the upper-level bleachers, called *arquibancada*. The price is US$8, unless it's a championship game, when it's more.

The metro is closed on Sundays, and taking a bus or cab can be a hassle. Getting to the stadium isn't too difficult: catch a bus marked 'Maracanã' (from the zona sul, No 434, 464 or 455; from Centro, No 238 or 239) and leave a couple of hours before the game is due to begin. Returning to your hotel by bus is often a drag. The buses are packed full and thieves set to work on the trapped passengers. Taking a cab is a possible alternative, but it can be hard to flag one down; the best strategy is to walk away from the stadium a bit.

Surprisingly, driving a car to the stadium is pretty easy. You should leave a couple of hours before kick-off and, for easy departure, park away from the stadium. The traffic isn't all that bad and if you arrive early you can watch the preliminary games.

HORSE RACING

There's lots to see at the racetrack. The Jóquei Clube, which seats 35,000, is on the Gávea side of the Lagoa Rodrigo de Freitas at Praça Santos Dumont 31 (take any of the buses that go to Jardim Botânico). It's a beautiful racetrack, with a great view of the mountains and Corcovado; it's rarely crowded and the fans are great to watch – it's a different slice of Rio life. It costs a few cents to enter the public stands and around a dollar to get into the members' enclosure. Foreign tourists are welcome in the members' enclosure, which has a nice bar and restaurant overlooking the track. Racing usually takes place every Saturday and Sunday afternoon, and Monday and Thursday night. The big event of the year is the Brazilian Grand Prix on the first Sunday in August.

MOTOR RACING

Brazilians love speed. Taxi drivers may give you a hint of it, and since the early '70s Brazilians have won more Formula One Grand Prix world championships than any other nationality. Emerson Fittipaldi was world champion twice in the '70s, Nelson Piquet won his third world championship in 1987, and Ayrton Senna took it out in 1988, '90 and '91. His death in 1994 was a national tragedy. The Brazilian Grand Prix traditionally kicks off the Formula One season around March each year. From 1981 to 1989 it was held at the Autódromo Nelson Piquet in Barra, near Jacarepaguá, but it's now held in São Paulo at the Interlagos circuit. Brazilians closely follow the Formula One and Formula Indy racing seasons. If you want to start a conversation, motor racing is a popular subject with Cariocas.

BEACH SPORTS

Surprisingly, volleyball is Brazil's second sport. A natural activity for the beach, it's also a popular spectator sport on TV. A local variation you'll see on Rio's beaches is volleyball played without the hands (*foot-volei*). It's quite fun to watch but it's bloody hard to play.

Peteca is a cross between volleyball and badminton, and is played with a peteca, similar to, but a little larger than, a shuttlecock. You'll see them being hawked on the beach. Peteca is a favourite with older Cariocas who are getting a bit slow for volleyball.

Usually played on the firm sand at the shoreline, *frescobal* involves two players, each with a wooden racquet, hitting a small rubber ball back and forth as hard as possible. Cariocas make it look easy.

JOHN MAIER, JR.

JOHN MAIER, JR.

Top: Football fans at an anxious moment
Bottom: Footvolei; volleyball without the hands

JOHN MAIER, JR.

JOHN MAIER, JR.

JOHN MAIER, JR.

Top: Fanatical football fans in Maracanã
Middle: Horse racing at the Jóquei Clube
Bottom: Motor racing is extremely popular

Shopping

Rio offers plenty of shopping opportunities for the visitor, including large department stores, gigantic shopping malls, fashionable streets with stylish boutiques and moveable fruit, flower and artisan markets with a genuine local flavour. Prices vary depending on the economic climate at the time, but it's safe to say that you can usually find yourself a bargain in Rio.

BARGAINING

Bargaining is not common in shops in Rio. If you want to have a go, ask if there's a *promoção*, or a discount for cash. Once you start buying on the street or at markets, it's a different story. Bargain as much as you can, but don't be surprised if the seller isn't always willing. Some are quite prepared to let you walk away if you don't meet their asking price. It just depends on what sort of day they're having.

SHOPPING AREAS

Centro

Clothing is a bargain in Centro, and you can get some things for a fraction of what you'd pay in Ipanema and Copacabana. The discount clothing shops are on Rua da Alfândega and Rua Senhor dos Passos. The further they are from Avenida Rio Branco, the cheaper they get. In Centro there are also a few craft shops on Rua Gonçalves Dias, an interesting street to wander along from the Largo da Carioca up to the flower market near Rua Buenos Aires.

Copacabana

Copacabana's main shopping drag is Avenida NS de Copacabana, one block in from the beach. We recommend walking from one end to the other just to watch the busy, lively way the Cariocas do their daily shopping. The high population density guarantees a lot of street action from dawn to dusk. The street has everything from souvenir shops to clothing shops as well as plenty of street stalls. Along Avenida Atlântica, you'll also find lots of vendors selling cheap souvenirs and beach items like shorts and towels.

Ipanema & Leblon

Much more stylish than Copacabana, this is where to find high fashion. The main shopping street in Ipanema is Rua Visconde de Pirajá and once again we recommend a stroll from one end to the other. There are lots of smaller shopping malls along the street containing chic boutiques, and some of the side streets are worth a look as well. The jewellery giants H Stern and Amsterdam Sauer are both here. Colourful markets in Ipanema include the Friday fruit and vegetable market on Praça N.S. da Paz and the hippy fair in Praça General Osório (see Copacabana map for reference) every Sunday.

In Leblon, the main shopping area is Avenida Ataulfo de Paiva. The shops are very up market.

MARKETS

Called feiras in Portuguese, there are several open markets where visitors can snap up a bargain, sample some traditional snacks, or just watch Cariocas.

The Feira do Nordestinho is held at the Pavilhão de São Cristóvão on the northern side of town every Sunday, near the Quinta da Boa Vista. It starts early and goes until about 3 pm. The fair is very Northeastern in character. There are lots of barracas (stalls) selling meat, beer and cachaça; bands of accordions, guitar and tambourine players performing the forró; comedy, capoeira dance/fight battles and people selling magic potions. It's a great scene.

Of course there's plenty to buy: besides food, they have lots of cheap clothes, some well-priced hammocks and a few good Northeastern gifts like leather vaqueiro (cowboy) hats. If you're ready for adventure it's best to arrive the night before the market. This is set-up time and also party time. At about 9 or 10 pm the barracas open for dinner and beer. Some vendors are busy setting up, others are already finished. Music and dance starts, and doesn't stop until sunrise. It's great fun so long as you're careful.

In Centro on Saturdays is the Feira de Antiguidades, the antique market in the Praça do Mercado next to the Niterói ferry terminal and the Restaurante Alba Mar. It goes from 9 am to 5 pm, and the stalls have a wide assortment of porcelain, glassware, plates, carpets, paintings and jewellery. Bargain hard here.

Also in Centro on Thursdays and Fridays is another hippy fair, in Praça 15 de Novembro. There are more than 300 stalls here, including many selling leather goods. It's not worth a special trip, as most of the items

JOHN MAIER, JR.

ANDREW DRAFFEN

ANDREW DRAFFEN

Bargains abound in Rio's open markets

can be found at the hippy fair in Ipanema, but if you're in the city, drop by and browse.

On Sunday in the Passeio Publico, Rio's stamp, coin and postcard collectors get together for a swap meet. If this is your thing, the 'action' starts at 7 am and goes to 1 pm.

In the zona sul, the most famous market is the Feira de Arte de Ipanema, better known as the hippy fair. There aren't many hippies there, but there is a lot of good souvenir material, like artwork, musical instruments, toys, leather goods and clothing. Make sure you have a look at the pewter designs of Michel, a Frenchman who lives in Rio. It's excellent work. In Praça General Osório, the market starts at 9 am and goes to 6 pm.

Also in the zona sul is the Feira de Antiguidades do Jardim de Alah, the antique market every Sunday from 9 am to 4 am in the Jardim de Alah between Ipanema and Leblon. It has plenty of porcelain, glassware etc. There's another antique fair going on at the same time on Avenida Borges de Medeiros, beside the lake in Lagoa.

In Copacabana every day between 5 and 9 pm, on the Avenida Atlântica median strip between Ruas Xavier da Silviera and Bolívar, opposite Posto 5, there's a market with lots of potential souvenirs and gifts.

SHOPPING MALLS

Brazilians, like Americans, seem to measure progress by shopping malls. They love to shop at these monsters. Rio Sul was the first mall to maul Rio. There are all kinds of shops, including the C&A department store, which has a good range of clothes and is inexpensive. Rio Sul is right before you enter the Copacabana tunnel in Botafogo. With over 400 shops, including restaurants and bars, Rio Sul is open from Monday to Saturday from 10 am to 10 pm. There are free buses from Copacabana. Close by is the recently opened Rio Off Price Shopping, with more than 100 shops including two cinemas, restaurants and a football club on the roof.

Gávea Shopping, in the suburb of the same name, is a smaller shopping mall with a number of high-fashion shops, art galleries and gift shops. It also houses three theatres and is open from Monday to Saturday from 10 am to 8 pm. It's at Rua Marquês de São Vincente 52.

Further out is the São Conrado Fashion Mall, close to the InterContinental and Nacional hotels. As its name suggests, there are a lot of clothing and accessory shops in the mall, as well as four cinemas and some excellent restaurants, including a branch of Guimas.

Barra lives up to its nickname as the California Carioca, with the biggest and what many shoppers consider to be the best mall in Rio: Barra Shopping. A huge complex at Avenida das Américas 4666, with over 500 shops beneath its roof, this place is mind boggling. It has eight cinemas, a theatre, a children's amusement park, an ice-skating rink and a bowling alley. There are plenty of eating options, from the golden arches to elegant restaurants. Buses run from most of the top hotels to the mall. It's open from Monday to Saturday from 10 am to 10 pm and Sundays from 3 to 9 pm. The leisure areas operate every day from 10 am until 2 am.

Close to Barra Shopping is Via Parque, at Avenida Ayrton Senna 3000, where many major shops operate factory outlets, so prices are lower here than at Barra Shopping. There are also six cinemas, lots of restaurants and snack bars, and the Metropolitan showroom.

THINGS TO BUY

Antiques

Apart from the antiques markets already mentioned, serious collectors could attend an auction in the zona sul. For times and locations, look in the weekend editions of *O Globo* and the *Jornal do Brasil* under *Leilões* (Auctions). The Rio Design Centre, at Avenida Ataulfo de Paiva 270, has a few antique shops, as does the Cassino Atlântico mall, under the Rio Palace Hotel.

Art

Colourful Brazilian art makes a great souvenir. There are lots of artists' stalls at the hippy fair in Ipanema. The artists paint what sells, so if all you're looking for is a gift or something to brighten up your home, you should find something you like. Those who would appreciate a little more originality might like to visit one of Rio's many galleries. Exhibitions are listed in newspapers and the weekly *Veja Rio* magazine. Shopping centres with a few galleries are Gávea Shopping and the Cassino Atlântico.

Art Supplies

Casa Matos is the big chain. There's a shop in Copacabana at Avenida NS de Copacabana 690. The small Arte Técnica shop is in Flamengo, at shop *Loga* (Shop) 119, Rua do Catete 228. It has better quality supplies and also sells poster tubes which you can use to carry home some of Rio's best gifts – art prints, giant photos, posters etc.

ANDREW DRAFFEN

Rio Sul, the city's first shopping mall

Books

Nova Livraria Leonardo da Vinci is Rio's best bookshop; it's at Avenida Rio Branco 185 (it's one floor down on the *sobreloja* level). It has a lot of books in French also. Edifício Marques do Herval (☎ 224-1329) is a serious bookshop, with Rio's largest collection of foreign books and a knowledgeable staff who, for a tidy sum, will order just about any book you want. It's open from 9 am to 7 pm Monday to Friday and 9 am until noon on Saturday.

Livraria Dazibão at Rua Visconde de Pirajá 571-B in Ipanema stocks many Penguin paperbacks. Livraria Kosmos, in Centro at Rua Rosário 155 and next to the Copacabana Palace Hotel, has many foreign-language books. Each of the Livraria Siciliana chain has a collection of paperbacks and current magazines in English, French and German. They are at Visconde de Pirajá 511, Ipanema, and Avenida NS de Copacabana 830, Copacabana.

Stúdio Livros at Rua Visconde de Pirajá 462 has current magazines and paperbacks in English. At the Leblon end of Ipanema, at Rua Visconde de Pirajá 640, there's a small used-book shop that has old, funky and cheap books in English.

Clothing

There are plenty of jeans and T-shirts everywhere. The big department stores, C&A and Mesbla, are good starting points for a clothes-buying expedition. Men will find lots of light, bright, sporty casuals made of cotton, linen and silk. Other shops to look for in the malls and along Rua Visconde de Pirajá include Eduardo Guinle, Giorgio Armani, Pullman, Mr Wonderful, Munis, Polo Ralph Lauren, Toulin, Elle et Lui (clothes), Via Veneto, Vila Romano (suits), Birelo and Mr Cat (shoes).

Carioca women dress to kill. You'll find sexy leather and suede gear, and lots of skirts, pants and tops in cotton, jersey, linen and silk. Have fun in Rua Visconde de Pirajá. Look for Folic, Elle et Lui, Blu 4, Yves Saint Laurent (traditional), Forum, Yes Brazil, Zoomp (boutiques), Bum Bum, Kitanga (bikinis), Victor Hugo, Louis Vuitton (bags), Pucci, Mariazinha and Sagaró (shoes).

Popular children's wear shops are Joana João, Pakalolo and Só Criancas. All have shops in the Rio Sul mall and various other locations in the zona sul.

Food & Drink

The local *supermercado* (supermarket) will fulfil most of your needs here. Even the smaller ones have a good variety. If you're just looking to put a few things in the fridge in your hotel room to avoid paying the hotel's hefty prices, stock up on *palmitos*, the delicious palm hearts that come in jars. Cold cuts and fresh cheeses are available at most supermarkets. So is alcohol – even imported stuff. Rio's major supermarket chains are Pão de Açúcar, Paes Mendonça, Zona Sul , Sendas and Carrefour. There's a branch of at least one in every major shopping centre.

Chocaholics must get to know the best chocolates in Brazil – Kopenhagen. Its Copacabana shop is at Avenida NS de Copacabana 583A. It also has shops in the big malls.

The markets that pop up in different locations every day are the best places to shop for fruit and vegetables. They're fun to check out even if you don't buy anything. In Copacabana, there are feiras on Wednesdays in Rua Domingos Ferreira, on Thursdays in Rua Belford Roxo and Rua Ronald de Carvalho and on Sundays in Rua Decio Vilares. In Ipanema, feiras are held on Mondays in Rua Henrique Dumont, on Tuesdays in Praça General Osório and on Fridays in Praça N.S. da Paz. Leblon's feira is on Thursdays in Rua General Urquiza.

Gifts & Souvenirs

Smart souvenir hunters can do well in Brazil, provided they know a little about Brazilian culture. Most people find the best souvenirs to be music, crafts and artwork.

The crafts of Brazil are as diverse and varied as the people themselves. The Northeast provides a rich assort-

ment of artistic items from which to choose. Salvador
and the nearby town of Cachoeira are notable for their
rough-hewn wood sculpture. Artisans in Fortaleza
and on the southern coast of Ceará specialise in fine
lace cloths. The interior of Pernambuco – in particular
Caruaru – is famous for wildly imaginative ceramic
figurines and traditional leather hats worn by the
sertanejos (Northeast cowboys). Functional and decorative hammocks are fixtures in most Brazilian homes.
They are indispensable to travellers and make fine
portable gifts. You'll see the hammock sellers on the
beach, near the major hotels and at the markets. Hammocks cost from around US$20 to around US$30. Have
some fun checking them out and bargaining with the
vendors.

Your best bet for local crafts are the artisan fairs, but
there are a number of shops with a fine assortment. A
popular gift item is the *figa*, a clenched fist with thumb
extended between the second and third fingers. Made of
jacaranda wood, gold, silver or bone, they come in all
sizes. Originally worn by black male slaves as fertility
symbols, they are now considered good luck symbols.
The good luck only comes when the figa is a gift.
Another favourite is the *penca*, a necklace or bracelet that
holds charms in the shapes of fish, coconuts, bananas
and other foods. Charms were originally given to slaves
for acts of good behaviour.

Pé de Boi (Bull's Foot; ☎ 285-4395) is a shop that sells
the traditional artisan handicrafts of Brazil's Northeast
and Minas Gerais, and it's all fine work. It has lots of
wood, lace, pottery and prints. It's not an inexpensive
shop – you have to buy closer to the source to get a better
price – but if you have some extra dollars – US$10 to
US$20 at a minimum – these pieces are the best gifts to
bring home from Brazil: imaginative and very Brazilian.
The small shop is worth a visit just to look around. Ana
Maria Chindler, the owner, knows what she's selling and
is happy to tell you about it. Pé de Boi is in Botafogo on
Rua Ipiranga 53. It is open Monday to Friday until 7 pm
and on Saturdays from 10 am to 1 pm.

Other places to try are the souvenir shops in Copacabana, on Avenida NS de Copacabana between the Praça
do Lido and Rua Paula Freitas. Rio Souvenirs Ltd at Rua
Fernando Mendes 28-C has a large selection of Bahian
costume dolls that are nice gifts.

Crystals, semiprecious gems and costume jewellery
make fine gifts and souvenirs. Those into the healing
power of crystals should visit Rising at Rua Santa Clara
50, room 301, in Copacabana. Its owner, Miumar Mothé,
is an expert on Brazilian crystals.

Kitsch souvenirs abound. They include the classic plastic TVs with scenic views, butterfly trays, lacquered piranhas, toucans carved from semi-precious stones and lots of T-shirts.

Finally, here are a few more ideas for the avid souvenir hunter. Coffee-table picture books on Brazil, videotapes of Carnaval and videotapes of highlights of the Brazilian national team and Pelé in various World Cup matches are hawked in the streets of Copacabana. Guaraná powder, a stimulant (said to be an aphrodisiac), is sold in health food shops and chemists around the country. Mounted reprints of old Rio lithographs are sold in Rio's Cinelândia district on the steps of the opera house. The smallest of Brazil's bikinis are sold at Bum Bum or Kitanga shops. Candomblé shops are a good source of curios, ranging from magical incense guaranteed to bring good fortune and increase sexual allure, wisdom and health, to amulets and ceramic figurines of Afro-Brazilian gods. If you are travelling in Brazil during Carnaval make sure you pick up a copy of the Carnaval edition of *Manchete* magazine.

Jewellery

If you're in the market for fine jewellery and precious stones, Rio is a paradise. Around 90% of the world's gemstones come from Brazil: amethysts, aquamarines, emeralds, opals, topazes, tourmalines and rubellites. Buy from a large and reputable dealer like Amsterdam Sauer, Roditi or H Stern. Stern is an international dealer based in Ipanema whose reputation for quality and honesty is beyond reproach. It isn't a discount shop, but its jewellery is less expensive in Brazil than in its outlets in other parts of the world.

Leather Goods

Brazilian leather goods are moderately priced, but the leather isn't particularly supple. The better Brazilian shoes, belts, wallets, purses and luggage are sold in the up-market shops of Ipanema and Copacabana. Brazilian shoes are extremely good value, but much of the best is reserved for export and larger sizes are difficult to find.

Music

Brazilian music is sure to evoke your most precious travel memories. The largest chain of music shops is Gabriella, with branches in most shopping malls and shopping areas. The latest releases can be found cheaper

JOHN MAIER, JR.

Rio is a paradise for jewellery lovers

at the large department stores, like Carrefours and Lojas Americanas. Magister, in Copacabana at Rua Miguel Lemos 53, is a cheap record shop that's recommended. There's a laundrette across the street, so you can go and listen to some music while your clothes spin.

Records are still widely available in Brazil, but CDs have become more popular. Records and tapes cost around US$10 and CDs are about US$20. Brazilian music videos are widely available. If you're not familiar with the artist, have a listen to the music on the shop's equipment.

Casa Oliveira is a beautiful music shop at Rua da Carioca 70 in Centro – Rio's oldest street. It sells a wide variety of instruments, including all the noise makers that fuel the Carnaval *baterias* (rhythm sections), a variety of small mandolin-like string instruments, accordions and electric guitars. These make great presents and it's a fun place to play even if you don't buy. You'll also find a good selection of instruments at the Sunday hippy fair in Ipanema.

Sporting Goods

High-quality, cheap, durable leather soccer balls with hand-stitched panels are sold all over Brazil in sporting goods shops. Inflated soccer balls should not be put in the cargo hold of a plane.

Excursions

The small state of Rio de Janeiro offers the traveller much more than just the Cidade Maravilhosa. Within four hours of travel from any point in the state are beaches, mountains and forests that equal any in the rest of Brazil.

Divided by the city of Rio and the giant Baía de Guanabara, which has 131 km of coast and 113 islands, there are two coastal regions: the Costa Verde to the west and the Costa do Sol to the east.

Along the Costa Verde, where the mountains kiss the sea, there are hundreds of islands, including Ilha Grande and the Restinga de Marambaia, which make for easy swimming and boating. There are beaches waiting to be explored, particularly further away from Rio city, where the coastal road stays close to the ocean and the views are spectacular. The most famous spots are Angra dos Reis, Parati and Ilha Grande.

To the east, the mountains begin to rise further inland. The littoral is filled with lagoons and swamp land. Stretching further from the coast are *campos* (plains) which extend about 30 km to the mountains. Búzios and Cabo Frio, famous for their beauty and luxury, are only two hours from Rio by car. Saquarema, one of Brazil's best surfing beaches, is even closer.

Driving due north from Rio city, you soon reach a wall of jungled mountains. After the climb, you're in the cool Serra dos Órgãos. The resort cities of Petrópolis and Teresópolis are nearby, as well as many smaller villages where Cariocas go to escape the tropical summer heat. Hiking and climbing among the fantastic peaks of the Parque Nacional da Serra dos Órgãos, outside Teresópolis, are superb.

The other mountain region where Cariocas play is the Itatiaia area, north-west of Rio city. This is a wonderful place to tramp around green hills, ride ponies up purple mountains, splash in waterfalls and blaze jungle trails without straying too far from civilisation.

ILHA GRANDE

Ilha Grande is what Hawaii must have been before the arrival of the British. It's all tropical beach and jungle. There are only three towns on the island. Freguesia de Santana is a small hamlet with no regular accommodation. Parnaioca has a few homes by a lovely strip of beach near the old prison. Abraão has a gorgeous, palm-tree-studded beachfront, plenty of pousadas, camping grounds and ferry connections to Mangaratiba and Angra dos Reis.

You can rent a boat in Abraão for US$8 per hour, and buzz around to Freguesia or Parnaioca. There are trails through the lush steamy jungle to various beaches around the island. For instance, it is a 2½-hour trek to Praia Lopes Mendes, claimed by some to be the most beautiful beach in all Brazil. Praia de Parnaioca also ranks up there. And these are only two of the island's 102 beaches!

There's a tourist information booth close to the dock that's open when the ferries arrive. The tourist office in Angra dos Reis also has information about Ilha Grande.

Change money before you get here.

Places to Stay

The cheapest option is to camp. *Camping Renato*, up a small path beside Dona Penha's, has well-drained, secure sites and basic facilities, as well as a café/bar onsite. It charges US$2 per person. *Das Palmeiras* is another camp site close to Dona Penha's.

Cerca-viva (☎ 551-2336) is a camp site and pousada combined. In a secure spot at Rua Getúlio Vargas 351, it rents small on-site tents for US$18/24 for two days. Quartos are US$32 a double for two days and apartamentos go for US$43 for two days. The prices go down if you stay longer.

The youth hostel, *Ilha Grande* (☎ (021) 264-6147) at Getúlio Vargas 13, is a good option here. Its staff are friendly and it's well located. It costs US$7 for members and US$10 for non-members. Reservations are a good idea here, especially on weekends and holidays.

Most of the pousadas in Abraão cost between US$30 and US$40 a double. A good option is the *Tropicana* (☎ 335-4572), at Rua da Praia 28. It's a very nice place, run by a French/Brazilian couple and has singles/doubles for US$30/40.

At right angles to the beachfront, Rua da Igreja is the second-most important street on the island. It features a white church, a few bars and the *Hotel Mar da Tranquilidade* (☎ 288-4162, or for reservations from Rio (021) 392-8475). The hotel has charming but expensive doubles with hot showers and includes breakfast and lunch for US$60. Singles are US$30. Around the corner in Rua Getúlio Vargas is *Hotel Alpino* (☎ (011) 229-1190), in a beautiful garden setting. Doubles are US$30 outside the tourist season.

Just before the Alpino is *Penhas*, the house of Dona Pena. Look for the yellow gate on the right hand side.

Dona Pena has gone upmarket in the past few years. Singles are US$20 and doubles go for US$25. Ilha Grande's most expensive hotel, *Paraiso do Sol* (☎ (021) 263-6126 for information and reservations), is minutes away by boat or two hours away on foot from Abraão at Praia das Palmas, on the trail to Praia Lopes Mendes. Doubles with full board are US$200.

Places to Eat

Restaurante Janethe's is a decent place that serves prato feitos with abundant portions of fresh fish (US$4). It's just around the corner from the church. *Casa da Mulata*, on the way to the old prison, also has good prato feitos for US$3. There are also lots of places along the beachfront.

Getting There & Away

Catch a Conerj ferry from either Mangaratiba or Angra dos Reis. If you take the 5.30 am bus from Rio to Mangaratiba, you can catch the daily 8.30 am ferry from Mangaratiba to Abraão. There are five buses a day from Rio to Mangaratiba: at 6 and 9 am, and 12.30, 3 and 7 pm. Outgoing bus schedules are similarly staggered, but begin half an hour earlier.

The boat returns from Abraão to Mangaratiba on Monday, Wednesday and Friday at 4.30 pm, on Tuesday and Thursday at 11 am and on Saturday and Sunday at 4 pm.

The ferry schedule from Angra dos Reis to Abraão is Monday, Wednesday and Friday at 4 pm, returning from Abraão at 10.15 am on the same days. It's a 90-minute, US$5 ride. If you miss the ferry you can hire a fishing boat to the island for about US$30 from either Mangaratiba or Angra.

PARATI

The colonial village of Parati is one of Brazil's most enchanting towns, set amid steep, jungled mountains that seem to leap into the sea, a scrambled shoreline with hundreds of islands and jutting peninsulas, and the clear, warm waters of the Baía da Ilha Grande, as calm as an empty aquarium.

Parati is both a great colonial relic, well preserved and architecturally unique, and a launching pad for a dazzling section of the Brazilian coastline. There are good swimming beaches close to town, but the best are along the coast toward São Paulo and out on the bay islands.

JOHN MAIER, JR.

JOHN MAIER, JR.

JOHN MAIER, JR.

Parati is one of Brazil's most enchanting towns

Parati is small and it's easy to find your way around, but one thing that becomes confusing is street names and house numbers. Many streets have more than one name, which has the locals, as well as the tourists, thoroughly perplexed. The house-numbering system seems totally random.

The Centro de Informações Turísticas (☎ 71-1266 extension 20) on Avenida Roberto Silveira is open daily from 7 am to 7 pm. The Secretaria de Turismo e Cultura (☎ 71-1256), in the Antigo Quartel do Forte near the port, is open daily from 8 am to 6 pm.

Paraty Tours (☎ & fax 71-1327), at Avenida Roberto Silveira 11, just before you hit the colonial part of town, is also useful for information. Its five-hour schooner cruises are US$18; with lunch they're US$30. It also rents bicycles for US$2.50 an hour or US$10 per day.

Churches

Parati's 18th-century prosperity is reflected in its beautiful old homes and churches. Three main churches were used to separate the races.

The **Igreja NS do Rosário e São Benedito dos Homens Pretos** (1725), Rua Samuel Costa, was built by and for slaves. Renovated in 1857, the church has gilded wood altars dedicated to Our Lady of the Rosary, St Benedict and St John. The pineapple crystals are for prosperity and good luck.

Igreja Santa Rita dos Pardos Libertos (built 1722 for freed mulattos), Praça Santa Rita, has a tiny museum of sacred art and some fine woodwork on the doorways and altars. Igreja de NS das Dores (1800), Rua Dr Pereira, was renovated in 1901. The cemetery is fashioned after the catacombs.

Matriz NS dos Remédios (built 1787 for the White elite), Praça Mons Hélio Pires, was built on the site of two 17th-century churches. Inside there is art from past and contemporary local artists. The construction of the church, according to legend, was financed by a pirate treasure hidden on Praia da Trindade.

Forte Defensor Perpétuo

The Forte Defensor Perpétuo was built in 1703 to defend the gold being exported from Minas Gerais from pirate attacks. The fort was rebuilt in 1822, the year of Brazilian independence, and was named after Emperor Dom Pedro I. It's on the Morro da Vila Velha, the hill just past Praia do Pontal, a 20-minute walk north from town. The fort houses the Casa de Artista e Centro de Artes e Tradições Populares de Parati.

Beaches & Islands

The closest fine beaches on the coast – Vermelha, Lulas and Saco – are about an hour away by boat (camping is allowed on the beaches). The best island beaches nearby are probably Araújo and Sapeca, but many of the islands have rocky shores and are private. The mainland beaches tend to be better. These beaches are all small and idyllic; most have a barraca serving beer and fish and, at most, a handful of beachgoers. See the Getting Around section for information on how to get to the less accessible beaches.

Praia do Pontal On the other side of the canal, 10 minutes away on foot, is Parati's city beach. There are several barracas and a lively crowd but the beach itself is not attractive and the water gets dirty.

Praia do Forte On the side of the hill, hidden by the rocks, Praia do Forte is the cleanest beach within a quick walk of the city, relatively secluded and frequented by a youngish crowd.

Praia do Jabaquara Continue on the dirt road north past Praia do Pontal, over the hill, for two km to Praia do Jabaquara, a big, spacious beach with great views in all directions. There is a small restaurant and a camping ground that's better than those in town. The sea is very shallow and it's possible to wade way out into the bay.

Festivals

Parati is known for its colourful and distinctive festivals. The two most important are the Festa do Divino Espírito Santo, which begins nine days before Pentecostal Sunday, and the NS dos Remédios on 8 September. The former is planned throughout the year and features all sorts of merrymaking revolving around the *fólios*, musical groups that go from door to door.

The Festas Juninas during the month of June are filled with dances, including the *xiba*, a circle clog dance, and the *ciranda*, a xiba with guitar accompaniment. The festivals culminate on 29 June with a maritime procession to Ilha do Araújo. Parati is a good option for Carnaval if you want to get out of Rio for a couple of days.

The Parati region produces excellent cachaça, and in 1984 the town council, in its wisdom, inaugurated an annual Festival da Pinga. The pinga party is held over an August weekend.

JOHN MAIER, JR.

JOHN MAIER, JR.

Top: Parati is architecturally unique
Bottom: Spectacular views are abundant around Parati

Places to Stay

Parati has two very different tourist seasons. From about October to February hotels get booked up and room prices double, so reservations are a good idea. Many places require the full amount to be paid in advance – usually placed in their bank account in Rio or São Paulo. This is often nonrefundable. The rest of the year, finding accommodation is easy and not expensive, the town is quiet and some of the boutiques and restaurants close for the winter. The prices quoted are off-season rates.

Places to Stay – bottom end

There are several camp sites on the edge of town, just over the bridge.

The *Pousada Familiar* (☎ 71-1475), at Rua José Vieira Ramos 262, is close to the bus station and charges US$9 per person, including a good breakfast. It's a friendly place, run by Lúcia, a Brazilian, and her Belgian husband, Joseph. Joseph speaks English, French, German, Spanish and, of course, Flemish, and is very helpful. The pousada also has clothes-washing facilities.

Another recommended place is the *Pousada Marendaz* (☎ 71-1369) at Rua Dr Derly Ellena 9. Run by Rachel and her four sisters, it's more of a family home than a hotel. They charge US$10 per person. Another cheapie is the pousada *Seu Walter* (☎ 712-341) at Rua Marechal Deodoro 489. Simple apartamentos without breakfast are US$8 per head.

The *Hotel Estalagem* (☎ 71-1626), Rua da Matriz, charges US$20/30 a single/double. Try and get the room upstairs – it has a great view. It also has kayaks for rent. The *Pousada da Matriz* (☎ 71-1610), Rua Mal Deodoro 334, is well located and has rooms for US$15 per person.

Places to Stay – middle

The *Hotel Solar dos Gerânios* (☎ 71-1550) on Praça da Matriz (also known as Praça Monsenhor Hélio Pires) is a beautiful old hotel with wood and ceramic sculptures, flat brick and stone, rustic heavy furniture and *azulejos* (Portuguese tiles). Rooms have hot showers. Singles/doubles start as low as US$15/25.

The *Bela Vista* (☎ 71-1429), Rua do Comércio 46, is a good choice with doubles from US$35 to US$40.

Located in the mountains 16 km from Parati is *Hotel Fazenda Le Gite D'Indaiatiba* (☎ 71-1218; fax 71-2188). Run by a French guy (if you have any trouble finding the place, ask for the French's hotel – everybody knows it), it has small bungalows in a beautiful setting with a great view. There are lots of activities, like horse riding, trekking, going to the beach. There's a good library of mostly French books. The cost is US$40 a night for a double during the week, a bit more on weekends. To get there by bus, take the Barra Grande via Grauna and get out at the last stop in Grauna. By car, head toward Rio for 12 km and turn off at the Fazenda Grauna road. Follow it for four km and you'll arrive.

Places to Stay – top end

There are three splendid, four-star, colonial pousadas in Parati. Owned by a famous Brazilian actor, the *Pousada Pardeiro* (☎ 71-1370; fax 71-1139), Rua do Comercio 74, has a tranquil garden setting, refined service and impeccable decor. This is one of Brazil's best pousadas, with singles/doubles for US$80/100.

The *Hotel Coxixo* (☎ 71-1460; fax 71-1568), Rua do Comercio 362, is just a notch below the Pousada Pardeiro, but it has some standard rooms that are a good deal at US$40. The pousada is cosy and colonial, with beautiful gardens and a pool, and the rooms are simple but comfortable and pretty. To get the US$40 doubles make reservations early. Most doubles go for US$70.

Pousada do Ouro (☎ 71-2033; fax 71-1311), Rua da Praia 145, is the kind of place where you can imagine bumping into Mick Jagger, Sonia Braga, Tom Cruise or Marcello Mastroianni, especially when you enter the hotel lobby and see photos of them posing in front of the pousada. The hotel has everything – bar, pool and a good restaurant. Doubles cost US$85 to US$105.

Places to Eat

Parati has many pretty restaurants that all seem to charge too much. To beat the inflated prices in the old part of town, try the sandwiches at the lanchonete on Praça da Matriz.

The best restaurants in the old town include the *Galeria do Engenho*, Rua da Lapa, which serves large and juicy steaks for US$10, and *Vagalume*, Rua da Ferraria. *Hiltinho*, Rua da Cadeia, at the edge of the Praça da Matriz, is more expensive, but there's a good menu and ample portions. Another recommended restaurant is *Pizzaria Bucaneiros* on Rua Samuel Costa. It has tasty pizzas.

Getting There & Away

The rodoviária (☎ 71-1186) is on the main road into town, Rua Roberto Silveira, half a km up from the old town.

There are six daily buses from Parati to Rio; it's a four-hour trip, with the first bus leaving at 3.30 am and the last at 8 pm. Buses leave Rio for Parati at 6 and 9 am and 12.30, 3, 6.20 and 8 pm. It's a US$10 trip.

There are 18 daily buses from Parati to Angra dos Reis; the trip takes two hours and costs US$3. The first bus leaves at 5 am, the last at 7.20 pm. There are two daily (11 am and 11.30 pm) buses for São Paulo which take six hours. Three daily buses go to Ubatuba (7 am, noon and 7 pm) and three more go to Cunha.

Getting Around

To visit the beaches that aren't easily accessible, many tourists take one of the schooners that leave from the docks. Departure times vary with the season, but the information is easy to get hold of. It costs US$18 per person. Lunch is served on board for an additional US$12. The boats make three beach stops for about 45 minutes each.

An alternative is to rent one of the many small motorboats at the port. For US$10 per hour (somewhat more in the summer) the skipper will take you where you want to go. Bargaining is difficult but you can lower the cost by finding travelling companions and renting bigger boats – they hold from six to 12 passengers.

PENEDO

Finnish immigrants, led by Toivo Uuskallio, settled Penedo in 1929. If the beautiful Scandinavian woodwork doesn't convince you of this, the number of saunas will. The Finns planted citrus groves along the banks of the Rio das Pedras, but when this enterprise failed they turned to preparing Finnish jams and jellies, home-made liqueurs and sauces.

Apart from jungle and waterfalls, there are not many attractions. The Museu Kahvila at Travessa da Fazenda 45 is a lanchonete which also displays Finnish clothing, books and photographs.

Things to See & Do

There are three waterfalls worth visiting. They are **Tres Cachoeiras** near Tião, **Cachoeira do Roman**, which is very pretty but on private grounds and 10 minutes uphill from the Pousada Challenge, and **Cachoeira do Diabo** right near the Pousada Challenge.

About 40 minutes of uphill hiking from Hans Camping takes you into very dense jungle, although there are trails inside. Hopefully you will run into the large bands of big monkeys and steer clear of the wild-cats. At the point where Penedo's main asphalt road turns to dirt you can hire horses for US$3 per hour, or a horse and carriage for US$6 per hour.

If you fancy a **sauna**, next door and across the street from the Clube Finlândia are the Sauna Bar and Sauna Finlandesa. The sweat shops are open to the public from early afternoon until 10 pm and later if there are enough people interested (US$3 admission).

Places to Stay & Eat

Hans Camping, several km up from the last bus stop, charges US$4 per person for camp sites and has a sauna, natural swimming pool, bar and a waterfall nearby.

Pousada Casa Grande(☎ 51-1383), close to the bus stop at Praça Finlândia 10, is the 200-year-old farmhouse where colonisation of the region began. It's a bit shabby, but the rooms are large and clean. Doubles are US$18.

The *Pousada Challenge* (☎ 51-1389), about a km up from Tião on the Estrada da Fazendinha, has very clean pre-fab chalets which sleep three. It costs US$40 for doubles and includes breakfast, lunch and use of the pool and sauna.

The *Hotel Baianinha* (☎ 51-1204), next to Tião on the Cachoeiras, asks US$12/15 for simple singles/doubles. The Baianinha kitchen specialises in fish and Bahian dishes which range in price from US$5 to US$12. The food is good and portions are huge. *Palhoça* at Avenida das Mangueiras 2510, has a good prato feito for US$3. *Casa do Chocolate*, at Avenida Casa das Pedras 10, has sandwiches, 50 different ice-cream flavours if it's hot, or hot chocolate if it's cold.

Entertainment

Among an assortment of Brazilian people there is now only a sprinkling of Finns, but they get together for polkas, mazurkas, *letkiss* and *jenkiss* dances every Saturday night at the Clube Finlândia. The Finnish dancers put on their Old World togs and do traditional dances (admission US$3, from 9 pm to 2 am).

Getting There & Away

From Resende it's much easier to get to Penedo and Itatiaia than to Mauá. There are 22 Penedo-bound buses daily from 6 am to 11 pm. The bus services the three-km main street and continues past the end of the paved road to Tião, which is the final stop. The Hotel Baianinha is the second-last stop. Pousada Challenge is a brisk 30-minute walk from Tião and Hans Camping is 20 minutes further up.

Itatiaia Turismo (☎ 511-1147), at Rua Visconde de Pirajá 540 in Rio, arranges weekend bus tours from Rio to Penedo, Mauá and Itatiaia.

VISCONDE DE MAUÁ

Mauá is prettier and a little more tranquil than Penedo, and harder to reach. It's a lovely place, with streams, tinkling goat bells, cosy chalets and country lanes graced with wildflowers. There are horses for hire by the footbridge for US$2.50 per hour, but some of them are pretty small.

Mauá is actually made up of three small villages a few km apart. The bus stops first at Vila Mauá, the largest village. Vila Maringá, on the other side of the Rio Preto, is actually in Minas Gerais, and has lots of restaurants and

JOHN MAIER, JR.

Waterfall slide in Mauá

places to stay. At the end of the bus route is Vila Maromba, which has restaurants and pousadas, but not as many as Maringá. Most travellers stay in Maringá or Maromba.

There are two places for tourist information: a cabana at the entrance to Vila Mauá, open from 8 am to 8 pm (closed for lunch) Tuesday to Sunday, and the Casa do Turista, one km further along the road to Maromba.

Things to Do

The **Santa Clara Cachoeira**, the nicest waterfall in the area, is a 40-minute walk from Vila Maromba. For a mini jungle experience, climb up on either side of the falls through the bamboo groves.

The young and the restless can follow the trail from Maromba to the Cachoeira Veu de Noiva in the Parque Nacional do Itatiaia. It's a full day's hike each way. It's possible to kayak the rapids of the **Rio Preto** if you are so inclined. The Rio Preto, which divides Minas Gerais from Rio, also has small river beaches and natural pools to explore.

If you get sick of walking, Bike Montanha, in Maringá, rents mountain bikes for US$2 an hour.

Places to Stay

Most pousadas offer full board with lodging. It's easy to find them because at each intersection there are lots of small signposts. If you don't want full board, you can bargain the price down quite a bit.

In Maringá, the cheapest place to stay is *Casarão* (☎ 54-3030). It's the youth hostel, camp site and regular pousada rolled into one. Small, simple apartamentos with veranda and hammock are US$28 a double. Camp sites are US$2 per person. The youth hostel costs US$8 and breakfast US$2. It also organises treks. The bus stops right outside.

Hotel Casa Alpininha (☎ 87-1292), in Maringá on the other side of the river, has doubles for US$30 including breakfast and lunch. In Maringá there are lots of places charging around US$40 a double.

In Maromba, there are a few cheap pousadas next to the bus stop. *Pousada Sonhador*, on the right side of the church, charges US$10/15 a single/double including breakfast. It also serves a good prato feito. Three km up from Maromba is *Pousada Tiatiaim*, which is in a great location and charges US$40 a double.

Places to Eat

Natural/vegetarian food is served at *Pureza* in Maringa. People here like brown rice, granola with tropical fruits and yoghurt mixed in, and caipirinhas with natural honey. The food is good, but expensive.

Renascer, also in Maringá, serves trout for US$4. Casarão also serves comida caseira. Its US$8 plate is plenty for two people.

Getting There & Away

The one daily bus from Resende to Visconde de Mauá (about 2½ hours on a winding dirt road, US$3) leaves Monday to Saturday at 4 pm, so you must catch the 1 pm bus from Rio to make it, or else hitch or pay for a taxi, which will cost US$35. The bus leaves for Resende at 8.30 am every day, except for Sunday when it leaves at 5 pm.

Itatiaia Turismo (☎ 511-1147), at Rua Visconde de Pirajá 540 in Rio, arranges weekend bus tours from Rio.

PARQUE NACIONAL DO ITATIAIA

This is a national park established in 1937 to protect 120 sq km of ruggedly beautiful land. It contains over 400 species of native birds, jaguars, monkeys, sloths, lakes, rivers, waterfalls, alpine meadows and primary and secondary Atlantic rainforests. Don't let the tropical house plants fool you: it gets below freezing point in June! Itatiaia even has a few snowy days some years!

Things to See & Do

The park headquarters, **museum** and Lagoa Azul (Blue Lake) are 10 km in from the Via Dutra highway. The museum, open Tuesday to Sunday from 8 am to 4 pm, has glass cases full of stuffed and mounted animals, pinned moths and snakes in jars.

Mountain climbing, rock climbing and trekking enthusiasts will want to pit themselves against the local peaks, cliffs and trails.

Every two weeks a group scales the **Agulhas Negras** peak, which at 2787 metres is the highest in the area. For more information call the Grupo Excursionista de Agulhas Negras (☎ 54-2587).

A walk to the **Abroucas refuge** at the base of Agulhas Negras is a 26-km, eight-hour jungle trek from the park entrance. The mountain refuge can sleep 24 people and is accessible by car from the Engenheiro Passos to São Lourenço road near the Minas Gerais and Rio de Janeiro border. Reservations are required. Call IBAMA in Resende (☎ (0243) 52-1461) and get maps and advice from the park IBAMA office before setting off.

Simpler hikes include the walk between Hotel Simon and Hotel Repouso (where the painter Guignard lived, worked and left a few of his paintings), and the 20-minute walk from the Sítio Jangada to the Poronga waterfalls.

Places to Stay

Camping is the cheapest option inside the park. There's a camp site, *Aporaoca*, four km from the main entrance to the park. When you get to the Gula & Artes store and the ice-cream shop, there's a signpost. The camp site is 200 metres up behind these places. Sites are US$3 per person.

Ipê Amarelo(☎ 52-1232) youth hostel is at Rua João Mauricio de Macedo Costa 352, in Campo Alegre, a suburb of Itatiaia. It has bicycles for rent.

Pousada do Elefante, close to the Hotel Simon, is the cheapest hotel in the park. It's basic but well located. It charges US$30/50 for singles/doubles with board. Other hotels are expensive, three-star Embratur affairs with saunas and swimming pools – like the *Hotel Simon* (☎ 52-1122), which charges US$90 for a double with full board. *Hotel do Ypê* (☎ 52-1453) charges US$80 a double or US$100 to stay in a chalet. Not far from the park entrance, *Hotel Aldéia da Serra* (☎ 52-1152) is reasonably priced, with chalets for US$45 a single and US$60 a double, all inclusive.

Getting There & Away

Every 20 minutes on weekdays and every 40 minutes on weekends (from 7 am to 11.20 pm), there is a bus from Resende to the town of Itatiaia. From Praça São José in Itatiaia, take the kombi with the 'Hotel Simon' sign in the window up to the park. It leaves at 8 and 10 am, noon, and 2, 5 and 7 pm. The ride is US$2, but you'll have to pay the park entry (US$1) as you go through the main gate. A taxi costs US$15.

Itatiaia Turismo (☎ 511-1147), at Rua Visconde de Pirajá 540 in Rio, arranges weekend bus tours from Rio to Itatiaia.

PETRÓPOLIS

Petrópolis is a lovely mountain retreat with a decidedly European flavour. It's only 60 km from Rio de Janeiro, making it an ideal day trip. This is where the imperial court spent its summer when Rio got too muggy. Petrópolis is still the home of the heir to the throne, Princess Isabel's grandson, 78-year-old Dom Pedro de Orleans e Bragança. He runs a real estate business and can often be seen riding his horse around town.

JOHN MAIER, JR.

JOHN MAIER, JR.

Top: Petrópolis' Museu Imperial
Bottom: Horse carriages in Petrópolis

Things to See & Do

Petrópolis' main attraction is the **Museu Imperial**, the
perfectly preserved and impeccably appointed palace of
Dom Pedro II. One interesting exhibit is the 1720-gram
imperial crown, with its 639 diamonds and 77 pearls.
The museum is open Tuesday to Sunday from noon to
5.30 pm; it costs 30c to get in.

You can visit **Casa de Santos Dumont**, the curious
home of Brazil's first aeronaut; open Tuesday to Sunday,
9 am to 5 pm. The **Palácio Cristal** is an iron and glass
structure built in France and imported to serve as an
orchid hothouse. You can also take a horse-and-carriage
ride through the city's squares and parks, past bridges,
canals and old-fashioned lamps.

Places to Stay

The *Hotel Comércio* (☎ 42-3500), at Rua Dr Porciúncula 56, is directly across from the rodoviária. Quartos are clean and cheap at US$5/7 for singles/doubles. Apartamentos cost US$14/18 a single/double.

If you want to spend a bit more, both the *Hotel York* (☎ 43-2662) at Rua do Imperador 78 and the *Casablanca Palace* (☎ 42-0162), Rua 16 de Março 123, have singles/doubles for US$25/30. The York is closer to the rodoviária.

The *Hotel Casablanca* (☎ 42-6662) is almost right next to the Museu Imperial, at Avenida 7 de Setembro 286, and has singles/doubles for US$40/45. Yes, the two Casablanca hotels are run by the same people.

There are some beautiful top-end hotels around Petrópolis. Elected the most charming in Brazil by the Guia Brasil 4 Rodas in 1995 is *Pousada Alcobaça* (☎ (0242) 21-1240) at Rua Agostinho Goulão 298 in the suburb of Corrêas. It has beautiful gardens crossed by a small river, as well as a pool, sauna and tennis court. Doubles go for US$100. The excellent restaurant is open to the public. Main courses are around US$15.

Places to Eat

Naturalmente is a good place to go for a healthy vegetarian buffet lunch. It's upstairs in the shopping centre at Rua do Imperador 288. You get all you can eat for US$5.

Rua 16 de Março has lots of places, like *Kafta*, the Arab restaurant at No 52, *Maurício's* seafood place at No 154 and the *Midas Steak House* at No 170.

Getting There & Away

From Rio, buses to Petrópolis leave every 30 minutes from 5 am onwards. The trip takes 1½ hours and costs US$2.50.

TERESÓPOLIS

Do as Empress Teresina did and escape the steamy summer heat of Rio in the cool mountain retreat of Teresópolis (910 metres), the highest city in the state, nestled in the strange, organ-pipe mountains of the Serra dos Órgãos. The road to Teresópolis first passes the sinuous curves of a padded green jungle, then winds and climbs past bald peaks which have poked through the jungle cover to touch the clouds.

The city itself is modern, prosperous and dull. The principal attraction is the landscape and its natural treasures – Teresópolis is the mountain climbing, rock climbing and trekking centre of Brazil.

There are extensive hiking trails in the region and it's possible to trek over the mountains and through the jungle to Petrópolis. Unfortunately the trails are unmarked and off the maps, but it's easy and inexpensive to hire a guide at the Parque Nacional, or go with a group organised by one of the hiking and mountaineering clubs in Rio.

Teresópolis is not simply for alpinists: it's a centre for sports lovers of all kinds. The city has facilities for motorcross, volleyball and equestrianism – many of Brazil's finest thoroughbreds are raised here – not to mention football. The city bears the distinction of hosting Brazil's World Cup football team; the national team is selected and trained here.

The Terminal Turistico tourist office is in Soberbo at the intersection with the road to Rio. It's open daily from 8 am to 11 pm and the view of Rio from the office is great. If you're travelling by bus, however, it's a hassle to get to, and you can pick up the same maps at the tourist stand on Avenida Lúcio Meira, which is open from Monday to Friday from 8 am to 5 pm.

Parque Nacional Serra dos Órgãos

The main entrance to the national park is open daily from 8 am to 5 pm (admission 25c). There's a 3.5-km walking trail, waterfalls, swimming pools, tended lawns and gardens. It's a very pretty park for a picnic. There are some chalets for rent at the park substation, 12 km towards Rio. There are also camp sites.

Other Attractions

The Mulher de Pedra (Rock Woman) rock formation, 12 km out towards Nova Friburgo, does indeed look like a reclining woman.

Colina dos Mirantes is a good place from which to view the Serra dos Órgãos range and the city. On clear days you can see as far as the Baía de Guanabara. To get there, take Rua Feliciano Sodré. The Quebra Frascos, the royal family of the Second Empire, lived in this neighbourhood. The best spot for viewing the Dedo de Deus peak is from Soberbo.

Places to Stay

The *Várzea Palace Hotel* (☎ 742-0878) at Rua Prefeito Sebastião Teixeira 41/55, behind the Igreja Matriz, is a grand old white building with red trim which has been a Teresópolis institution since 1916. Can this be a budget hotel? Cheap and classy singles/ doubles without a bath are US$15/19. With a bath they cost US$18/28.

Other relatively cheap hotels are nearby, including the *Center Hotel* (☎ 742-5890) at Sebastião Teixeira 245, which has singles/doubles for US$17/23. The *Hotel Avenida* (☎ 742-2751) is in front of the Igreja Matriz, at Rua Delfim Moreira 439. Singles/doubles here cost US$20/28.

The more expensive hotels are out of town. *Hotel Alpina* (☎ 742-5252) is three km on the road to Petrópolis and has singles/doubles for US$45/60. There's a golf club across the road. At km 6 along the Teresópolis to Nova Friburgo road is *Pousada Vrajabhumi* (☎ 742-3011). Run by Hari Krishnas, this place is in the middle of a forest reserve and has chalets and natural swimming pools. Rates start at US$60 a double including all meals, which are vegetarian. The restaurant is open to the public for lunch and dinner. At km 27 is *Hotel Rosa dos Ventos* (☎ 742-8833), the only Brazilian hotel in the international Relais & Chateaux chain. It has everything except youth. No-one under 16 is permitted to stay here. Daily rates with breakfast and lunch included are between US$110 and US$250.

Places to Eat

Restaurante Irene (☎ 742-2901) at Rua Yeda 730 (parallel to Rua Sebastião Teixeira) basks in its reputation for Teresópolis' best haute cuisine. It's expensive, and reservations are required.

Cheiro de Mato at Delfim Moreira 140 is a decent vegetarian restaurant. *Bar Gota da Água* at Praça Baltazar da Silveira 16 is also known as *Bar do Ivam* and is a comfy little place which serves trout with a choice of sauces for US$7. Try it with alcaparra, a bitter pea-like vegetable, or almond sauce. For dessert have some apple strudel and Viennese coffee a few doors down at *Lanches Mickey*. *Tudo em Cima*, Avenida Delfim Moreira 409, serves an admirable soufflé of bacalhau for US$6. *O Tigre de Papel* is a good Chinese restaurant in the centre at the end of Rua Francisco Sá.

Getting There & Away

The rodoviária is on Rua 1 do Maio, off Avenida Tenente Luiz. It has buses to Rio every 30 minutes from 5 am to 10 pm (US$4, 1½ hours, 95 km). There are seven buses to Petrópolis (from 6 am to 9 pm) and plenty to Nova Friburgo.

Getting Around

To get to the park from the centre, take the 'Albequerque Soberbo' bus for 50c. It runs every hour and its last stop is the Terminal Turistico in Soberbo.

NOVA FRIBURGO

During the Napoleonic wars, Dom João II encouraged immigration to Brazil. At the time people were starving in Switzerland, so 300 families in the Swiss canton of Friburg packed up and took off for Brazil in 1818. The journey was horrible; many died, but enough families survived to settle in the mountains and establish a small village in the New World.

Like Teresópolis and Petrópolis, Nova Friburgo has good hotels and restaurants as well as many lovely natural attractions: waterfalls, woods, trails, sunny mountain mornings and cool evenings. (It's chilly and rainy during the winter months from June through August.) The Cónego neighbourhood is interesting for its Germanic architecture and its apparently perpetually blooming flowers.

The tourist office on Praça Dr Demervel B Moreira is open daily from 8 am to 8 pm. As well as maps it has a complete list of hotels, including the cheapest, with updated prices.

Things to See & Do

Most of the nice sights are a few km out of town. Scout out the surrounding area from **Morro da Cruz** (1800 metres). The cable-car station is in the centre at Praça do Suspiro. Cable cars to Morro da Cruz run from 10 am to 6 pm on weekends and holidays. **Pico da Caledônia** (2310 metres) offers fantastic views and jump-off sites for hang-gliders. It's a six-km hike uphill, but the view is worth it.

You can hike to Pedra do Cão Sentado, explore the Furnas do Catete rock formations or visit the mountain towns of **Bom Jardim** (23 km north on BR-492) and **Lumiar** (25 km from Mury and a little bit before the entrance to Friburgo). Hippies, cheap pensions, waterfalls, walking trails and white-water canoe trips abound in Lumiar.

Places to Stay

Fabris Hotel (☎ 22-2852), at Avenida Alberto Braune 148, asks US$12/14 for clean singles/doubles. *Hotel*

Montanus (☎ 22-1235), at Rua Fernando Bizzotto 26, has simple singles/doubles for the same price, but can be bargained down. The *Avenida Hotel* (☎ 22-1664), at Rua Dante Laginestra 89, is a bit cheaper, with quartos for US$10/14 a single/double.

A good mid-range place in the centre is the *Sanjaya Hotel* (☎ 22-6052) at Avenida Alberto Braune 58. It charges US$30 a single and US$35 a double.

In Lumiar, try the *Pousada dos Gnomos* (☎ (021) 256-3926 in Rio), with a nice waterfall close by, a good breakfast and rooms for US$35 a double.

Rates at the top hotels are all for double occupancy and include full board. *Sans Souci* (☎ 22-7752), in town at Rua Itajai, charges US$110. *Hotel Garlipp* (☎ 42-1330) is in Mury, 10 km out on the road to Niterói, and charges US$110.

Places to Eat

If you want to eat very well, try one of the two Swiss/German delicatessens on Rua Fernando Bizzotto for a hefty cold-cut sandwich on black bread with dark mustard. The other deli, *Oberland* (☎ 22-9838) at No 12, doubles as a restaurant. It's a very cosy wood-panelled room where the menu is short and the food is great. Try the weisswurst (veal sausage) with sauerkraut for US$4 and the chocolate cakes for dessert.

The *Churrascaría Majórica*, in the centre at Praça Getúlio Vargas 74, serves a decent cut of filet mignon for US$15 – it's enough for two. *Walisau*, a small shopping complex on the other side of Praça Getúlio Vargas, has a few bars and cafés on the 1st floor. It gets crowded in the evenings.

Getting There & Away

Nova Friburgo is a little over two hours (US$6) by bus from Rio via Niterói on 1001 Lines. The ride is along a picturesque, winding, misty, jungle road. From Novo Friburgo, buses to Rio leave every 30 minutes to one hour from 5.40 am. To Teresópolis there are four daily buses, at 7 and 11 am and 3 and 6 pm. The two-hour trip costs US$4. If you're heading to the coast, an adventurous trip is to catch a bus to Lumiar and from there catch another to Macaé.

Getting Around

The local bus terminal is behind Praça Getúlio Vargas. Local buses go to just about all the tourist attractions. Ask for details at the tourist office.

SAQUAREMA

Saquarema, 100 km east of Rio de Janeiro, sits between long stretches of open beach, lagoons and jungled mountains. It's still possible to find sloths and bands of monkeys in the jungles, and the fish and shrimp are abundant in the lakes and lagoons. The long shoreline of fine, white sand and clean water attracts surfers, sports fishers and sun worshippers.

Saquarema is a horse-breeding and fruit-growing centre. You can visit the orchards and pick fruit, or hire horses and take to the hills. Adventurers who tramp the jungle trails in search of the elusive micro-leão marmoset are sure to discover beautiful waterfalls, if not primates.

The beaches – Bambui, Ponta Negra and Jaconé, south of town – are long and empty save for a couple of fishing villages. The waves are big, particularly in Ponta Negra and three km north of Saquarema in Praia Itaúna, where an annual surfing contest is held during the last two weeks of May.

Saquarema hosts the NS de Nazaré Mass on 7 and 8 September. It attracts 150,000 pilgrims.

The best place to go for information, especially about places to stay, is Saquatur Toulouse Lagos Turismo (☎ & fax 51-2161) at Avenida Oceânica 165 in Itauna.

Places to Stay – bottom end

The youth hostel *Ilhas Gregas* (☎ 51-1008) is excellent. Only 100 metres from the beach at Rua do Prado 671 in Itaúna, it has bicycles, a swimming pool, a sauna and a bar/restaurant. It's easiest to get a taxi from the bus station in Saquarema, but if you feel like a hike, get off the bus at the petrol station 'Sudoeste' and walk for 30 minutes along Avenida Oceânica until you get to the centre of Itaúna (where there are lots of bars and kiosks on the beachfront). Go along Avenida NS de Nazareth and enter the second street on the left (Rua das Caravelas), then enter the first street on your right, which is Rua do Prado.

Pousada da Mansão (☎ (021) 259-2100 in Rio for reservations), at Avenida Oceânica 353, has rooms in the old mansion that go for US$10 a single and US$20 a double, and there's camping there too. Sonia, who runs the place, speaks English and French. The *Hotel Saquarema* (☎ 51-2275) is right at the bus stop. It charges US$15 per person, but stay there only as a last resort. It's OK, but there are better places for the same price.

Pousada da Titia (☎ 51-2058), at Avenida Salgado Filho 774, is a good alternative, with quartos for US$14 a double and apartamentos for US$20. *Barra Bel* (☎ 51-2322) at Avenida Oceânica 1028 in Itaúna, is also recommended.

Places to Stay – top end

There are stacks of places charging around US$40 a double. A couple of popular ones are the *Maasai Hotel Club* (☎ 51-1092) near Itaúna beach, *Pousada dos Socos*, at Rua dos Socos 592, and *Pousada Pratagi* (☎ 51-2161) at Avenida Salgado Filho 4484.

The *Hotel Fazenda Serra da Castelhana* (☎ 719-0412) charges US$75 a double with full board and its food is very good. It's in the suburb of Palmital.

If you're thinking of staying in one of these places, go and see Conceição at Saquatur. She has brochures and all the latest details. It'll save you a lot of legwork.

Places to Eat

For prato feito, *Pensão Tia Tiana* is a favourite with locals in town. There are lots of lanchonetes at Itaúna. *Pinhos'* at Rua das Pitangas 145, is a family-run place that's cheap and highly recommended by hungry surfers. Ilhas Gregas also has a decent restaurant. You might also like to try *Berro da Agua* at Avenida Oceânica 165, and the restaurant at the Barra Bel.

Getting There & Away

From Rio to Saquarema there are seven buses a day from 6.30 am to 6.30 pm (8.30 pm Friday to Sunday). The same number go the other way from 5.30 am to 5.50 pm (7.50 pm Friday to Sunday). The two-hour trip costs US$4. To get to Cabo Frio, take a local bus to Bacaxá. From there, buses to Cabo leave every 30 minutes.

BÚZIOS

Búzios, a lovely beach resort, is a peninsula (scalloped by 17 beaches) which juts into the Atlantic. It was a simple fishing village until 'discovered' by Brigitte Bardot and her Brazilian boyfriend in the early '60s. The village is now littered with boutiques, fine restaurants, fancy villas, bars and posh pousadas. It's twice the price of the rest of Brazil during the holiday season.

Búzios is not a single town but three settlements on the peninsula – Ossos, Manguinhos and Armação – and one further north on the mainland called Rasa. Ossos (Bones) at the northernmost tip of the peninsula is the

JOHN MAIER, JR.

JOHN MAIER, JR.

JOHN MAIER, JR.

Top: One of the 17 beaches in Búzios
Middle: Búzio's seagulls enjoy a day on the boat
Bottom: Young lovers taking an afternoon stroll

oldest and most attractive. It has a pretty harbour with a yacht club, a few hotels, bars and a tourist stand. Manguinhos at the isthmus is the most commercial and even has a 24-hour medical clinic. Armação, in between, has the best restaurants, along with city necessities like international phones and a bank, petrol station, post office and pharmacy. North-west along the coast is Rasa and the island of Rasa, where Brazil's political dignitaries and rich relax.

The Secretaria de Turismo (☎ 23-1143) is at Praça Santos Dumont 111 in Armação, but it's not worth a special trip. The Ekoda Tourist Agency (☎ 23-1490), in Armação at Rua das Pedras 13, is open seven days a week from 10 am to 8 pm. Staff change money, represent American Express and arrange accommodation (except at the cheaper places) and tours.

Boat Trips

The schooner *Queen Lory* makes daily trips out to Ilha Feia, Tartaruga and João Fernandinho. There is a 2½-hour trip which costs US$15 and a four-hour trip for US$20. These trips are good value, especially since caipirinhas, soft drinks, fruit salad and snorkelling gear are included in the price. To make a reservation, ask at your pousada or visit Queen Lory Tours, Rua Angela Diniz 35.

Beaches

In general the southern beaches are trickier to get to, but they're prettier and have better surf. The northern beaches are more sheltered and closer to the towns.

Working anticlockwise from south of Manguinhos, the first beaches are Geribá and Ferradurinha (Little Horseshoe). These are beautiful beaches with good surf but the Búzios Beach Club has built condos here.

Next on the coast is Ferradura, which is large enough for windsurfing, and Lagoinha, a rocky beach with rough water. Praia da Foca and Praia do Forno have colder water than the other beaches. Praia Olho de Boi (Bull's Eye) was named after Brazil's first postage stamp. It's a pocket-sized beach reached from the long, clean beach of Praia Brava by a little trail.

João Fernandinho and João Fernandes are both good for snorkelling, as are the topless beaches of Azedinha and Azeda.

Places to Stay

If you want to camp, *Geribá* (☎ 23-2020) at Rua da Ânchora 1, Praia da Geribá, is a good spot. It's 150 metres from the beach and charges US$9 per person. It also rents basic quartos for US$16 per person.

Zen-Do (☎ 23-1542), Rua João Fernandes 60, is a private home with rooms to let. Yesha Vanicore runs a progressive household and has doubles for US$25 in the off season. Yesha, a friendly lady, speaks English and is an excellent vegetarian cook. *Pousada Mediterrânea* (☎ 23-2353) at Rua João Fernandes 58 is a white-washed and tiled little hotel. Off-season doubles with a lovely inland view are US$30. *Pousada la Chimere* (☎ & fax 23-1460), Praça Eugênio Harold 36, is an excellent splurge: it has a lovely courtyard and large well-appointed rooms with a view over the square. Low-season doubles are US$45, high season US$60. Close to the bus station, *Don Quixote* (☎ & fax 23-1487), Estrada da Usina Velha 300, is good value, charging US$30 a double in the off season.

In Armação, try *Pousada do Arco Iris* (☎ 23-1256; fax 23-2148) at Rua Manoel Turibe de Farias 182, with US$20 doubles in the off season, and US$40 in the high season.

Places to Eat

For good cheap food, have grilled fish right on the beaches. Brava, Ferradura and João Fernandes beaches have little thatched-roof fish and beer restaurants. Most of the better restaurants are in or about Armação. *Restaurante David* in Armação, on Rua Manoel Turibe de Farias, has good cheap food. An ample US$6 prato feito usually includes shark fillet (cassão) with rice, beans and salad. *Gostinho Natural*, also in Armação, is very popular and its servings are huge.

Búzios is also a good place to indulge in some fancy food. *Le Streghe* (The Witch) in Armação, on Rua das Pedras, has great pasta and northern Italian dishes, but obsequious service. *Au Cheval Blanc*, a few doors down, has a reputation for fine French food. Both have main courses starting at US$12.

Chez Michou Crêperie, also on Rua das Pedras, is a popular hang-out because of its incredible crepes. Staff will make any kind of crepe you want, and the outdoor bar has delicious pinha coladas for US$3. On Avenida Beira Mar, between Ossos and Armação, are *Satíricon*, with overpriced Italian seafood, and *Orient Express*, a flash Japanese sushi bar and steak house.

Getting There & Away

From Cabo Frio to Búzios (Ossos) take the municipal bus for a 50-minute, 20-km bone-crunching cobblestone run. There are four direct buses daily to Rio from the bus stop

JOHN MAIER, JR.

JOHN MAIER, JR.

Top:　Men at a bar in Búzios
Bottom:　Café with interesting menu, Búzios

on the Estrada da Usina Velha. The three-hour trip costs US$7, with the first bus leaving at 7 am and the last at 6 pm (8.45 pm on Sunday).

Getting Around

Cycling is a good way to get around the area.

Rent A Bike, at Avenida José Bento Ribeiro Dantas 843, and Casa Central Bicicleta at Rua Lúcio Quintanilha 152, both in Armação, rent bicycles for around US$20 a day.

Index

Maps

JOHN MAIER, JR.

Street Carnaval

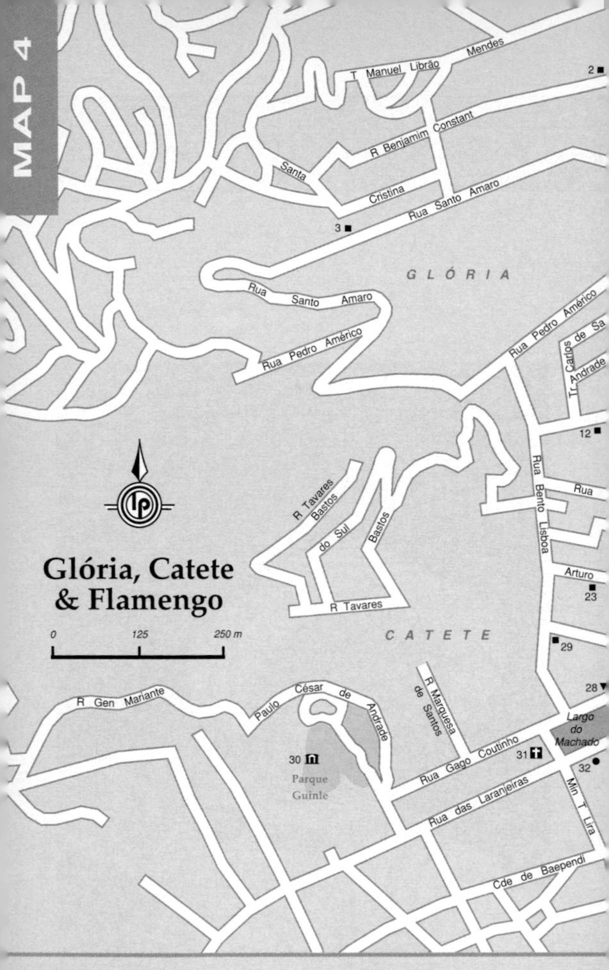

MAP 4

Manuel Librão Mendes

2 ∎

R Benjamim Constant

Santa

Cristina

Rua Santo Amaro

3 ∎

GLÓRIA

Rua Santo Amaro

Rua Pedro Américo

Rua Pedro Américo

Rua de Sá

Tv Cattete

Andrade

12 ∎

Rua Bento Lisboa

Rua

R Tavares Bastos

Bastos

do Sul

Arturo

23 ∎

Glória, Catete & Flamengo

0   125   250 m

R Tavares

CATETE

29 ∎

28 ▼

R Gen Mariante

Paulo

César de Andrade

R Marquesa de Santos

Largo do Machado

30 🏛

Parque Guinle

Rua Gago Coutinho

31 🏧

32 ●

Min T Lira

Rua das Laranjeiras

Cde de Baependi

PLACES TO STAY	PLACES TO EAT
2 Hotel Benjamin Constant	22 Restaurante Amazónia
3 Hostel Bello	27 Casa dos Galetos &
4 Hotel Turístico	Pizzaria Machado
5 Best Western Golden Park Hotel	28 Adega Portugália
6 Hotel Glória	33 Salé & Douce Ice
9 Flamengo Palace Hotel	Cream & Delicatessen
10 Hotel Novo Mundo	34 Churrascaria Majórica
11 Hotel Inglês	38 Café Lamas
12 Hotel Hispánico Brasileiro	
13 Hotel Monte Blanco	**OTHER**
16 Hotel Vitória	
17 Hotel Imperial	1 Marina da Glória
18 Hotel Flórida	7 Teatro Glória
19 Hotel Ferreira Viana	8 Bosque Escultura
20 Hotel Mayflower	14 Museu da República &
21 Regina Hotel	Palácio do Catete
23 Monterrey	15 Museu Folclorico Edson Carneiro
24 Hotel Rio Lisboa	26 Museu de Telefon
25 Hotel Rio Claro	30 Palácio das laranjeiras
29 Flamengo Rio Hotel	31 Igreja Nossa Senhora da Glória
35 Hotel Venezuela	32 Dantur
36 Hotel Paysandú	37 Teatro de Marionetes e Fantoches

R da Glória

Ⓜ Glória

Avenida Beira Mar

1

Lad da Glória

4

5

6

7

8

Antônio M Campos

Al Almões

Orlando

Rangel

Golfacases

Rua do Russel

Pertence

Catete

Ⓜ

Silveira

Rua

9

11

10

Martins

Parque do Catete

🏛 14

🏛 15

13

16

17

Ferreira

19

Viana

18

20

21

Correla

Dutra

Praia do Flamengo

Infante Dom Henrique

22

Bernardes

25

24

R Buarque de Macedo

Catete

26

27

Rua 2 de Dezembro

Baía de Guanabara

Rua Machado de Assis

Largo do Machado

Ⓜ

33

Rua Almt Tamandaré

Praia do Flamengo

FLAMENGO

Praia do Flamengo

Br do Flamengo

34

35

36

To Museu Carmen Miranda

S. Salvador

38

Paiçandu

Sen Vergueiro

37

Igreja Nossa Senhora da Glória

JOHN MAIER, JR.

MAP 5

MAP 3

Jardim Botânico

Jóquei Clube

Avenida Borges de Medeiros

Jardim Botânico

Marqués de São Vicente

GÁVEA

Avenida Rodrigo Otavio

4 ✚

Mario Ribeiro

● 6

● 3

5 ●

Avenida Pe Leonel Franca

Avenida Bartolomeu Mitre

Gilberto Cardoso

Avenida Atlantico de Melo Franco

Humberto de Campos

● 16

Avenida Visc de Albuquerque

Ferreira

João

José

Cupertino

Carlos Góis

Almirante

14 ★

Dias

7 ▼

13 ▼

15 ■

8 ▼

Rainha Guilhermina

Gen Urquisa

Venâncio Flores

Ataulfo de Paiva

Durão

Guilherm

Aristides Spinola

Avenida

12 ■

San Martin

LEBLON

Rita Ludolf

Avenida Gen

Lira

Linhares

10 ● 11 ●

Avenida Delfim Moreira

Praia do Leblon

ATLANTIC

OCEAN

Estrada do Vidigal

Av Niemeyer

9 ■

Ipanema & Leblon

0   250   500 m

Ilha Piraqué

Lagoa Rodrigo

de Freitas

Ilha dos Caiçaras

Avenida Epitácio Pessoa

MAP 6

Avenida Epitácio Pessoa

Alm Saddock de Sá

Alberto Campos

Nascimento Silva

I P A N E M A

Avenida Borges de Medeiros

Jardim de Alah

Avenida Epitácio Pessoa

Durmont

Barão

Henrique

Anibal Mendonça

Garcia d'Avila

Torre

Maria Quitéria

Joana Angélica

Vinicius de Moraes

Praça N.S. da Paz

Visc de Pirajá

Prudente de Morais

Avenida Vieira Souto

Praia de Ipanema

Farme de Amoedo

PLACES TO STAY

9 Sheraton Hotel
10 Marina Palace
11 Marina Rio
12 Hotel Carlton
15 Leblon Palace Hotel
18 Praia Ipanema
24 Hotel São Marco
25 Marlpanema
30 Everest Rio
31 Caesar Park
32 Everest Park Hotel
35 Ipanema Inn
38 Sol Ipanema
44 Hotel Vermont

PLACES TO EAT

7 Celeiro
8 Restaurante Bozó
13 Sabor Saúde
19 Chez Michou
21 Delicats
22 Boni's
29 Kabuki Japanese Buffet
33 Banana Café
36 Sabor Saúde

37 Chaika's
39 Esquina
41 Porcão
42 Natural
43 Bar Bofetada
45 Sindicato do Chopp
46 Via Farme
47 Alberico's

OTHER

1 Clube Navel Ilha Piraqué
2 Parque Carlos Lacerda
3 Estácio de Remo
4 Hospital Miguel Couto
5 Planetário
6 Clube de Regatas do Flamengo
14 Rio Tourist Police
16 Scala
17 Clube Monte Líbano
20 Lord Jim's
23 Clube dos Caiçaras
26 Museu Amsterdam Sauer
27 Museu H. Stern
28 Post Office
34 Casa de Câmbio
40 Garota de Ipanema

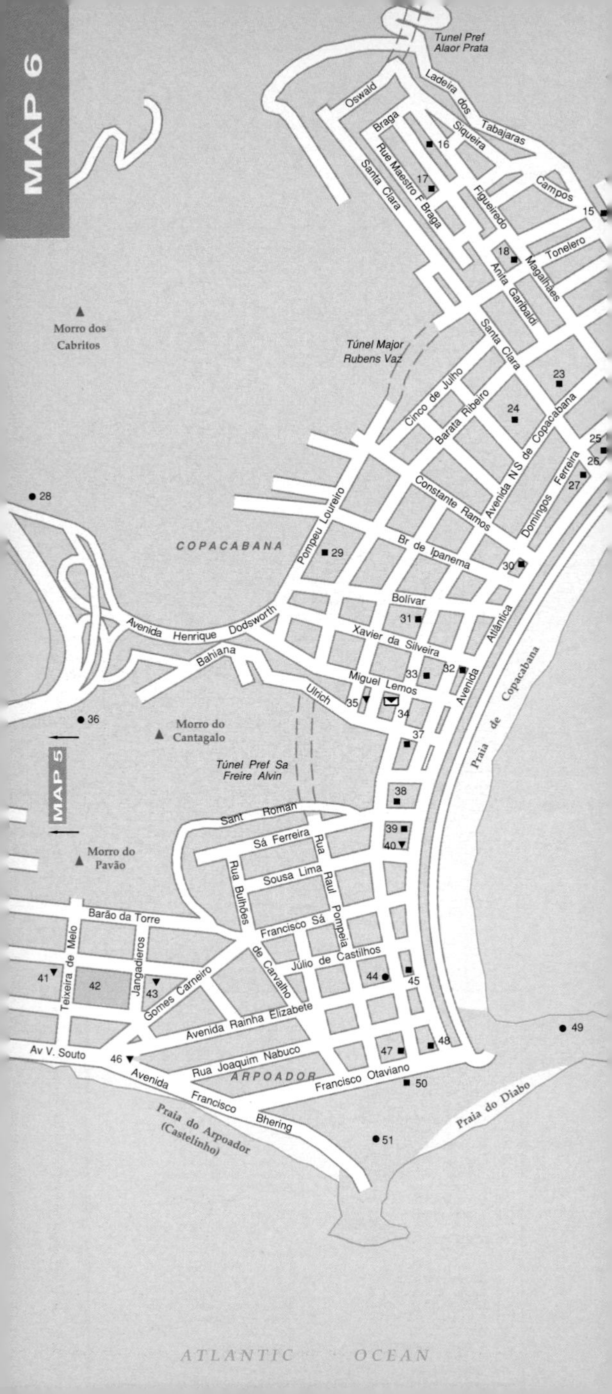

MAP 6

Túnel Pref
Alaor Prata

Ladeira dos
Oswald
Tabajaras
Braga
Siqueira
16
Rua Maestro F Braga
Figueiredo
Campos
17
Santa Clara
15

18
Tonelero
Anna Garibaldi
Maganhães

Santa Clara

Túnel Major
Rubens Vaz
Cinco de Julho
23

24
Barata Ribeiro
25
Constante Ramos
Avenida N.S. de Copacabana
26
Domingos Ferreira
27

Morro dos
Cabritos

Pompeu Loureiro
Br de Ipanema
COPACABANA
29
30
Bolivar
28
31
Xavier da Silveira

Atlântica
Avenida Henrique Dodsworth
33
32
Bahiana
Miguel Lemos
35
34
Ulrich
37
36
Morro do
Cantagalo
38

MAP 5
Túnel Pref Sa
Freire Alvin
39
40

Morro do
Pavão
Sant Roman

Praia de Copacabana
Sá Ferreira

Rua Bulhões
Sousa Lima
Raul Pompéia
Rua
Barão da Torre
Francisco Sá

Teixeira de Melo
de Carvalho
Julio de Castilhos
41
44
45
42
Jangadeiros
Gomes Carneiro
43
Avenida Rainha Elizabete
Av. V. Souto
Rua Joaquim Nabuco
47
48
46
49
ARPOADOR
Avenida
Francisco Otaviano
50
Francisco
Bhening
51
Praia do Arpoador
(Castelinho)
Praia do Diabo

ATLANTIC   OCEAN

Copacabana from the top of Pão de Açucar

CHRIS BEALL

Copacabana

0   250   500 m

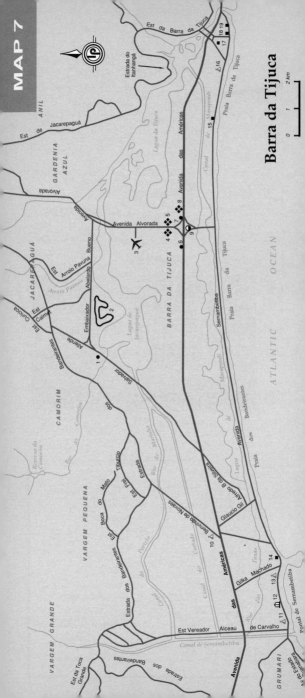

MAP 7

Barra da Tijuca

0   1   2 km

Map 7
Barra da Tijuca

PLACES TO STAY

10 Camping Novo Rio
11 Camping CCB RJ-10
13 Camping Ostal
14 Hotel Atlântico Sul
15 Golden Green
16 Camping CCB RJ-9
17 Hotel Entremares
18 Tropical Barra
19 Praia Linda

OTHER

1 Riocentro Convention Centre
2 Autoódromo Nelson Piquet
3 Aeroporte de Jacarepaguá
4 Via Parque Shopping
5 Casa Shopping
6 Bosque da Barra
7 Carrefour Supermarket
8 Barra Shopping
9 Urban Bus Terminal
12 Museu Casa do Pontal

JOHN MAIER, JR.

Barra da Tijuca

Rio's most fashionable suburb, Barra da Tijuca

MAP 8

Ilha de Paquetá

Praia do Lameirão

Praia Catimbau

Praia Pintor Castagneto

Cerqueira

Dos Irmãos

F. Borges

Luz

Cerqueira

Morro do Castelo ▲

Thomás

Maestro Aracildo

Alamban

Morro de São Roque ▲

P. Juvenal

Morro da Covanca

Praia Dr. Arédio

Morro do Costallat ▲

Ilha de Brocoió

Piriche Regente

Praia dos Tamoios

To Rio de Janeiro

Morro das Pedreiras ▲

Dr. Lacerda

Ilha dos Lobos

Praia José Bonifácio

Pinheiro Freire

Praia Grossa

Morro das Paineiras ▲

Manuel de Macedo

Luis de Andrada

Morro da Cruz ▲

Morro da Veloso ▲

Morro do Vigário ▲

Praia das Gaivotas

Praia da Imbuca

Ilha das Fôlhas

Praia M. Luis

0   200   400 m

JOHN MAIER, JR.

JOHN MAIER, JR.

Left: Hanging out on Ilha de Paquetá
Right: The island is free of cars

MAP 9

FLORESTA DA TIJUCA

Morro do Andaraí

Caveira

Exce

Pedra do Ce

Pico da
Tijuca

FLORESTA DA TIJUCA

Caminho do Pico da Tijuca

Papagaio

Im. do bom Retiro

Bom Retiro

Caminho do Bico do Archer

Pico do
Archer

Ruínas do
Archer

Restaurante
A Floresta

Estrada do Excelsior

Furna Luís
Fernando

Gruta da
Saudade

Furna
Belmiro

Estrada do bom Retiro

Lagoa das
Fadas

Gruta Paulo
E Virgínia

Cascata
Gabriela

Alto da
Boa Vista

Cascata
Diamantina

Restaurante
Os Esquilos

Barracão

Bico do Papagaio

Est Escragnole

Meu Recanto

A Fazenda

Açude da
Solidão

Capela do
Mairynk

PARQUE   NACIONAL

Estrada Visc. do Bom Retiro

DA   TIJUCA

Est da Cascatinha

Entrada da
Floresta

Morro da Taquara
da Tijuca

Cascatinha
de Taunay

Estrada do Açude

Floresta da Tijuca

0   0.5   1 km

ANDREW DRAFFEN

ANDREW DRAFFEN

Top: Rio from Floresta da Tijuca
Bottom: Drinking fountain in Floresta da Tijuca

Top: Cabo Frio, north of Rio
Bottom: Snorkelling is good near Rio

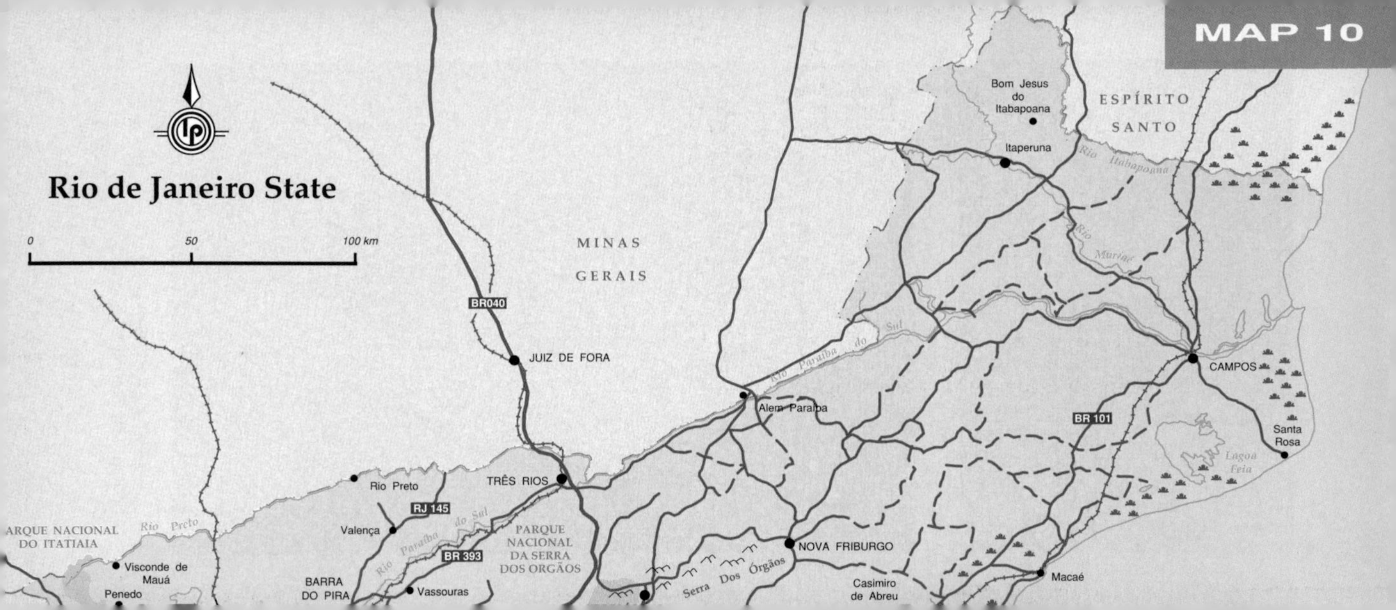

MAP 10

Rio de Janeiro State

ESPÍRITO SANTO

MINAS GERAIS

Bom Jesus do Itabapoana
Itaperuna

CAMPOS
Santa Rosa

Lagoa Feia

BR 101

Macaé

JUIZ DE FORA

Aleia Paraíba

NOVA FRIBURGO

Casimiro de Abreu

PARQUE NACIONAL DA SERRA DOS ÓRGÃOS

Serra Dos Órgãos

TRÊS RIOS

BR 040

BR 393

Rio Preto

RJ 145

Valença

Vassouras

BARRA DO PIRAÍ

PARQUE NACIONAL DO ITATIAIA

Visconde de Mauá

Penedo

0   50   100 km